Praise for
On Campaign with the Army of the Potomac

"Dodge's regiment was in the Union wing crushed by Stonewall Jackson's attack. Dodge's acuity makes invaluable his perspective on the Army of the Potomac's nadir, its string of defeats in 1862–1863. The privations of campaigning, the loss of companions, and even the life of camp rumors Dodge records enable his journal to conjure a vivid, you-are-there aura."
—*Booklist*

"Dodge includes a lot of information in his journal, especially concerning the differing qualities of the officers, both general and regimental, under whom he served. His comments shed much light on the inner workings of the army in 1862–1863. For those interested in the Army of the Potomac, Chancellorsville, and Gettysburg, this work, ably edited by Sears, is well worth a careful reading." —*Blue & Gray*

"The first-ever publication of Dodge's meticulous journal gives a fresh and incisive look at military events from the 1862 Peninsula Campaign through the 1863 showdown at Gettysburg. This is a first-rate personal narrative."
—JAMES I. ROBERTSON, JR., author of *Stonewall Jackson*

"Brilliant, brutally forthright, and fervently devoted to the Union, Dodge personified the very best of the younger officers who proved essential to the Army of the Potomac's fighting prowess. Dodge's recently discovered journal already ranks as one of the finest personal accounts of military life and combat in the Civil War." —T. MICHAEL PARRISH, editor of *Brothers in Gray: The Civil War Letters of The Pierson Family* and author of *Richard Taylor: Soldier Prince of Dixie*

"Under even the most trying conditions, Dodge kept his journal faithfully. His accounts of Chancellorsville and the march to Gettysburg, where he lost a leg, are crisp and detailed. Dodge's journal also answers succinctly the question: why would men stand before such withering fire?" —*Concord Monitor* (New Hampshire)

"Dodge's own experiences at the Battle of Chancellorsville and throughout the other famous campaigns in the Virginia theater afford great reading and important historical evidence, all edited with the sure skill of renowned historian Sears." —ROBERT K. KRICK, author of *Stonewall Jackson at Cedar Mountain* and *Lee's Colonels*

On Campaign with the Army of the Potomac

The Civil War Journal of Theodore Ayrault Dodge

Edited by Stephen W. Sears

Cooper Square Press

First Cooper Square Press paperback edition 2003.

This Cooper Square Press paperback edition of *On Campaign with the Army of the Potomac* is an unabridged republication of the hardcover edition first published in New York in 2001. It is reprinted by arrangement with the editor.

Published by Cooper Square Press
A Member of the Rowman & Littlefield Publishing Group
200 Park Avenue South, Suite 1109
New York, New York 10003-1503
www.coopersquarepress.com

Distributed by National Book Network

The Library of Congress previously cataloged the hardcover edition of this book as follows: 0-8154-1030-1 (cloth: alk. paper)

Dodge, Theodore Ayrault, 1842–1909.
On campaign with the Army of the Potomac : the Civil War journal of Theodore Ayrault Dodge / edited by Stephen W. Sears.
    p. cm.
Includes index.
ISBN 0-8154-1266-5 (pbk.: alk. paper)
    1. Dodge, Thedore Ayrault, 1842–1909—Diaries. 2. United States. Army. New York Infantry Regiment, 101st (1861–1862). 3. United States. Army. New York Infantry Regiment, 119th (1862–1865). 4. United States. Army of the Potomac. 5. New York (State)—History—Civil War, 1861–1865—Personal narratives. 6. United States—History—Civil War, 1861–1865—Personal narratives. 7. New York (State)—History—Civil War, 1861–1865—Regimental histories. 8. United States—History—Civil War, 1861–1865—Regimental histories. 9. United States—History—Civil War—1861–1865—Campaigns. 10. Soldiers—New York (State)—Diaries. I. Sears, Stephen W. II. Title.

E523.5 101st .D63 2001
973.7'447—dc21   00–53501

Contents

Introduction

In 1898, reading over the manuscript volumes of his Civil War journal for the first time in thirty years, Theodore Ayrault Dodge cast his historian's eye on them and was pleased. "I took them up last evening," he explained in a letter to his brother, "and was very much interested." Theodore Dodge was speaking from a secure place as one of America's leading military historians. On the Civil War he had written two major works, as well as numerous articles, and he lectured frequently on the subject. Furthermore, he was well embarked on an ambitious "Great Captains" project, with biographies already published on Alexander, Hannibal, Caesar, and Gustavus Adolphus, and with a multivolume life of Napoleon on the horizon. Yet now he took time out to relive the long days and the hot moments of his own fighting career in the great war of 1861–65.

Back in 1868, Dodge had drafted a sort of private memoir, based on his wartime journal, labeling the manuscript "The Camps and Campaigns of Adjutant Arrow." It would never see the light of day, and was later destroyed in a fire. In 1899, a year after rediscovering and reappreciating this record of his Civil War experiences, he wrote a little volume of anecdotes loosely based on the journal, calling it *Army and Other Tales* and publishing it privately. But Dodge's original journal, one of the best and brightest records we have of life (and death) in the Army of the Potomac, is deserving of a wider audience.

From the Peninsula to Gettysburg, Theodore Dodge "journalized" (as he put it) with remarkable dedication. He scarcely missed a day. At one point, after a wound and typhoid fever immobilized him, he dictated a careful narrative based on notes he had somehow managed to scribble during his trials. From his perspective as a regimental adjutant, Dodge always seemed to know (and to record with candor) exactly what was going on *inside* this great army, whether it was in camp or on campaign or in battle—and at the same time confessed his frustration, as do all soldiers, at the unknowns pressing down on the army from *outside*. The frustration for the reader is that this remarkable journal ends all too soon. As a lieutenant, then as a captain, Dodge always took his post with his men at the center of the fighting. He was wounded once slightly, a second time seriously, a third time so seriously as to lose a leg. His fighting career, and his journal, ends on the bloody field of Gettysburg.

When Theodore Dodge went to war for the Union as a first lieutenant at age nineteen, he brought certain special qualities to the job. He had been born in 1842 in Pittsfield, Massachusetts, to a family of some means. His father, Nathaniel S. Dodge, was a manufacturer who would later operate the Copake Iron Works, to the south and west just over the New York border. His mother, Emily Pomeroy Dodge, was a woman of culture. Pittsfield, in the Berkshires, was popular with artists and writers of the day (among them Herman Melville and Oliver Wendell Holmes), and young Theodore was raised in an atmosphere of learning. For his education he was sent abroad—to schools in Berlin, to the University of Heidelberg, and to University College in London, from which he graduated in 1861. His stay in Berlin included military schooling, with tutoring by a certain General von Froneich of the Prussian Army.

When the very well educated Dodge returned to America at the outbreak of the rebellion, he spoke German and French fluently and had a grounding in the military arts—not in battle, to be sure, but certainly in military administration. A regimental adjutant's job is to manage the regiment, and Theodore Dodge did not have to learn that skill on the job. He was in effect a seasoned adjutant right from the start.

Young Dodge was very much the gentleman officer, not entirely comfortable in the company of rough-and-tumble volunteers. "American volunteer soldiers might be the best in the world," he said, "but they were still volunteers." He also had the attitudes and prejudices that marked many of his class and background. In his journal he is casually anti-Semitic and he evaluates people of color merely as servants—but was much dependent on them for the quality of his life in camp and field. He regarded the Emancipation Proclamation as useless. But Theodore Dodge was strongly committed to the cause for which he was fighting. "I fight because having once gone into it, I will not back out," he wrote, and on campaign he demonstrated that he meant it. He was one of those wholly dedicated, indispensable company and regimental officers who composed the iron backbone of the much-abused Army of the Potomac during this crucial period of the war.

Nineteen-year-old Theodore Dodge was mustered into the 101st New York volunteers on February 13, 1862. The 101st had opened recruiting the previous September in the area of Syracuse, but under inept officers its ranks were slow to fill. Dodge's enlistment coincided with the arrival of a new colonel, Enrico Fardella, late of the Sardinian Army, who reinvigorated the 101st. It was moved downstate to Hancock, near the Pennsylvania border, and there consolidated with another half-recruited unit. The 101st New York entered federal service on February 28, 1862, at Hancock. Dodge, who put on his service record that he had helped in the recruiting process, was appointed first lieutenant in Company G.

The regiment joined the Army of the Potomac at Washington in early March, but when McClellan took the army to the Peninsula that month, the 101st remained behind to help man the capital's defenses. It was garrisoned at Fort Lyon in Alexandria until June, at which time McClellan called for reinforcements for his final drive against Richmond. On June 6 the 101st New York embarked for the Peninsula, and Lieutenant Dodge started his campaign journal.

As Dodge later explained, it became his habit "to jot down things" in a small pocket diary, and at the first opportunity to expand the notes into journal entries, "written at odd times on scraps of paper, which, in due season, got mailed home." He also carried on a regular correspondence with his family in New York. Often these journal "scraps" would be mailed along with the letters. At times a journal entry appears to serve as a letter, or a letter as an entry; in the following pages it is not always possible to distinguish between the two. In any event, each served the same purpose. His family had urged him to keep a running journal-type account of his campaign experiences, an age-old soldierly tradition, and he was more than willing to oblige. From New York both journal and letters were then sent on to Theodore's older brother George, living in London.

Even before the 101st New York left Alexandria, the captain of Company G resigned, and so on the Peninsula Lieutenant Dodge served as acting captain of the company. At Oak Grove, the first of the Seven Days' Battles, posted in Philip Kearny's famous division, Dodge led his company into its first fight. "We have been in a very confused state of dangers," he wrote the next morning, "which I will tell you about as near as I can make out." He did remarkably well in making out what had happened in his first battle.

Through that tumultuous last week of June, Dodge records the fighting and the marching. Although the 101st was engaged at Glendale on June 30 and at Malvern Hill on July 1, it is the bewildering, exhausting flight to the James—which Dodge believed at the time to be yet another of McClellan's maneuvers—that he renders best. Although deeply disappointed at the outcome of the campaign, Dodge was not disillusioned with General McClellan. Indeed, he never became disillusioned. As late as the week before Gettysburg, when Meade replaced Hooker as head of the Army of the Potomac, Dodge exclaimed, "Oh! that Little Mac were the man!"

At Harrison's Landing on the James, while the army sweltered though the hot summer and argument raged about what to do with it, Dodge moved up to be adjutant of the 101st New York. By all accounts he managed the regiment very well, certainly better than his predecessor. His superior told him he "was the only officer in the Regiment who would make a good Adjutant," and so it appeared.

The Second Bull Run campaign was the last for Adjutant Dodge in service with the 101st New York, and indeed it was the last campaign for the regiment itself. Badly worn by disease and straggling, the 101st was severely decimated in the Bull Run fighting. Following the campaign, another regiment absorbed the 101st, but before then Dodge had resigned as adjutant. The campaign had almost decimated him as well. On the first day of the Second Bull Run a piece of shell had bruised his right arm, and at Chantilly at the close of the campaign he took a bullet through the left thigh. In addition to these wounds, he was suffering severely from typhoid fever; it was November 1862 before he rejoined the army.

The period from the evacuation of the Peninsula through Second Bull Run is the only time that Dodge was unable to keep up a daily journal. He did maintain his pocket diary, however, and during his recuperation he carefully reconstructed a journal-*cum*-narrative from these notes. In doing so, he did not succumb to hindsight and second-guessing, but reported events as they had seemed to him at the time.

His new regiment, the 119th New York volunteers, set Theodore Dodge on a very different road from what he had been traveling. Earlier he had been part of a superior brigade, David Birney's, in a crack division, Phil Kearny's. Now he was among what the rest of the army came to call the black sheep—the "damn Dutchmen" of the Eleventh Corps.

The 119th New York was organized in New York City in response to the president's appeal for fresh troops following the failure of the Peninsula campaign. The colonel of the new regiment was a Dodge family friend, Elias Peissner, a professor at Union College in Schenectady along with Lieutenant Dodge's uncle. The 119th's new regimental quartermaster was the lieutenant's father, Nathaniel S. Dodge. For a wounded veteran without a regiment, the berth of regimental adjutant was the answer to a prayer. Indeed, he had been angling for a post in the new regiment since his days at Harrison's Landing. The 119th New York was mustered in on September 4, 1862, and the healed Lieutenant Dodge joined the regiment in the field on November 21.

Fluent in German, Dodge was a natural choice for adjutant in the half-German 119th, assigned to a largely German division under Carl Schurz. Although Dodge's tolerance for the Germans of the Eleventh Corps proved to be limited, he offers a fascinating insider's look at the workings of this hard-luck corps, fated to serve with the Army of the Potomac in only two campaigns, Chancellorsville and Gettysburg. Afterward, the Eleventh transferred to the western theater, no doubt as much to its relief as to the relief of the Potomac army.

Dodge's journal for the winter and spring of 1863 offers a very knowing look at how a Civil War army was operated, both in camp and on campaign. It is made evident here that the management of a regiment was only as good as its adjutant and its quartermaster. To be sure, in the case of the 119th New York, that meant the journal's author and his father; nevertheless, the details are clear and the conclusions obvious.

Adjutant Dodge is informative in small matters as well. Civil War drummer boys, for example, have a warm, cozy reputation, typically described (and pictured) as innocent heroes. In the 119th, at least, that was hardly the case. Dodge described the regiment's drummers as "wretched little villains," and at one point during the march to Gettysburg he had the entire drum corps tied to trees in punishment for their depredations against civilians. There is logic here. The regiment was recruited from the streets of New York City, and who more likely to sign up (for the enlistment bonus) as drummers than streetwise urchins?

In the ten-day Chancellorsville campaign Dodge is the knowledgeable and inquiring observer. Certainly no eyewitness better described the ordeal of the Eleventh Corps as it was victimized by Stonewall Jackson's flank attack. Dodge blamed the generals for the surprise, but he is blunt about the skedaddle ("to use a very vulgar word") among the routed troops. As he wrote his brother, "The panic among the Dutch was fearful." He insisted the scene would never have taken place in Phil Kearny's old division. At least, he said, the 119th New York had attempted a stand in the midst of the chaos, and Colonel Peissner died waving his sword, trying to rally his men. As for himself, he was satisfied. "I know that I did my duty—that is enough."

Dodge's riveting experience at Chancellorsville resulted in his first book when he embarked on a postwar career as a military historian and analyst. The considerable authority evident in *The Campaign of Chancellorsville* (recently reprinted in paperback) owes much to its author having lived the battle and having recorded his impressions even as the bullets flew.

While the Army of the Potomac licked its wounds after the Chancellorsville defeat, the bloodied 119th New York was brought back up to standard by the dedicated efforts of a new commander, John T. Lockman, and the hard work of Adjutant Dodge. The journal for this period offers a textbook example of restoring morale in a battle-torn Civil War regiment. But the respite between campaigns proved to be not even a month as General Lee turned the war on a new course by striking north across the Potomac toward Pennsylvania.

On June 12, 1863, the Eleventh Corps set out on the road toward a deadly July 1 appointment at Gettysburg. Theodore Dodge's account of the last twenty days of his fighting career is highly informative and carefully detailed.

From the beginning he had intended his journal primarily as a campaign chronicle, and for this campaign, his last one, he is at his best. He describes the sights of the march with a full appreciation for getting it as right as he possibly could.

There is also here a sense of his own maturity as a soldier and an officer. In the earlier pages of his journal the youthful Dodge sometimes reveals a streak of the martinet, an impatience with the frailties of those in the ranks who fail to live up to his ideal of the disciplined soldier. On the road to Gettysburg that June the troops endured long, hard marches in brutal heat, and straggling was widespread. When Dodge braced one of the 119th's stragglers, the man briefly "brought his piece to a 'ready' against me." On the evidence of the journal to this point, that was a gesture meriting instant arrest and court-martial. Instead, Dodge recognized it merely as an exhausted man's momentary impulse—"He was so sorry for it afterwards"—under exceedingly trying circumstances, and looked the other way. This is one more piece of evidence suggesting that Theodore Dodge would have made an able officer at higher command levels had a Confederate bullet not interfered.

That bullet shattered his right ankle, necessitating amputation, during the battering of the Eleventh Corps on July 1, 1863, the first day of Gettysburg. For the duration of the great battle Dodge lay in enemy hands, but he was left behind when the Confederates retreated back to Virginia. With the amputation of his leg, Dodge marked an end to his journal and letter writing from the front.

He was not done with army service however. On his recovery he served in the Veteran Reserve Corps in Washington, and during the latter half of the war headed (at age twenty-two) the Enrollment Branch, then the Deserters Branch of the Provost Marshal General's office. On August 17, 1864, Dodge was promoted to major, the rank he had kept hoping would be his earlier, during his field service. Such were his administrative talents that after the war, in 1866, he was appointed captain in the regular army and remained serving in Washington. He took retirement as a brevet lieutenant colonel in April 1870, just short of his twenty-eighth birthday.

Theodore Dodge then took up residence in Cambridge, Massachusetts, and embarked on a business career with the purpose (as his Civil War colleague Thomas L. Livermore put it) "of gathering a fortune which should leave him free for the more congenial pursuit of letters." He soon enough achieved his goal. As president of the Boston Woven Hose Company, a major producer of rubber products and of tires, Dodge succeeded in business with one hand while with the other he indulged himself in that more congenial pursuit.

In 1876 he became one of the founding members of the Military Historical Society of Massachusetts, to which he would deliver three papers on the Battle of Chancellorsville. These became the core of his *The Campaign of Chancellorsville* (1881 and 1886 editions), for three decades the standard work on the subject. *A Bird's-Eye View of Our Civil War* (1883 and 1897, recently reprinted in paperback) also enjoyed standard status as a general military history. In addition, Dodge delivered a series of Lowell Lectures in Boston with the Civil War as one of his topics. Among his several war articles was "Left Wounded on the Field," published in *Putnam's Magazine* in 1869, a personal account of Gettysburg drawn in part from his wartime journal and included here as an appendix.

By the 1890s Dodge was well begun on his "Great Captains" biography series. He traveled widely in the Old World to study the battlefields made famous by his subjects, and during the last decade of his life he settled in Paris to focus his researches on Napoleon. He died in 1909 and was buried in Arlington National Cemetery.

Theodore Dodge's Civil War journal is transcribed here from a wartime copy made under the direction of his brother, George

P. Dodge. Theodore's journal and his letters had been forwarded by his family in New York to brother George in London, who for safekeeping arranged for their transcription by a copyist. This proved to be a fortunate precaution, for the original journal and letters, after their return to Theodore in Boston, were destroyed by fire. Another casualty of the fire were the notes in Dodge's wartime pocket diaries. This transcription is taken from the microfilm copy of the journal in the Manuscript Division of the Library of Congress, placed there through the courtesy of Colonel Clarence C. Clendenen on behalf of Theodore Dodge's grandson. The editor acknowledges the kind assistance of Jeffrey M. Flannery of the Manuscript Division, Library of Congress, in sorting out the journal's provenance.

In 1898, when Theodore Dodge took up the copy of his journal for the first time in three decades, he made note that "there are too many copyist's errors to make it possible to correct them all." Nevertheless, he marked corrections as he read over the journal, and added marginal comments on a number of points and events. It does indeed appear that the 1860s English copyist had to guess at some of Dodge's admitted scrawlings, and in the bargain took liberties with his spelling and habits of capitalization. Guided by Dodge's injunction about the copyist's many errors, the present editor has rescinded the more obvious of these liberties and corrected the spelling of persons and places. The chapter divisions are the editor's as well, and the explanatory headnotes make use of Dodge's marginal notations. Fuller identification of many of the regimental officers mentioned can be found in the index.

It is readily apparent, in reading this journal, that it is the work of an unusually intelligent and inquiring mind. It is equally apparent that in June 1862 Theodore Ayrault Dodge deliberately set about composing a first draft of the war's history as he was experiencing it. The result is a superb record of the most critical year in the Army of the Potomac's four-year history.

CHAPTER ONE

Off to the Wars

June 7 to June 24, 1862

General *George B. McClellan's Peninsula campaign was in its fourth month by the time the 101st New York joined the fray. The Grand Campaign, as it was labeled, was designed by McClellan to capture Richmond by way of the Virginia Peninsula, between the James and York Rivers. By early June, the Army of the Potomac had fought its way from Fortress Monroe, at the tip of the Peninsula, to within sight of the Confederate capital. Along the way there had been a besieging operation at Yorktown, a sharp rear-guard action at Williamsburg, and, a week before Lieutenant Dodge's first journal entry, a pitched battle at Fair Oaks, or Seven Pines. The fight at Fair Oaks was indecisive, its most noteworthy result being the elevation of Robert E. Lee to command the Confederate army defending Richmond. For his part, McClellan called on Washington for reinforcements to brace his climactic effort to capture the enemy's capital and break the back of the rebellion. "The final and decisive battle is at hand," he announced.*

James Wadsworth, Washington's military governor, contributed the 101st New York to this effort, and Theodore Dodge was able to record in his journal, almost with relief, "So at last I have got off to the wars." In command at Fortress Monroe was Major General John A. Dix, who promptly forwarded the 101st to McClellan's supply base at White House on the Pamunkey. Dodge's first three journal entries describe his regiment's passage from Alexandria to White House aboard the Hudson River steamer North America.

Potomac River, June 7, 1862

We started from Fort Lyon at 5 P.M. yesterday & embarked on board the "North America" transport, lately on North River. Owing to delay about the baggage we did not leave Alexandria until 4 A.M. this morning. As you may well imagine, 800 men with baggage & all the necessaries of life take up much room, & a more crowded, filthy place than this boat you can scarce imagine. The Adjutant has put me on as Officer of the Day today, and I have but little time to look around.

The banks are pretty & green, but do not present any very interesting point. The water of the river is very muddy, owing to the late heavy rains. We had considerable difficulty in getting the men on board; many got drunk & were very noisy; four tried to run away by jumping overboard.

We are all very glad to get out of Genl. Wadsworth's clutches. Genl. Dix is I think a good man. We shall be near McClellan.

Sunday morning 8th June [1862]

Anchored in York River last night from dark till daylight, to avoid a heavy sea in the Bay. Have just now arrived & wharfed opposite Fortress Monroe. They say we shall not stop here, but go on further. Many troops are embarked on transports all around us. I was relieved by Captain Sturges as Officer of the Day at 8 this morning, it being now 1/2 past 9. We came to the wharf between the Rip Raps & the Fort. Many gunboats are lying about. I always thought Norfolk was visible from the Fort, but I cannot see it.

It is rumored that we are to go to Norfolk & beyond—to Weldon Junction to cut off the retreat from Richmond. I cannot yet give you the proper nomenclature of the places, but will when I get acquainted with them. Fortress Monroe is a *real* fort, of stone, with guns mounted in casements.

The Colonel has just been to report to Genl. Dix, who says Genl. Wadsworth is an ass for sending us here. It is McClellan who wants all the men & we are going to the "White House," Genl. McClellan's Head Quarters. So at last we have come to some fighting. I don't exactly know what to do with my big trunk, but guess I can take care of it somehow. I hear it can be sent back to Government Storage in Washington.

Monday [June 9, 1862], 8 A.M.

Owing to conflicting orders about baggage we did not get off yesterday, but anchored in the Bay opposite the Fort

4

overnight. The wind blew a hurricane & is still so strong this morning that I don't know when we shall get off. If Genl. Wadsworth had known what he was about he would have sent us to Genl. McClellan at once, instead of here to Genl. Dix, who says he does not want us; but McClellan does. We are to go to the "White House," Genl. McClellan's Head Quarters up the York River, in this boat, & from there by cars to the battlefield. I have packed my change of clothes in the little green bag. Shall carry my blanket on my back & my provisions in my haversack. My boy is strong & will be of great service. My trunk will be kept at White House, or sent back to Washington.

Transports are worse than camps, dirty, crowded, & with nothing to eat or drink. They have breakfast, dinner & supper for the officers on board, for which they charge 50¢ each, and for this they don't give you anything to eat.

So at last I have got off to the wars. Well, I'm glad. I don't suppose I should relish being shot more than anyone else, but if I'm a soldier, a real soldier I want to be.

Left Fort Monroe & had a windy sail up the York River. Though we are so far south, it is colder than where you are. We passed Yorktown some time ago. It is a miserable little place, with only some 20 houses in it. The entrenchments are not very formidable as seen from the river; at least, I should not say so. Everybody is delighted at the idea of going to Richmond. White House is on the Pamunkey River. We shall reach there tomorrow.

The York River is broad with wooded banks, & every now & then a beautiful plantation, looking so inviting after being on board the transport. These Virginia homesteads are indeed beautiful. How much I wish you could get one. The green of the woods & grass is similar to that of England, so soft & velvety. We passed West Point about half an hour ago, & are now in the Pamunkey River. It is about as broad as the Thames at Richmond, with the banks as beautiful as you could wish.

We could not get a pilot at West Point, and are therefore steaming along without one. The men are in fine spirits, singing & chatting merrily. We occasionally see some negroes, but no white people at all. West Point consists of some 6 to 10 houses & the places marked on the map are nothing but plantations.

White House, Monday 9 1/2 P.M.—

We arrived here some two hours ago, but shall not disembark tonight. Tomorrow we shall go on by rail to the advance. Richmond is not yet taken, but there will be a great battle before many days, in which we shall take part, & I suppose we shall be in the city among the first. They are using up at the rate of 5 or 6 regiments a week, not counting battles. Boat after boat of sick & wounded pass down the river. I hope I may not be among them. The Colonel is in splendid spirits. Nothing could make him resign now. We did not think 5 days ago that we were to be in the Grand Army of the Potomac, & directly under Genl. McClellan.

The sail from Fortress Monroe is very beautiful. I have thoroughly enjoyed it. By the way I swapped my revolver the other day for one of Colt's double Navy, carrying the minié rifle ball. I gave $2.50 to boot, & have now a better weapon than at first. It is as powerful as a rifle.

McClellan's supply line ran by water up the York and Pamunkey Rivers to White House, the plantation of General Lee's son, W. H. F. "Rooney" Lee. From there Union engineers had put the York River Railroad back in service, rebuilding the trestle at Bottom's Bridge across the Chickahominy, to carry supplies right to the gates of Richmond. By June, following the Fair Oaks battle, the Army of the Potomac lay due east of Richmond, straddling the Chickahominy and, as Dodge notes, nearly within easy cannon range of the capital.

Colonel Enrico Fardella's 101st New York was assigned to David B. Birney's brigade (led pro tem by Hobart Ward) of Philip Kearny's division of Samuel Heintzelman's Third Corps. Dodge's journal entries here take the 101st to the battle lines, where optimism ran high and, by rumor at least, Richmond appeared about to fall.

Near White House, Tuesday June 10 [1862], 4 P.M.

Well, here I am & I feel as jolly as a lark. I am sitting under an apple tree here, with thousands of green apples over my head & many strewing the ground in company with bean & corn stalks. Over in front of me is the line of men, with arms stacked & resting at ease behind them. We have just disembarked from the North America, drawn 3 days' rations, & come out here to get our tents, stay overnight & prepare for our march of 26 miles to the left of the line before Richmond tomorrow. We are assigned to Genl. Kearny's division of Genl. Heintzelman's Corps, which is on the extreme left. We are going into hot work, and much danger, but I am happy to lay down my life for my Country if need be.

It has rained hard all day & the ground is very damp, but we are to have some shelter tents made of India rubber blankets, & I don't think we shall suffer. The Officers are not allowed to take any baggage, & I have sent to Copake Iron Works, per Adams' Express, my trunk, only taking change of underclothes. My boy carries plenty of blankets, & I shall get on well.

I have just had Henry (my boy) put up a tent for me. It is composed of 3 sheets of canvas with buttons & button holes along the edges. Upright sticks, to be cut anywhere, about 3 feet high, stand as the nave, & the blankets stretch down slanting on either side. No ridge pole is necessary. A third blanket goes behind. Three men tent together, each carrying a sheet. They are of course very small, but only meant for crawling under at night.

They say a battle is imminent. I shall I suppose bear a part in it. It seems that the bad luck of the 101st has at last turned & brought us in at the death. I hear Richmond is being shelled. If so the Rebels must at once either evacuate or make a sortie with all forces as a last struggle. May our arms be victorious!

I am in very good spirits, despite my uncomfortable life. So we all, especially Col. Fardella. The only way to get on here is to have nothing but cash—eat on cash, sleep on cash & live on cash generally. Oh, that I had plenty!

The camp has been put up, each 3 men pitching their tent where most convenient. It has a singular appearance. At a distance the tents look as if they were of the usual size, 9 feet high, but the men walk among them like so many giants, half their bodies above the highest of them. The space inside them is rather cramped, but better than open air.

You would laugh to see me sometimes at dinner—today, for example. Of course my dinner had to be produced from my haversack. It consisted of some biscuits (crackers), a can (hermetically sealed) of beef a la mode, & a bottle of currant jelly. My plates, or rather my cover, consisted of one cup & a pocket penknife. With these & my natural chopsticks, I fell to, drinking water from my hands. All this, under an apple tree. Or now, as I am "scrouched" underneath a tent (similar to those we children used to make in bed, or with chairs & a blanket thrown over them) writing by the light of a candle, on the ground.

Our changing quarters & baggage was so sudden, that there are many things in my trunk I ought to have with me, such as needles & thread & such like, but I can easily supply the loss.

I hope you got my remittance of $150. You had better direct to 101st N.Y., Kearny's Division, Heintzelman's Corps, Army of the Potomac.

Is there anything in these scraps likely to interest George? If so, please send them on. I cannot write to him or Mrs. G. very often now.

Near White House, June 11, 1862

We march in about half an hour. It is a beautiful day, but they say the road is very bad indeed. Partly, our route is on the Railway.

White House is a plantation belonging to Genl. Lee of the C.S.A. It was confiscated by the Government. His house is the only one near & is Genl. McClellan's Head Quarters when he is not with the advance, where he is now. I think it is going to be very hot today.

Near Genl. Kearny's division hospital, near Bottom's Bridge—

Only one word. I am writing by a camp fire and shall sleep out tonight. We have marched since noon some 15 miles & have arrived here 10 miles from Richmond. We go to the Division to-morrow.

Many troops are arriving. Genl. McClellan is said to have advanced 2,000 yards today. We hear heavy firing—shelling pickets. We shall probably be in a battle in a couple of days.

Thursday [June] 12th [1862], 5 A.M.

I think I made a mistake in saying Genl. Kearny's Division was on the left. Our Adjutant says it is in the centre. We shall march to Head Quarters today.

Our Army is now between 3 and 4 miles from Richmond. If Genl. McClellan only goes a mile farther, he can plant his mortars & shell the town out. They say he has already two batteries on the right and left for this purpose.

The road we came was excellent, all along the Railway through the woods. We passed several large & beautiful plantations, now deserted by their owners who have fled to Richmond. One house, close by where we are camping, was set fire to & burned by the proprietor before fleeing before our Army to Richmond. The people seem to have a most exaggerated idea of our cruelty. I was talking to a soldier last night, who was in the

9

battle of Sunday week. He says he saw the Rebels bayonet two men of his company lying wounded on the field. He believes that the stories of their maltreatment of our wounded are true.

Last night we encamped for supper on the battlefield of Bottom's Bridge, a large piece of woodland. They have already built the bridge again over the Chickahominy Creek.

The Railway is being employed in carrying stores to the Army & in bringing back the sick & wounded. Frequent trains full of the poor fellows come over the road. There are only 3 stations between White House & Richmond, each a large plantation. On the map they are marked with capital letters, though there are scarce 3 houses in any one.

Near Heintzelman's Head Quarters, 7 miles east of Richmond—

Have just come from Bottom's Bridge & have encamped on a muddy piece of ground. The Officers however will be in a pine wood which is nice and dry. From the appearance of the environs I should think that scarcity abounds. My provisions have nearly run out since day before yesterday and I don't see any way to procure more. However I guess I can forage. We are near the battlefield of Fair Oaks. I shall go over and see it bye and bye. There is no news today that I can hear. New York papers sell for 10 and 20 cents. I know nothing of the prospects of a fight. It looks as if Richmond would be evacuated, in which case we shall have some fun, rejoicing in all manner of niceties, tho' I fear it is pretty well cleaned out.

The battle "of Sunday week" was Fair Oaks, fought on May 31 and June 1 in the immediate vicinity of the 101st New York's posting in the line. Dodge's mention of a gallant charge by the Irish Brigade in this action was probably culled from an imaginative newspaper account; the Irish Brigade's role here was comparatively minor. The tales of the enemy bayoneting wounded were equally imaginative.

Thursday June 12th [1862], 7 P.M.

Did you ever think your Son would be in want of a piece of bread? I did not. But here I am, hungry, and without a morsel to slake it, and furthermore no money can furnish bread. Here we are half a mile from the enemy, our 3 days' rations gone, no sutler near us, & nothing to eat. However I hope that we shall soon be able to get something, by hook or by crook.

Our pickets were driven in a few hundred yards this morning, but the Rebels did not advance. I think the lesson they got on Sunday week is enough for them. I rather think they will evacuate Richmond. At all events, in case of a battle, they will be beaten. Our men have learned one thing, that it is cold steel that carries the day. They never stand our charges. We are encamped on the battlefield of Fair Oaks. Quarter of a mile from us, the woods are full of half buried Rebels and Union graves.

There is no doubt that the Rebels treat our wounded shamefully. We honor our dead soldiers with a head stone. The gallant charge of the Irish Brigade that decided the Battle of Fair Oaks, was made over a swamp, into which every step you sink half way to the knees. It is wonderful how they could charge at double quick over this ground!

Old Genl. Kearny inspected us today, but was very gruff— probably in a bad humor. He lost his left arm in Mexico. The Rebels call him the "one-armed-devil."

Col. Ward's Brigade, left centre advance.
Before Richmond Sunday morning June 15 [1862]

We marched forward to take our position with the Brigade to which we have been attached, & pitched our tents. Genl. McClellan was to have been here to review us, and we marched out to the line to receive him, but he did not come. He has gone to Washington. This was yesterday morning. In

11

the afternoon we cut a road through the woods, & built entrenchments in case of attack. They are simple breastworks, mounting some brass field pieces, to protect us from musketry. We expected an attack last night or today—or rather we made ready for one. The enemy is concentrating in force on our left—his right. Several Brigades have lately been moved there. I am within half a mile or so of the 2nd Excelsior Brigade and shall go and see Robert Brewster, if possible. They told me he had been made Captain.

I am Officer of the Day today, and my company and Lieutenant are on fatigue. I am getting on very well, tho' my style of living is rather meagre, consisting generally of "hard tack" and coffee—sometimes salt bacon (broiled) and, as a rarity, beans. We draw a ration of whiskey and quinine every day. If you can send parcels as far as this, which I will ascertain, I should like some one of you to make some purchases in the shape of delicacies for me, perhaps in cases hermetically sealed, & send them. We shall probably however be in Richmond in a fortnight. My health is most excellent & spirits high; am only temporarily depressed during the middle of the day by the heat, which is intense. The Colonel suffers dreadfully from the heat. Mosquitoes are here as big as moths, and moths fly into our candles which are as big as birds. They generally put the candles out in their insane attempts to burn off their heads.

The enemy beat the long roll last night, thinking we were attacking them.

Monday, June 16th [1862]

We moved with our whole brigade back to our old camp yesterday morning, and are now very near the centre. In the afternoon our pickets were driven in and the whole Brigade immediately fell out under arms. However we were not called upon. In the skirmish we took a Colonel & a Captain & 4 privates prisoners. We lost some 8 or 10 men & Capt. [Joseph L.] Palmer, A. A. Adjutant General of Sickles' Brigade. He was ordered to reconnoitre, and unnecessarily exposing himself, was shot by 4 bullets thro' the head. This morning, about an hour before daybreak, there was some sharp firing along the pickets.

I have just been relieved as Officer of the Day. I had a hard time of it, for we had a heavy thunderstorm yesterday afternoon. I lay by a camp fire all night and did not feel well this morning, but a good breakfast (the first since I left Fort Lyon) of eggs restored me. If we are not called out today, I shall try and go over to see Bob Brewster. Our Regiment is thought much of for a new one here. The 40th and 38th New York Volunteers, which are on our left and right and in our Brigade, say they like the spirit of our men. If the Officers only do their duty, "we shall come out at the big end of the horn." The old Regiments here turn out under arms in precisely the same mood that they turn out for meals. They are fine fellows. I have not yet received letters of later date than the 3rd inst. [instant; the present or current month]. I hope you have received my remittance of $150 and my trunk. I have journalized only & sent regularly at intervals. Have you received my letters?

Tuesday June 17th [1862]

Nothing of importance occurred yesterday. I am under the impression that the Rebels will evacuate Richmond. I saw Elly Whittlesey & Bob Brewster yesterday, and had a long talk with both. They are both within a 1/4 of a mile of me. The ration of whiskey with quinine in it does our men much good these cold mornings.

The two last days have been warm but not hot. During the night it has been cool and refreshing. We have had very warm weather, almost suffocating, when the perspiration runs down like water. I expect it will begin again. Give my best love to all.

Dodge's characterization of McClellan as Fabius-like is both apt and observant. The Roman general who constantly harassed Hannibal but studiously avoided battle with him did indeed seem a model for McClellan in his glacial march on Richmond in these weeks. Clearly, Dodge has no reservations about McClellan's approach, and no doubts about the ultimate outcome of the campaign. The twenty-year-old lieutenant also reveals an observant eye for a well-run military administration. His own talents in that area would soon be recognized.

Wednesday 18th June [1862]

No news of importance. We rather expected an attack, and do expect it now within a couple of days. The weather is pleasant—not too hot. The acting appointments have all been made and nobody has been placed over me. After Richmond has been taken, I think there will be many resignations. I am anxious to hear from you. My last date is the 5th instant.

We have just moved a mile or two forward to help throw up breastworks. We shall stay two days I believe. Genl. McClellan is another Fabius. You see he will not attack the Rebels until he has completed his grand line of forts and breastworks, on which to fall back in case of disaster. This line extends from the James River to the Chickahominy east of Richmond. This line is occasionally strengthened with forts, one of which we are now about to build. I don't think they will send us out on picket, but will choose older Regiments which have got used to the work, but if a fight comes on, our Brigade will have its share to do and it will do it nobly, I know. It is wonderful how admirably the Regiments of our Brigade are disciplined. When orders come to turn out under arms, not a word is said, nor a sound heard, but the men fall into their places almost as by magic, and in less time than 3 minutes the line is formed. They strike tents, pack knapsacks and move in 1/4 of an hour.

It seems as if meeting the enemy was akin to eating dinner, so quietly & systematically do they go to work. The Colonel (Fardella) says they are as good soldiers as he ever saw in his life. Our men, when they turn out, seem to think that they are just going out to fire at the Rebels, who at once run away; but when they have been into one or two actions, they will find that turning out to fight is not so pleasant a duty. They are good men however—the bad ones have nearly all got worked out. I am quite confident they will do their duty. But I have a sort of an idea that the Rebels are evacuating Richmond, tho' everybody says there will be a big battle before they leave. If they do fight and we whip them, it will be so thoroughly that the Rebellion will be virtually at an end, but if they again retreat they will prolong the war in the Southern States. I hope they will fight—I am confident of victory.

They have attacked our pickets and, as it is a rainy and stormy night, we shall probably have a fight. But "let them come and be damned! Battalion left face!" as our Brigadier said some days ago, all in the same breath, as the Rebels were coming down the Railway; and drawing his command in line across the track, they thought it prudent to retire.

Thursday June 19th [1862]

We fully expected an attack in force last night, and slept on our arms ready to fall out. The life of a soldier is indeed a hard one, and if it were not for the honor of the profession, few would choose it. We have to carry all our kit and house upon our backs, and often our means of subsistence for four days as well. Talk of living on bread and water! We have now mostly to live on hard sea-crackers and water. Then again one don't feel much like carrying more than one blanket on his back and in consequence at night one must sleep often cold, and wet if it rains. And then you are so dirty. I don't get a good wash more than once a week, and I feel grubby all over. But after all there is a strange fascination about the life of a soldier, which despite all his privations makes him love his calling above everything else. An old soldier can never be anything but a soldier and he always returns to it when he is able. It is a life of alternate work and laziness. The work is done when it comes and the very dangers and hardships undergone render the *dolce far niente*, succeeding doubly pleasant. Then it is at once a dependent and an independent life; one must be deferential to superiors in the strongest way, but the frequent change of scene, work and climate (though each man is dependent on each other man in the Army) makes one feel independent and free as the mountain air.

I don't think the enemy will attack us again—I think they know we are too strong for them. If however they do not leave Richmond before many days, we shall attack them. We expect to celebrate the 4th of July in that city.

Thursday 9 A.M.—

Men, men, men, men, nothing but men, male sex predominant entirely; females excluded. It is a wonderful thing to see so many men. Where is there such another machine as the human body and where such a machine of machines as an Army? It is wonderful. You see a Regiment march up all order, every man in his place; they break ranks, all is confusion; one word and all is order again. Here are 2 Regiments, some 800 strong, at work on a redoubt, ours included. We have thrown up a beautiful one mounting siege guns, 32 pounders, in two days. Everything is well organized. Here come 36 men carrying a log (a whole tree) which they place just in the right place, whilst others cover it over with earth. Some 600 men are handling picks and shovels, all working in order. One vast distinction there is between the component parts of an Army, i.e. Man, and an Army itself. The one is rendered comparatively unfit for service by any part being disabled, but how many blows can an Army suffer in the destruction of its numbers without apparent slack in the working of its machinery.

The country round Richmond is made up of patches of wood and plain alternating at distances of about 1/4 mile. Scientific battles are therefore impossible, but a scientific siege is truly going on here. The more I see here, the more I am assured of the talent of McClellan, and it would convince any one. He is the only real General in our Army.

Theodore Dodge reveals himself here as something of a gentleman soldier, impatient with the often haphazard ways of the volunteer army. His appeal for a post with the Regulars was directed to his father, Nathaniel S. Dodge, who seems to have known of strings to pull with the military in Washington.

Friday June 20th [1862]

We worked at the breastworks, or rather the redoubt, by relief till midnight last night, which made us sleep very soundly. I slept under a tree with one blanket, but as sound as a mouse. Henry brought me a good dinner yesterday, and ditto breakfast this morning. He managed to get me some dried apples, and made some apple fritters—quite a delicacy, I can assure you.

They say trains have arrived every 5 minutes during the night in Richmond, which strengthens my belief that the evacuation of the place is going on. I don't believe they wish to fight. It may be however reinforcements they are bringing in. I saw Robert Brewster last evening—he looks very poorly. He ought to take a furlough as soon as we get into Richmond. The Colonel will undoubtedly resign when we get Richmond.

17

How about my getting a place in the Regular Army? I shall have to look to your strategy, as I can only bring a Commission and a Certificate from Colonel Fardella to bear. I would rather have a 2nd Lieutenancy in the Regulars than a Captaincy in the Volunteers. I am sick of seeing boors in the places which gentlemen alone can, and ought to occupy. Our Regular Army is as good as that of any country in the world. Our Volunteers are far better than those of any other country; but Volunteers are Volunteers, and I don't wish to stay with them, if I can get a place with the Regulars. What influence do you think you can bring to bear in my favor? If I can once get a place in the Regulars, I am confident I can work my way up, and a better life than that of a soldier I don't desire. If possible, after Richmond is taken, I shall get a short furlough, for fight or evacuate, when Richmond is in our hands, the Summer Campaign is at an end.

We have just returned to our old camp. Before leaving however the Rebels treated us to 30 or 40 shells, which all fell short. Their nearest was 20 rods. The boys crowded to the breastworks, and we had a hearty laugh at their bad marksmanship. They had probably mounted some new guns and were trying them. Not more than 4 out of 5 of their shells burst; they are or seem to be of very poor manufacture. They use a slow match instead of a fuse, and do not cut them accurately.

We have made a very pretty redoubt, mounting 9 guns. The Rebels will have hard work to take it. Genl. [Hiram] Berry planned it. It was only 3 days' work—600 men were at work all the time.

I have had no letter since the 5th instant, before we left Fort Lyon. I am of course very anxious to hear from you. I send letters regularly, but somehow don't get any.

One-armed Phil Kearny, Dodge's divisional commander, was probably the most fabulous figure in the Potomac army. Independently

wealthy, Kearny had attended the French cavalry school at Saumur and took up the life of a soldier of fortune. He fought with the Chasseurs d'Afrique, lost his left arm in Mexico, and led cavalry charges at Magenta and Solferino in the Italian War. Dodge came to admire him greatly, but realized, too, the tests that Kearny demanded of his men. Dodge's own colonel, Enrico Fardella, was also a much traveled veteran soldier, having served in the Old World in the Sardinian Army's campaigns and as an aide to Garibaldi. Dodge did not lack for colorful characters to chronicle in his journal.

Sunday morning June 22nd [1862], 5 A.M.

Yesterday we marched again to the front, and built or helped to build another battery.

The Rebels threw some shells in the morning at a venture; one gun, getting the range very nicely, threw 3 or 4 shells very close to us. One struck the ground in the front of the battery we built two days ago and jumping over a man's head who stood on the parapet bounded right among us. Fortunately it did not explode. I was sitting in the woods at the time. The next one fell within 20 yards of me and exploded. It made me jump, for it was the first shell I had seen explode; it tore the trunk of a tree all to pieces, but hurt no one. We worked hard all day and all the thanks we got was "That we did not work well," from Genl. [John C.] Robinson, who was superintending the building of the battery.

About 6 P.M. the Rebels made a reconnaissance with about 200 men, and succeeded in driving in our pickets far enough to see where we had been at work and what we had done. We of course fell under arms the instant that the firing, which was very heavy for a moment, began; and in less than five minutes, more than 10,000 men were in line behind a front of 1/4 mile. It was almost instantaneous; our Regiment was in advance, at work on the battery, and of course had the front post; and our boys, who have not yet been under fire, were very anxious for a fight, but as soon as we found out it was only a reconnaissance, we broke ranks. I only conjecture they accomplished their object by finding out our battery. They made a similar movement to the right with two Regiments, and we took 500 prisoners. In the evening we marched back to our camp in the Reserve, where we now are, about a mile behind the advanced pickets. Early in the night, the Rebels made another attack on our pickets, and this morning about one another again. This makes me sure they will not attack us, altho' it is Sunday, else they would have kept quiet till they were ready to begin.

It is curious how they like to attack on Sunday: Bull Run, Ball's Bluff, Williamsburg, Fair Oaks, were all fought that day. It is said that because Genl. McClellan approves of keeping the Sabbath, they always attack on Sunday, hoping to find us unprepared. I trust they will give me time to take a wash and change my clothes today. I heartily wish we could get a mail. I have not heard from you since the 5th.

The weather is very fine—not too hot and generally breezy; when it is hot, it is hot with a vengeance, but it has been very cool and nice lately. You probably know that the 101st is in the fighting division of the Army. Genl. Kearny is called by the Rebels "the one-armed Devil" and they believe that they cannot shoot him. He rides into the thickest hail of bullets, always in full uniform (he is a splendid looking man, tall and straight, with a fierce mustache and imperial) with his reins in his right hand or on his horse's neck. He lost his left arm in Mexico. At Williamsburg the Rebels cried, "Come on you damned Yankee!" He answered, dropping his reins and shaking his fist at them, "I'm coming, you devils, and you'll be sorry enough to see me there!" The 38th and 40th New York Volunteers are in his Brigade, the best Regiments in the Army.

Genl. McClellan sent a dispatch to Kearny yesterday, asking if he could hold his position (the left centre) while he

(McClellan) swung his right round towards Richmond. "I can hold hell against the devil" was his reply. Several prisoners we have taken say that they have taken deliberate aim at him (he is a conspicuous mark) but that they believe it to be impossible to hit him. He sends his aides into equally the same dangers he goes himself. They say one has to be servile as a Chinaman to be one of them. I am glad we are in his Division, for it is the post of danger and of honor; rather than give up he would see his whole Division cut to pieces.

Sunday P.M.—

Verdi (my 2nd lieutenant) has just received a letter from his brother, in which he says that you wrote him saying you had not heard from me. I have journalized daily since I left Fort Lyon, and sent letters regularly. You ought to have heard up to the 17th. I have been under the impression that you heard from me regularly, and knew all about my movements. I am sorry about it.

Dodge's witty description of the self-proclaimed professor Thaddeus S. C. Lowe was right on target, for the aeronaut was known to inflate his claims along with his war balloons. In a later marginal notation alongside this journal entry, Dodge explained that Lieutenant Colonel Johnson B. Brown of the 101st, and his son, "have been the head and front of most of the disagreement. Low vulgar fellows!"

Monday noon June 23rd [1862]

We turned out for inspection by Genl. Kearny this A.M., but it was postponed till tomorrow. A camp rumor (which you must know means nothing) says Prof. Lowe discovered this morning that the Rebels had evacuated Richmond, which was in flames. By the way this said Professor Lowe is a "bigwig"—rank of Colonel, pay ditto. Shoulder straps of bullion with balloon on them in rich silver. Swell trains carrying inflators, 100 men at his disposal, hand and glove state of amity with Little Mac, fine cloth coats and little boots (so as not to weigh down the balloon, I suppose), handsome horses, wall tents, and commander in chief of Balloon Department of the Army of the Potomac!! Fine high position whether up or down, is it not?

Col. Fardella doesn't believe in balloons, but in reconnaissances rather. He don't trust in the professor at all; but I think balloons are a great idea. Three Companies of our Regiment went out picketing yesterday but saw nothing of importance. Capt. Allen took charge of a scouting party and went 1 1/2 miles beyond our pickets, but did not meet a single Rebel.

We are getting quite used to turning out under arms now, being called out on an average of between three and four times a day. We send daily three or four Companies out on picket. My turn comes tomorrow. We had Brigade drill this morning, and as several of our Companies were on picket duty, each Regiment numbered only 8 Companies, and I was detached to drill with the 10th. The 101st did not do over well, on account of the Colonel's not understanding the commands of the General.

There seems to be a growing dissatisfaction in the Regiment, why I don't know. The numbers do not seem to agree. It is said that the Browns, father and son, have been indicted before the United States Court for fraud in Syracuse about rations for their men. I don't know the truth of the report. Don't talk of my coming home if I get ill, when we have to get a pass from the War Department to leave the Regiment for even a few hours; but I am very well, though I am now lying in the water writing this.

Tuesday morning June 24th [1862]

I was Officer of the Day yesterday, relieving Capt. Bradt, who was ill. (By the way, Genl. Kearny has appointed "Acting Captains" in the place of those resigned.) All went smoothly till night, the afternoon being rather rainy; firing along the pickets was strong all day. About 10 P.M. it began to rain hard, and at midnight the most violent thunderstorm arose I ever saw—5 out of 6 of all our tents were blown down and perfect rivers ran though the camp. I was visiting the guard with my overcoat on and in less than 5 minutes I was as wet as a rat. It was pitch dark, and I could only advance a few steps at a time, and wait for the lightning, which was very vivid, to show me where to step next. The storm lasted 2 or 3 hours.

Tuesday afternoon—

Just received yours of the 7th, 13th, 16th & 19th, and the Colonel yours of the 7th. This is our first mail. My address now is "Birney's Brigade, Kearny's Division, Army of Potomac." I hope we shall now get a mail regularly. Love to all dear ones. How often I think of you, you don't know.

CHAPTER TWO

The Seven Days

June 25 to July 4, 1862

The Seven Days' Battles opened on June 25, with what McClellan intended to be his first step forward in laying siege to Richmond. The fight that day became known as the Battle of Oak Grove. That was as far as McClellan got, however. On June 26 General Lee seized the initiative and for six days attacked repeatedly and relentlessly. On the 26th, at Beaver Dam Creek, the Confederates were beaten off, but on the 27th, at Gaines's Mill, Lee broke the Federal right wing— and broke McClellan's spirit. Little Mac put his army into flight toward the James River, with Lee in pursuit. There was scattered fighting on June 28 and 29, and a pitched, drawn battle at Glendale on the 30th. On July 1, at Malvern Hill overlooking the James, Lee's final attack was driven back. But McClellan was beaten, if his army was not, and he fell back down the James to a secure base at Harrison's Landing. Richmond was redeemed.

The 101st New York, in Kearny's division, had its baptism of fire on the first of the Seven Days', at Oak Grove. In common with most new regiments, it was a rough baptism, but in the final count it lost only three killed and seven wounded. In the two following journal entries, Lieutenant Dodge records his impressions of his regiment's (and his) first battle.

Of Oak Grove, Colonel Fardella of the 101st wrote General Kearny, "I hear that it has been reported to you that my regiment broke in the presence of the enemy. This report, general, I must assure you is incorrect." Kearny endorsed the colonel's explanation favorably, and added that Fardella "is a noble and brave old soldier. His only difficulty is that he does not speak English fluently."

Wednesday 25th June [1862], 6 A.M.

My Company fell in for picket, when the order was countermanded, and the whole Regiment was ordered to move in an hour. The Brigade is to be ready, and I think the whole Army makes an advance. If so, we shall have a bloody day. I feel confident, and sure that we shall be victorious. Your dear letters make me feel sure of myself, for if you are happy and content to leave me in the hands of Providence, how can I feel anything but confident and happy? My boys, with only two or three exceptions, have hearts like lions, and would follow me anywhere.

There is heavy firing in front, seemingly along the whole line. Love to all. My breast pocket is so full of your dear letters that I scarce think a bullet could go thro' it.

3 P.M.—

Kearny had a sharp action this morning at 10, in which he was driven at first and we (who had been in the Reserve) were ordered up to reinforce him. However, before we got up, a charge drove the Rebels back. We have again returned to the rescue. Our Brigade is supporting a battery, which is throwing shell & spherical case into the Rebel entrenchments. They were driven back some half mile this morning, and they say have retired to their entrenchments.

We are expecting every moment to be ordered up. I was really disappointed this morning that the engagement was not general, for we all have an ardent desire to march into Richmond, which outweighs all other thoughts. We have not yet had a chance to fire a shot, but hot work will come, I expect. We all came out in battle array, I with sword and pistol, haversack with rations for two days, cartridges for pistol in one pocket, and tourniquet and old handkerchiefs in the other, when we went up to reinforce Kearny. The wounded men were lying on the ground, or slowly creeping to the rear; poor fellows, they looked bright and cheerful, despite the pain of their wounds. The Colonel was anxious to get in, and I was almost more so. Hearing the bullets whistle and the rattle of musketry makes one want to be engaged in it. The Rebels do not answer our fire at all. I do not know how successful our artillery was. I should like to know when McClellan is going to make the general attack. There are 9 days before the 4th of July, which we must celebrate in Richmond.

Thursday June 26th [1862], 8 A.M.

Well, here I am safe and sound! But I don't want to be any nearer seeing my Regiment cut up than I have been since yesterday at noon. We have been in a very confused state of dangers, which I will tell you about as near as I can make out.

We were ordered forward in the afternoon again, to help Kearny drive the Rebels out of some woods in the advance. We went in, drawn up in line, and before we knew much about who was firing (we were in an undergrowth where you could not see 3 yards) "chick, chick, chick," came the balls through the leaves, and two men on my right hand fell dead. Everybody stopped at once, and crash went our volley through the trees. We could not see ahead, and it happened that another of our Regiments was in position to our right front. Some of our fire therefore went on our own men, with what result I don't know. We drove the Rebels out of the wood, however, in fine style. Our men stood the fire well. Somehow or other, I had not the slightest thought of the danger I was in, I was so occupied with my boys; but the first bullet which "chicked" through the leaves made me "down" rather fast into a safer position.

The Rebels shoot round balls, not conical as we do, and instead of the fearful "zish" our fire makes, theirs is scarcely heard—only the cutting of the leaves in the wood. After the Rebels had been driven out of the wood, we were moved by one of Birney's aides, and finally brought back to the clearing, when we slung muskets and took picks and shovels to cast up breastworks behind our advanced pickets some half a mile in front. Here, all of a sudden, the enemy, who had been reinforced, poured a fearful volley into our pickets, who retired upon us in confusion, passed through our ranks and left us between them & the Rebels. At the moment we could not see exactly what had happened, and the order to fall back at double quick was given. It was more of a run for a few moments than a retreat.

However, my Company was retreating pretty well, I behind trying to make them "halt." This I soon succeeded in doing, and after we had gone through the "slashing" (a wood cut down and not removed, but lying in confusion) about a furlong, I rallied them and marched them quietly in retreat about 200 yards farther, where the Regiment was rallying on the colors, which the Major held up as high as he could whilst mounted on a stump.

After we had again formed, we marched back to the clearing and recovered our tools which the boys had thrown away when we were attacked. You see we were a fatigue party and not ready to meet such a heavy fire. Genl. Kearny abandoned the idea of throwing up breastworks, & ordered us forward to relieve the 13th Massachusetts and some other Regiments on the advanced pickets; so out we went and relieved them. This was about 10 P.M.; we were close enough to the Rebels (who were in great force before us) to hear them talk, give commands and converse about "driving" in the morning. About 1 or 2 this morning Genl. Kearny found out that the Rebels were too strong for him to hold the post we had gained by the charge of yesterday and again gave orders for the flanking Regiments to retire. They retired accordingly, but the order did not get to us. During the night the Rebels poured several volleys into us, which we only partially answered. I and my men were protected by a strong fence, behind which we lay in security from the bullets.

About 3 A.M. an aide rode up to the right of our line and said to Capt. Allen, "For God's sake retire at once or you will be cut off." So Captain Allen (Co. A of the 101st) gave the order to retreat, and to pass the order down the line. The order came as far as the Company to my right but no farther; and I saw all on my right falling back, but receiving no order I kept my place, together with the Company on my left and the Colonel and Major.

Lieut. Col. Brown had gone to see after three other Companies who had been sent on picket about a mile on our left. We were only 7 Companies all this time. About 15 minutes after the Companies on our right had retired, a man came up with orders from Genl. Kearny to retire at double quick, or we should be cut off. We at once obeyed, and as we started, up rose the Rebels on our right and left, and poured a volley into us. They were not more than 100 yards off, and in 3 minutes more we should all have been taken prisoners or killed.

Fortunately we just escaped. We formed in rear of the other Regiments of our Brigade and here we are again behind our own redoubts, resting. Kearny will act in the defensive all day, I believe. The Rebels are in too great force in front to admit of an attack by us. The casualties in the Regt. I do not as yet know. My acting 1st Lieut. Eagan, and my orderly, were wounded; also Lieut. Carter in the head. We have probably lost some 6 killed and 10 or 12 wounded. One thing is certain, that three minutes more of delay and I and my Company would have been in Richmond as prisoners. Genl. Kearny received us when we retired to the beginning of the clearing, and said, "I expected you all to have been killed." When we retired and were fired upon, we could see the wretches rise from the bushes, with their tall hats, and brown coats, looking as if they would like to cut our livers out; but we are safe, all but the poor fellows who are killed. God have mercy on their souls.

For all I have written I cannot certify to the accuracy. I write simply what I have seen. But now it is all right, and tho' I am sorry the Regiment had to retreat, it was not our fault so much as that of our guides, who placed us in so exposed a position. I tried to do my duty and did stick to my Company and brought it out all right and safe. Some men who had lately been ill dropped out of the ranks from fatigue; but they are now here. Bullet holes through clothes are plenty, among which I will mention Lieut. Miller who had a bullet through the seat of his trousers, as he was facing sideways to the enemy. Lieut. Verdi lost his watch, cap, sword & pistol and finally his Company (he is now with me) and I was alone with my men. I lost nothing but my India rubber blanket which I forgot to pick up when bringing my Company out of our sad scrape.

I hope you receive my leaves regularly—if so, you will find I have journalized whenever I had not something else to do. Love to dear Mother, Polly (who I hope is having a good time in Albany), Roy and all.

In these entries for June 28–30, Dodge reflects the puzzlement of many in the Army of the Potomac over the unexpected turn of the campaign. Kearny's division, of the Third Corps, had been posted in the lines south of the Chickahominy, and so was unaware of what had transpired north of the river during the two previous days—and certainly unaware of McClellan's mental collapse. Dodge wonders here if this is all a grand maneuver by the general, and speculates that they may still march into Richmond by the Fourth of July. Rumor, of course, abounded. The report on the 29th that Ambrose Burnside's force was on the way from the Carolina coast was true enough, but (as Dodge suspects) that Henry Halleck's army was on the way from the western theater was a pipe dream.

Saturday 28th June [1862]

I have just mailed a letter to say that we have just come back from picket duty. Probably this will reach you at the same time as the other. We are going out now only half an hour after we came in tired from picket, to fatigue work on the redan, and this evening we are going to make a forced march, where I don't know, only I suppose it is for the best. It is pretty hard work however. We shall probably double quick it, off and on, all night. What movement this is I don't know. Good bye. Love to all dear ones.

Sunday 29th June [1862]

We have fallen back about two miles, and as yet the pickets have not begun to fire. I cannot imagine that we shall really have to retreat, and am of opinion that this movement is some ruse or other. Talk goes among us of a junction by Burnside and Halleck—but that the latter should be near us is improbable. The wagons have carried a little valise for me. My sash, Commission, glass, revolver & sword I carry with me, and 3 days' rations of hard bread, with pen, ink and paper, 2 or 3 pocket handkerchiefs, a pair of stockings &c [old form of etc.] in my haversack. Henry (my servant) carries my overcoat, blankets and some rations.

One of my poor boys was just shot by accident, whilst we were in line. We buried him, poor fellow, right on the spot, and put a little board with his name &c at the head of the grave. The ball, which one of his companions shot off, went right through his head. You have no idea of what we have left behind. Blankets, overcoats, knapsacks, guns and *omnia militis* shew the way. One thing however is apparent, that they are all destroyed before leaving them. All things we could not take with us I took an axe and cut to pieces, and in the operation destroyed the axe.

I should like to know the meaning of all these movements—they are very incomprehensible. Genl. Kearny is off on a hill, disposing his troops. I guess he means to invite a battle here. The ground is open and good, so that we should have a chance of charging on the Rebels. In bushwhacking I think they beat us; but they can't stand our cold steel. The Colonel has been very highly complimented for his picket duty of the other day. Our Regiment occupied a line of 2 1/4 miles, & the Colonel disposed his men very well. Kearny is much pleased with him. This movement is certainly very queer. I wish I could find out how matters stand. As usual when anything is to be done, I am the only officer in my Company fit for duty.

But never mind! I'm up to work, and have spirit to do all my muscles can stand.

Sunday 5 P.M.—

We are marching towards the James River, and have done already some 6 or 7 miles from our last resting place.

Monday 30th June [1862], 4 A.M.

A call to attention brought the above to a close. To continue: On the road we met thousands of stragglers & thousands of dollars worth of property destroyed. On the West Point Railway a train of 25 cars were burning; near it a huge pile of the knapsacks of a whole Regiment blazing and crackling; everywhere tents & boxes of stores on fire. You could see fine solid leather hunks cut to pieces with axes, and boots, shoes, pantaloons, coats, underclothing and all manner of traps lay strewn around destroyed. (Such is the waste of war!)

After we left this place, we took a road leading round White Oak Swamp. Infantry predominated in the columns, but as the artillery was the first thing to be protected, we made room every now and then for the guns to gallop by. Genl. Kearny rode along from front to rear, from rear to front, alive to the welfare of his men. A more stirring and clear-headed man you could not see. Straight, soldier-like figure with grey hair and beard *a l'Americaine,* his armless sleeve flapping up and down, he inspires the confidence of all his men.

The load of 150 rounds of cartridges, which the men had to carry, broke many of them down; and the intense heat melted them. Under these circumstances it is not to wonder that many should have fallen out. At one time, I had almost 20 stragglers out of my Company alone, but they all joined again. Once, on the road, our Brigade lost its way and had to march half a mile through a swamp, the best road through which, and the one I took, was along the bed of a little stream, with the water above our knees. After all we had to retrace our steps, march through the swamp again and regain the right road. We lost some two hours by this diversion. We marched on till about 9 P.M., when we halted in column with our left resting on the road, and laid down on our arms. Of course we were all wet below by wading, above by perspiration, and most of the men had thrown away their overcoats, blankets and all. I had my India rubber blanket and overcoat, and slept like a log. Some of the boys almost froze.

We started again this morning, about an hour and a half ago and here we are in a large field, arms stacked in line of battle, and with the James River some 8 or 10 miles off. I hope we are all right. I can scarcely believe but what this retreat is a flank movement. I suppose we are now south of Richmond. Tomorrow is the 1st of July. Shall we be in Richmond by the 4th?

With the exception of a few shots we have not been disturbed. Our Regiment got a volley when we marched through the swamp. I am rather wet as to legs and feet, for I have forded another brook this morning, but I feel as well and better than ever. I fear you will lose some of my letters; but it don't make much difference. I wish I had more to write about, for I like to think of and write to you; but I have detailed all but the number & description of the holes I fell into on the road in the dark.

But all's well that ends well. I have just taken breakfast with great delectation. Unsling haversack and canteen, squat down & place the former between my knees and the latter resting against the former; open the haversack, extract a brown cartridge paper, which unroll and find a chunk of boiled beef; cut therefrom one third of a day's ration, take also 2 sea-crackers and begin to eat, drinking splendid fresh spring water from my canteen. Suddenly says Verdi on my right, "Want a piece of balogna?" and cuts a slice off the same, whose spicy juice would raise the dead! What breakfast could possibly compare with this—hard crackers, boiled beef

35

(2 days in the haversack) and balogna sausage (ditto). Think you, you ever fare so sumptuously? It is now 5 1/2 A.M.

9 A.M.—

I have just had a most delicious feast of blackberries. About half a mile in front of us there are bushels of them, and one of my boys just brought me a great cup of them. They only lacked a little sugar. I think our Brigade is stopping here to hold this position until part or whole of the Army passes, but of course I don't know. No order to march.

At Glendale on June 30, Phil Kearny wrote, the Rebels came on "in such masses as I had never witnessed." Theodore Dodge's imagery was more imaginative: "The Rebels were as thick as blackberries." The 101st New York was posted on the fringes of that battlefield and escaped the worst of the fire. Again, at Malvern Hill on July 1, the postings of the 101st through the day (which Dodge records in detail) were equally fortuitous. At Malvern it was the Union artillery that was primarily responsible for the decisive repulse of the Rebel attacks. Dodge succumbed to exhaustion during the battle (as his mother later wrote), with "two on his immediate right and under the same tree being hit with a shell whose explosion never woke him."

Tuesday July 1st [1862]

Paper getting scarce, so must be brief. Our Brigade came near having an engagement yesterday afternoon, but the Rebels retired on a few shells being thrown into them. We were ordered into the line from a position 1/4 of a mile in the rear, where we were awaiting some Rebel cavalry, and the order came to leave knapsacks and all, and double quick up. We started and formed up, where we stayed 2 or 3 hours; we then changed our position about 1/2 mile, to protect our column (which was in motion along the Charles City Road) from a flank movement of the enemy. We marched into the woods and drew up in line, where we lay quietly for a couple of hours, when our batteries began shelling the enemy, who had gone into the fields we had just vacated and were taking possession of the things we had been obliged by the order to leave behind.

Shortly musketry opened on our side. The Rebels were as thick as blackberries. I forgot to mention that when our Regiment took its position in the wood, I threw out my Company as skirmishers and scouts, covering its front and joining with those of the Regiments on our right and left. The firing continued, waxing hotter and hotter. The artillery played superbly. The Rebels now opened batteries and began shelling us. The grape and canister flew in torrents in our direction, but none harmed me or my Company. The musketry on our right did not open near enough our Regiment to provoke a reply from us, but it was very sharp. It lasted till nightfall, when it slackened and suspended. I have not ascertained our losses.

About 9, I was relieved by another Company and I fell back on the Battalion. I was very tired & the darkness prevented my finding Henry, who had my blankets, and so I was obliged to sleep without any covering whatever. I rested well. This A.M. at 2 o'clock, the enemy appeared on our flank and we were obliged to draw back. We regained the road and marched unmolested with the rest of the column (the Rebels had retired) to the James River, where we are now encamped with the greater part of the Army, on a huge plain, where was fought yesterday's battle. I made my breakfast this morning off wheat ears which had been trampled down over hundreds of acres. But now we have got our baggage, and are where there is plenty to eat.

10 A.M.—

We are having a little play with artillery at the Rebels and they have just skedaddled out of the woods in fine style. Birney's (ours) Brigade is supporting the batteries. I don't think, after the taste they got of us yesterday, they will attack us, or make a very obstinate resistance if attacked. The 101st is in the Reserve. Hundreds and hundreds of acres of ripe wheat are trodden down here, and we are marching through it without thought.

10 1/2 A.M.—

The enemy have opened upon us with shell and the pieces are falling about us everywhere. They don't aim as well as we do. Our gunboats are also shelling them. Their shots are accurate. You can scarce imagine such a hissing. All the men are lying down till the musketry commences. It is a good thing to accustom the men to the fire.

12 A.M.—

The firing of artillery has ceased, and I think in a little while the Rebels will commence an attack. We are all behind a wood as reserves to a line of skirmishers, which we shall relieve when needful. We lost some 3 or 4 men wounded by the shelling this morning. Nothing serious however occurred. It is very hot. The gunboats will be a valuable aid if we fight here.

1 1/2 P.M.—

We have moved to the right a little into a clearing. The Rebels can be seen very plainly planting batteries about 1/2 mile distant. Our boys have torn down a fence and built themselves a nice barricade. Now let them come! Our batteries are on a height about 60 or 80 yards behind us, ready to pour canister and grape into the Rebels if they come.

5 P.M.—

We have had a very sharp artillery engagement, we supporting the battery. They had a pretty good range. One shell burst and scattered the dirt all over me. No man was injured in my Company. I think today the Union loss was heavy, for a good many wounded are coming in. Some artillerists have been killed. I guess we shall stay here all night.

The Army of the Potomac pulled itself together at Harrison's Landing (labeled City Point on Dodge's less than accurate map), thanks in part to a major resupply effort. In the margin of his journal next to his record of Company G's losses during the retreat, Dodge later wrote, of the thirteen missing, "4 were killed, 7 wounded & 2 unaccounted for." He was the only officer remaining of his company, but his optimism and his resolve remained firm. "I believe Richmond will soon be taken," he wrote; ". . . we are working in a good cause." He faithfully recorded the latest camp rumors. A substantial part of Irvin McDowell's corps had already reached McClellan, although not under the command of either McDowell or Nathaniel Banks. The rumor of consolidation of the 101st New York, started here, would become a continuous plague on regimental morale. Colonel Fardella was already resigning, and the officers from the 101st's original organization, in Hancock, New York, were threatening to do so. Dodge, too, began seriously to cast his eye on a new posting.

Thursday July 3rd [1862], 6 P.M.

Paper all gone. Scraps only left.

On the 1st inst. had a heavy affair on our left—lost considerably. Firing very heavy—drew in pickets and left at one o'clock A.M. Marched till 9 A.M. thro' heavy rain, when we reached City Point, where we now are. Of course we had lost all blankets &c, and as it rained all last night and all day we were really uncomfortable.

Here the trials of a soldier's life cropped out. On the march I had got as wet as a rat, and the rain ran down my body under my shirt in streams. When we got near City Point, we camped in a pine wood, 3 feet deep in mud. A more uncomfortable day I never spent. Last night I rolled 2 big logs together and slept in the hollow between them, covered by my India rubber blanket.

I unfortunately broke my spectacles during the night and am again reduced to double glasses. Yesterday we had no rations and Genl. McClellan gave permission to kill the cattle on a large estate hard by. There was at once beef, mutton, pork, turkeys, chicken, quail & everything we wanted but bread. Of the mud you can form no idea at all. Every step without exaggeration one sinks in above the ankles. The worst is that one has no place to dry one's self afterwards, for if it rains and one has no tent it is impossible to get dry by the fire. I have now some conception of the self-sacrifice of a soldier. It is real patriotism to be in the Army of the Potomac, and especially in Kearny's Division. Since just one week ago today the Brigade, in which the 101st is, has been at work and we have had not one minute's rest.

"Little Mac" came past yesterday and said, amid our hearty cheering, "We are all safe now, boys, and have got 50,000 fresh troops and plenty of rations for you." But since I began this scrap we have been ordered out under arms, to go where I don't know, so that Little Mac's rest, which he promised us, seems to be a fiction. Of course the papers give you a better insight into the strategic part of this move, than I can, as here all is conjecture. We know nothing. I only write about myself. My Company has lost since the 25th, which was our first engagement, 2 wounded and 13 missing.

I often think of you all and know you think of me. I have as yet received but one mail from you. I am glad you cannot see me just now, such is the state of filth in which I am, not having washed since yesterday week. I have also no change of clothing, and my stockings I have not changed since we left our breastworks in front of Richmond. You certainly would not know me. I fear my letters are almost wholly unintelligible, as I perceive the rain and mud has damaged the last scraps. These scraps are only crumpled bits of paper, brown as the Virginia mud can make them, Mother.

I have almost spoiled my Commission by the wet and I shall send it home by the first chance. I still have the key of my trunk in my pocket. I believe Richmond will soon be taken, as it must eventually, and then I shall get a furlough if I can. If not you will come on and see me, and we can right many things which may now be wrong. But how many poor fellows will not live to see Richmond! If you could see the heaps of dead men I have seen, who were swept down by artillery and musketry, by grape and canister, you would shudder.

You should have seen the boys posting after the sheep and oxen yesterday. It was real fun and they enjoyed it. They must have taken some 100 head of cattle and double the number of sheep and hogs killed. Such a country for productiveness I never saw. Grasshoppers as big as canaries and moths gigantic in size. Wild turkey and quail run through our camp all the time. Grain was ripe long ago, and the second crop of Indian corn is growing. The country is woody but very beautiful; however in such a march one has not much time to observe this. It is only now and then that I look around.

I have been writing while the men are standing under arms and now we have broken into column, stacked arms and been told to put up tents. Company G (mine) is situated in a mud hole which tons of gravel would not improve. How we are to camp here, I don't know. Oh for a fine day!

I am going to try to send you a letter today. Please buy me a pair of spectacles of the number of glass enclosed, as soon as possible. Love to Father, Mother, Polly, Roy and all. When you write to George, tell him I would write him if I could.

Friday 4th July [1862], 4 A.M.

Well! this is tough work. Yesterday the Rebels began to shell us in our camp & got the range very accurately. Two shells burst right over the left of our Regt. The pieces (or rather the bullets, for it was canister) whizzed round merrily.

A battery of ours was ordered out and almost at once the Rebels withdrew. About 5 P.M. we moved down into the woods, where we threw up barricades, and where we spent the night.

I told you about the fresh bread we had two days ago. It was a great change from the pilot bread and water, and we all ate heartily. I, for one, took beef, mutton, lamb, chicken, pork, turkey and everything indiscriminately. I put the meat on the end of a stick and roasted it at the fire. Last evening the colic took me very bad. I felt as if I could not keep up with the Company, but as I was the only officer in the Company (as usual) I was bound to do so. When we got to our place in the line of pickets, I lay down and slept it off. I feel better this morning. We had to march through a stream yesterday and I am still very wet, but Henry lighted a fire and I am trying to get dry. The fact is that this is the third day since I wet my feet, on the march from our last picket to City Point, and they have not been dry since. I slept in my overcoat without an India rubber blanket. The dew fell pretty heavily and you can imagine I am not very dry, even now. You have no idea how grateful the fire feels. This country, which is nothing but woods, is a terrible place to conduct a campaign in. In Europe there are highways, villages, and many large plains. This work is harder than I imagined it would be. Fort Lyon would be a paradise to it.

I am very sorry to say that Capt. Beckwith, Lieuts. Hinds, Verdi, Catlin, and Ford have disappeared since before our artillery fight of the other day. It was rumored that they went to Fortress Monroe; Verdi was not well, but not sick enough to ask for leave of absence at such a time. They say he got one from McClellan. He was trying to get a place as surgeon somewhere in the Army. As for the others, I consider what they have done as simple cowardice. But what is cowardice in some is bravery in others. I could no more skulk off to Fortress

Monroe or any other place away from my duty just now than I could fly. I should never be able to look my parents or brethren in the face again.

There is also a rumor of consolidating the 38th N.Y. with the 101st. The former has about 200 men, we 500. The senior Colonel, who is Hobart Ward, would take command. Col. Fardella told me this morning that such a step had been proposed to him by Genl. Kearny. He said he had just as lief leave now as when we get to Richmond. I am convinced that the Col. don't please here—he don't understand this fighting in the woods, and they prefer an American officer. I don't think the Colonel is the man for this country. I am sorry for him, for he is a very good friend of mine; but he is not happy here and wants to get home.

Our boys are cutting down trees fast to make barricades. We must make them head high. We are in a pine wood, with thin underbrush, of which there are so many in this country. On our left is a lake, on our right Hooker's Division, I believe. I don't know whether it is the wet has stretched my belt, or that I am getting thin: I have just taken it in 1 1/2 ins. more than I ever wore it before. I just heard one of our boys who wanted something to eat ask another for a cracker in imitation of a parrot: "Polly wants a cracker." How it reminded me of old times and Polly at home!

I have a little diarrhoea. Sleeping on the ground makes one liable to a looseness of the bowels. My bed last night was made up of leaves covered with an India rubber blanket—head against a tall fir tree. I think tonight I shall nestle close up to a recumbent log for warmth. I fancy it will be warmer.

The liability of attack from the Rebels from minute to minute, the extreme posts being only 300 or 100 yards distant, makes picket duty harassing when extended over as long a space as ours has been. I wish Kearny's conscience would let him alone.

I am short of paper; I am afraid these scraps are almost illegible. Next campaign I shall have a patent knapsack made according to my own ideas. I pretty well know what is wanted now. It will not be for clothes, but for necessaries of life, eatables, with a touch also of the drinkables. How much I should like some of that cherry brandy; but it is no use wishing. At length, by dint of holding myself in all the excruciating positions the human body is capable of, and by severe muscular exertion of preserving it perpendicular, of excoriating by heat (which was intended to dry) most of my lower extremities, and by keeping Henry at work (myself assisting) to expose each successive part of my garments which the wet had drenched, to the red glare, I have succeeded in making myself dry. With my body more comfortable, my sprits have become more buoyant. Tended by a wash out of a tin cup & a wipe on a cotton handkerchief, I again feel as if I could enjoy another 4th of July. Oh! how hard I am working this 4th. One year ago in peace, now in war, and such a terrible war—a war truly to the knife! You who read the papers, and see & rejoice over a glorious victory, little know at what an amount of human suffering it is won.

I have run out my shoes entirely & don't know where to look for another pair. I must try to send down to the Landing to see about some.

About the consolidation—people talk as if it were a certain thing. Almost all the Hancock officers talk of resigning if it takes place. The Colonel has sent in his resignation, and the Quarter Master also, I believe. I don't see how it is to be managed. I shall by no means resign, with a foe in our front. A foreigner may do so at any time; as an American I should not except under very peculiar circumstances. How about a place in the Regulars? I would rather be 2nd Lieutenant there than Captain here. I am confident I could work my way up. I am only 20 years old and have plenty of time if God spares my life. But we are working in a good cause, and we shall prosper.

This Brigade has done a very great deal of hard work since we left Fair Oaks; we have done more towards protecting the movement than any other equal number of men. We have lost heavily, but we have worked hard. We used to think it hard if we had to do picket duty 3 times in a fortnight; and since last Wednesday week we have been on picket all the time.

But it is cheering to know that matters are prospering. I heard yesterday that Burnside was on the other side of the river with 75,000 men, and that McDowell's Corps, under command of Banks, was also here. So it would seem as if all troops were being concentrated here. I hope the matter will be decided here. I feel confident we shall win; but you don't want to hear platitudes from me.

About getting into the Regular Army, I am in earnest. I don't like Vols. at all & shall stay with them no longer than I can help. Now I stay because I am serving my country. I do not want money. I have some $30 yet, and do not spend much, for there is little to buy here. I eat with the men & draw an extra ration for the Company, as all officers do here. I believe all sutlers are sent away from the Landing at City Point. About the Col.'s papers—there is no magistrate here at all. What shall be the substitute? He expects to be in New York in a few days if his furlough is granted.

6 P.M.—

We have passed a very quiet 4th. The national salute has been fired, and the bands have, by Genl. McClellan's order, again begun to play. I hope they will relieve us from picket to-morrow, as for the last 10 days we have had no rest. Genl. Kearny is, I beg to say, a conscience-stricken man & has to work incessantly to keep his mind quiet. Hence the work heaped on his Division, by his own wish. I had my hair cut today by Lieut. Miller's boy, who is a barber by trade; he cut it à la Zouave, and it is very comfortable. It does not matter how one looks here and I intend to pass a good night.

CHAPTER THREE

Waiting at Harrison's Landing

July 6 to August 4, 1862

Harrison's Landing on the James, some twenty miles southeast of Richmond, was so well guarded by artillery and gunboats that Lee set a watch on it and fell back to recruit the Army of Northern Virginia in preparation for the Federals' next move. That move was a matter of hot debate. McClellan, imaginatively doubling the actual count of the enemy he faced, demanded vast reinforcements. President Lincoln brought Henry Halleck from the western theater to be general-in-chief. Halleck argued for abandoning the Peninsula campaign in favor of combining the Army of the Potomac with John Pope's newly formed Army of Virginia in front of Washington.

While this high command argument raged, Lieutenant Dodge and his comrades waited in ignorance and in general discomfort in the Harrison's Landing camps. In his July 7 journal entry Dodge speaks of being inspirited by McClellan's July 4 address to his army, an address that transmuted a headlong retreat into a change of base "by a flank movement." This and the other fictions studding the address served at least to raise morale in the sweltering camps. Dodge also mentions writing to his father, who was aboard the Euterpe, *a vessel bound for the Peninsula with a cargo of medical supplies under the charge of the elder Dodge.*

Sunday July 6th /62

Received your welcome letters of the 26th, 30th & 1st yesterday. They of course afforded me the greatest joy. Lieut. Verdi has disappeared since the 1st. I have written to his brother. Lieut. Catlin, a relative of Kearny's, ditto. Genl. K. appointed him Provost Marshal of the Division, but on finding he had been absent without leave at once told him he must undergo a court martial or resign: he has done the latter. The same is here concerning several other officers who were the bragging portion of the Regiment. About the consolidation of the 101st and the 38th nothing further has transpired, nor about the Colonel's resignation. I sincerely hope Father can come on here and see me. I should be in ecstasies to see him again. This life makes one think much of home.

Our Division is still in the same position in the advance. Each Regiment has intrenched itself and covered its front with pickets thrown out some half a mile, so that we are often called under arms. We are getting rested, however. By the way, our address is "101st N.Y., Birney's Brigade, Kearny's Division, Army of the Potomac." It is useless to put in "Heintzelman's Corps." I received yesterday letters from Mrs. G. and Mr. G. of the 1st ult. [ultimate; the previous month]. I wrote the few words I sent you yesterday before receiving the letters, which please tell them when you write.

The weather is hot, but I do not suffer at all from it. The wagons have come and I have got my blankets and things, so I shall be more comfortable now. About my diet. I find that living upon hard bread, crackers and meat is very healthy. My bowels were never in better order than when I live like this.

This morning the Regiment went out on fatigue, I, though unwell, going with Company G, as there is no other officer. I had to come back, however. I have a little touch of bilious diarrhoea and fever, and must be careful of myself. Sick men cannot, except under stringent conditions, leave the Army. Capt. Mitchell is very unwell but cannot procure a furlough. If possible, if I get ill, I shall make for the "Euterpe." At all events, I will write Father, who can do much. But don't be alarmed, I shall not suffer.

Henry has gone to the Landing to buy me a pair of boots, mine being all worn out. I wrote you to send me instanter, by mail or express, a new pair of "specs," as mine, which were slender, have broken, and I have to wear glasses. Do send them at once. They must be strong, but not too heavy. Henry is a good honest boy, and takes great care of me. He is fully worth $15 per month.

Do as Roy does and look on the bright side of things. I love to have you cheer me. If you feel down-hearted, it makes me so too. All the news we get, we get from New York papers, and we look anxiously for them. I will send you letters often; you do the same. Tell me if my journal is broken off anywhere, as in that case a letter must have been lost. Don't be alarmed at my having a little fever. It will pass off by tomorrow. Dr. V. takes good care of me. Have Dr. Westlake put me up some more of the pills, and send them: they are admirable. I have just got a cup of lemonade—how good and refreshing it tastes!

I hope the war will soon be over now, so I can see you all again. You are much on my heart. Being in danger makes me love to think of you. I think the Rebels have something else to think of than attacking us here. How splendidly our men fought all the week of the retreat! They are heroes. The Colonel says he never saw such bravery. The loss of our Regiment was only some 120. But the Rebels fought most desperately too. Write me nice long cheerful letters. Love to all dear ones.

Monday July 7th [1862], A.M.

This is a very quiet place, where we are getting quite a rest. It is very seldom we have to fall to arms during the day. Only every morning, at 2 1/2 till daylight, we have to be in line to prevent surprise, just those couple of hours being the time most appropriate for attacks. I wrote Father yesterday on board the "Euterpe." I don't know whether he will get the letter. I feel much better today, and think that I shall soon be all right again. I intended sending the scraps yesterday, but delayed. I think I shall write a few words to Charley Dewey. I am waiting with the utmost interest the arrival of the New York newspapers; as through them alone can we obtain any substantial information.

4 P.M.—

I feel quite well this afternoon and have eaten a good dinner. It has been very hot and I have taken a good bath, which has tended to refresh me. It is universally acknowledged that the last fortnight's work has been the severest campaigning done yet on the Peninsula, but we are rewarded by knowing that we have made a successful flank movement, which places us in a better position than before. We have just received Genl. McClellan's order of the 4th inst., which is very inspiriting.

We are in a very nice quiet place though in the advance. We send out one Company every day to protect our front as a picket, how far out I don't know as my Company has not yet been out. I wish we could have more officers. You see that I have so much to do, being all alone in my Company, that when I feel at all unwell it is very hard on me. I have a sort of feeling as if Father would come on and see me. I much desire it. I think the Colonel's resignation will be accepted. I am sorry and if Brown is to be in command, I shall feel very much like resigning too. If I could get a place elsewhere I most certainly should, but I shall not be rash and besides it don't look well to resign in front of the enemy.

My stock of clothing has run short through these forced marches. All my silk handkerchiefs, all but two pair of socks &c &c are gone. I shall have to refurnish when we get thro' with this campaign.

The resignation of Enrico Fardella as colonel of the 101st dismayed both the regiment and Lieutenant Dodge. His appraisal of Fardella suggests that this old veteran of Europe's wars was not at ease commanding American volunteers—and, as Kearny noted, he had a language problem. In addition to the military treatise Dodge mentions, the colonel presented his lieutenant with a testimonial praising him as "a gentleman and a soldier in all your actions. You have guided

your Company with intelligence in its administration, and with courage and coolness in 3 battles." The G. F. Train who Dodge cites from his newspaper reading was George Francis Train, a loud and eccentric promoter who had aligned himself with that noted military eccentric, General Benjamin F. Butler.

July 8th [1862], noon

Well, Col. Fardella has gone! We have been under an ill star ever since we started and this is the culminating point. The 101st is doomed. Lieut. Col. Brown took the Regiment out on picket this morning and said no good bye to Col. Fardella. Almost all the officers (the old Hancock officers I mean) stayed behind to see the Colonel off. As the picket where we are is not hazardous, I stayed back because I am very weak. The Colonel sold his horse this morning to the Adjutant of the 40th New York Volunteers, for $150. He took a very kind leave of all of us. I had the last shake of the hand and word with him. He gave me a book, the "Secondary Operations of War," in Italian, which I have often spoken to you about as a good book to translate. I prize it much. He seemed in good spirits about seeing Italy again, but not about leaving us all.

Col. Fardella is a man whom I respect, and love much as a friend. I honor his integrity which was white as snow. I love his good qualities which were many. He was very kind to me at all times, though, since I have been alone in my Company, I have not been so much with him as in the beginning. He is a man of undoubted merit as a gentleman and a soldier; he is noble and full of courage. Nevertheless, though his perception is keener than that of most men, he never thoroughly (except in a few points) understood the American character. This was the reason he was not appreciated here. Everyone who talked with him acknowledged his merits fully, but generally he did not do as we American officers do. Show Col. Fardella the enemy and he would beat twice the number he himself had;

but put in woods as we continually have been, and not know-ing—as most Colonels do not—the position or strength of the enemy, he was not in his element. On the plains of Europe he has won renown; in our American forests he could not do his best. But be all this as it may, he was a gentleman and a man of justice, kindness of heart, honor; and as a friend I honor and love him. I hope to see him in Italy again, if it be best. I shall write to him.

I feel much better though yet weak. I shall soon get strong again. That terrible fortnight's work was enough to kill a horse. Read the *Philadelphia Enquirer* of the 5th inst. It gives the best account of what I saw and experienced of any paper I have seen. Do you see that G. F. Train has been coming it strong again? But he defends Genl. Butler, though he don't need any defense, very well.

I think we shall stay here some time. Now that Colonel Fardella has gone, I hope we shall be consolidated with the 38th. Again I say, do try and get me a place in the Regular Army, if you can; I don't like to be with the Browns'. Just think of Brown's never taking leave of or noticing Col. Fardella; it was so mean an action: after all the Colonel's kindness and friendly actions towards him. I guess Brown has an evil eye on me. In a few weeks I think all the old Hancock officers will re-sign; they say they will accept them in a few weeks' time.

The announced consolidation of the 101st and 38th New York regi-ments, of Birney's brigade, would not in fact be effected. Colonel Ward's direction of the 101st was only a temporary arrangement until a new colonel was appointed to replace the resigned Fardella. It would be under that new regime that Dodge would accept the post of regimental adjutant. The Elias Peissner he mentions was a family acquaintance, who was indeed just then raising an infantry regi-ment in New York. During Lincoln's visit to Harrison's Landing on

July 8, McClellan claimed that he had to order the troops to cheer the president; by Dodge's testimony, no such order was necessary, at least for Birney's brigade.

July 9th [1862], 8 A.M.

It was read at dress parade to the 38th yesterday that the consolidation of the 101st had been effected. Well, I am glad, though it lessens my chance of promotion.

Old Abe passed our camp last evening and was heartily cheered by those who remained there, tho' the Regiment mainly were on picket duty. He was accompanied by a large suite; he bowed graciously.

I feel pretty well this A.M. though not so strong as usual. I took a strong dose of medicine yesterday and it drove away my complaint, which is probably the result of our late fatigue and exposure. I received your letter of the 3rd yesterday. Do not fear for me. I have been in very little danger compared with some of our brave boys, but I have seen enough to know what war really is.

I am on guard but the duties are not arduous. Lieut. Colonel Brown asked me to be Adjutant in place of Lamont, which position I shall decline. We are going to send recruiting officers to New York; I should not mind going.

It is wonderful how want of eatables quickens the inventive faculties in cooking. For example, I had on hand for my breakfast this A.M. 12 pilot crackers, 1 lump of salt fat pork, coffee and sugar. With this my darkie presented me the following bill of fare: fried pilot crackers, made by soaking said crackers 2 hours in water and then frying them in pork fat, with salt and pepper, which I assure you was quite palatable. Breakfast cakes made of soaked pilot crackers fried in fat and eaten with sugar—all washed down with some good coffee but without milk. Don't I live well? For dinner I hope to secure a piece of ham, to which I trust to add some stewed apples.

Yesterday my boy managed to secure me a salt mackerel; how delicious it tasted you can't imagine. My table is the ground, my table furniture a pocket knife, fork, spoon and cup, and several pieces of board off which I eat. Sometimes, when gravy accompanies the dish, I eat out of the frying pan (which is borrowed for the occasion, there being but one in the Regiment). This is hand to mouth living I reckon. In Europe campaigning is different—there one can probably get anything, owing to the fact that large towns and villages abound; but in this vast & thinly populated region, it is almost impossible to get what you want. If you buy of the sutlers, you have to pay the most extravagant prices. For instance, $2 for a shilling bottle of pickles, and other things in proportion. It is very hot. We have no thermometer but the perspiration rolls out of every pore, even when one sits still, running down in streams under our clothes.

July 9 P.M.—

Things look as if we were going to stop here for some time. I wish more would transpire about this consolidation. Col. Ward issued an order taking command, saying that divisions (every 2 Companies in line make a division) must be consolidated into Companies, "Senior Officers to take command." Now if Companies G and H are consolidated, there are 5 officers: two Captains, two 1st Lieutenants and one 2nd ditto, of which I am 4th in seniority. What position would I hold in the consolidated Company? One thing is certain, I have my Commission as 1st Lieutenant and I shall not act at any lower grade. But wait and see—wait and see. I have sent my boy down to the Landing to see if he can procure anything for supper. I hope he will.

July 10 [1862]

Last evening, after dress parade, Col. Ward called the officers of the 101st to him, and told us that the organization of our Regiment was to remain entirely intact under command of Brown; that consolidating two Companies into one was simply making divisions act as Companies in field evolutions. Thus my chances of promotion are not destroyed. He also assured us that he should exact the most rigid discipline from the officers and men. The state of the 101st under our present commander is dubious indeed. Again I beg you to try and get me a transfer into some other Regiment. I should like immensely to be with Peissner; can't it be done?

My period of guard is drawing to a close, and I can have a rest. Last night it was a lovely moonlight. It was warm and I spread my India rubber under a tree and lay down, the moon shining full in my face. I have often heard of the influence of the moon on a person sleeping. I fell asleep and for two hours had the most erratic, wild and terrifying visions conceivable; it is useless to try and tell you of them. I awoke with a start, the muscles of my face contracted, my eyes almost blinded and weary and weak. I changed my position to the shade: my visions became varied and changeable, none were of war, all of them peaceful and quiet.

10 A.M.—

A change has taken place in the Regiment. Adjutant Lamont has thrown up his position and his resignation has been accepted. After this was done, Capt. Allen (acting Major) came to me with the order to proceed at once to fill the position vacated by Lamont.

I went to Lieut. Col. Brown and, thanking him for his kind intentions in appointing me on his Staff, begged leave to decline his offer. Of course I did this most politely. Brown told me he thought he was advancing my interests in making me his Adjutant and had therefore done it; and moreover said I was the only officer in the Regiment who would make a good Adjutant. I thanked him again for his kindness, but told him I was attached to my Company and did not want to leave it. I should like to be Adjutant above all things with a Colonel for whom I have some respect, but not under Brown. He seemed considerably annoyed at my refusal. I should like much to be Peissner's Adjutant; and, if he raises a Regiment, will willingly exchange with any Lieutenant in it.

I am quite well again, so don't be alarmed about my health. I am candid and tell you all, so don't imagine all sorts of troubles for me.

Nathaniel S. Dodge was a man with good connections, and he wrangled a civilian pass to Harrison's Landing to see his son by conducting what he described as "1,000 valuable cases" of medical supplies to Fortress Monroe aboard the steamer Euterpe. *In a letter home, the elder Dodge observed of the Harrison's Landing encampment, "Poor fellows, they are nearly starved and are living like pigs." Soon enough, however, Lieutenant Dodge reported his lifestyle considerably improved, and joked about his resemblance to Bombastes Furioso, the bombastic general in William Barnes Rhodes's 1810 burlesque opera. General Kearny's crackdown, mentioned in the July 15 entry, was an attempt to rein in abuses of sick leave by which thousands evaded further army service.*

July 12 [1862], morning

Yesterday was the first day since I left Fort Lyon that I have not written a journal; and yet it was the most important one. Father was here!!! I felt so much satisfaction in seeing him, that the desire of communicating with you, which journalizing satisfies, did not arise within me.

We have had a thoroughly rainy day, and now again must look for some severe hot weather. Father will tell you about our mode of living &c. Capt. Lyle expressed it well. He said in reply to someone who said we were living like swine: "Why I am ashamed to look a well nurtured hog in the face. The swine at home have good beds, comfortable meals, and shelter. Oh! that I was a hog in my Father's pen!"

I managed before the rain of day before yesterday to secure an old condemned tent from the Brigade Q. M. and erected therein a bed. I can scarce give you a description of the beauties of this arrangement, but Father will perhaps be able to discourse upon its superior qualities. It is fabricated of 4 upright crutch sticks, about 2 feet from the ground, which represent the posts. Across these are two poles, one at the head and one at the feet and from one to the other are laid supple young trees so that the horizontal section on which I lie is something like a mattress—as you can imagine, a most soft and flexible couch.

Yesterday we (Lieut. Miller and I, who have lately struck up a tacit sort of friendship) managed to secure some dried apples, and Henry made us a large dish of stewed apple, which I assure you was acceptable. Lieut. Col. Brown is going (I hear) to open a sutler's store, and vend wares himself.

July 13 [1862], noon

The hurrah! of my last was well timed. Lieut. Col. Brown has proved himself in one thing a brick! He went down to the Landing and bought (by permission of the Provost) on board a boat, a wagon load of good things, and sold them to us officers at nil profit. Miller and I dined last night off mutton and currant jelly, bean soup, apple fritters, and washed all down with a bottle of good claret! How good it was you can't imagine unless you have fasted as long as we have. It really was very good of Col. B. to take all that trouble for us. We have now bread and butter, which I have not tasted before since we left Fort Lyon; vegetables, including potatoes, carrots, onions, and peas, meat *ad libitum*, preserves, and claret, together with an assortment of cakes. All these at reasonable prices for this place.

59

We were mustered for pay yesterday afternoon, but will not be paid probably till after the end of August. I have been writing all the A.M. making out my pay rolls. I wish I could go to church with you today. We have no service here. Love to all. Has Polly come home from her gay tour yet? How I wish I could fly home for a day or two. Oh! that I had the wings of a dove &c &c.

Monday July 14th [1862], 4 P.M.

We have marched out on picket for 24 hours, and are posted half a mile beyond the swamp which protects our camp, the Reserve being at a large farm house. I am luckily today in the Reserve, for I am by no means well and could scarce do my duty thoroughly in the advance. My long living on crackers and water has so weakened my digestive organs that almost all my food passes my bowels in a crude state. I told my boy to get me some dandelions today, and I shall try Father's dandelion cure.

The weather is warm, but very agreeable. My Company has stacked arms in the farmyard and I have ensconced myself in an old wagon full of corn stalks, which will make a capital bed for the night. In the farm house (whose owner is in Richmond) there is a little boy, a nephew of the owner, the only white inhabitant. Besides him there are only negroes.

I received today 2 letters from Father, from Fortress Monroe, and yours and Polly's of the 10th and 11th. I am glad you have received my journal. It is as complete as circumstances would allow, for I have kept a daily record of events. Lieut. Col. B. is ill and not able to be out today. Ditto Major Sniper, so that the command devolves on Capt. Allen. I am happy to hear that you, dear Mother, are so well. Roy must take great pleasure in his aides. I hope Polly will have a nice visit in Pittsfield.

I am the most unlucky of mortals; today I lost my pocket knife and my gold pencil and holder, which are not replaceable here. I hope to find them again, however. I also lost the brass point off the end of my scabbard, so that my sword protrudes like that of Bombastes Furioso. This is the greatest of the losses, but I shall institute a strict search for it.

You ask me if I am acting Captain. Certainly, Lieut. commanding means that; and I have had no Captain in Company G since I last saw you. I have been Captain all the time, with the exception of not having the Commission; and worse, have never had a Lieutenant to assist me, have done the work of three officers myself. Only on one occasion have I had any help—when Verdi was in my Company at the Battle of White Oak Swamp, and then he lay behind a stump all the time, and I was continually running from right to left of the Company (those deployed as skirmishers in the wood in front of the Division) and back again. Verdi may be a nice fellow, but he can't stand fire, I'm very sorry to say.

July 15 [1862], 4 A.M.

We sent out a scouting party yesterday, who met a party of our cavalry, who had been all the way to Bottom's Bridge over the Chickahominy without seeing a Rebel; so you see our picketing here is not quite so dangerous as it used to be. The cavalry party came across a herd of cattle, some 15 head and some calves, which they drove within our lines. This was quite a godsend. I hope they will give us some of the fresh beef.

When you once get used to it, you have no idea how delicious it is to sleep in the open air on these beautiful summer nights. I tried to sleep under a shed last night in the wagon referred to above, but before midnight I was fain to change my couch to beneath a tree, where I enjoyed a sweet delicious sleep. Of course you know a portion of the Reserve is allowed to sleep, one third of them watching all the time, and hence one can sleep without anxiety.

10 A.M.—

We were relieved this A.M. by the 3rd Maine and came into camp. I am a good deal better, but have not yet found the dandelions to effect the cure of my system. I think however a dollar will fetch them somehow. The trouble is the fields are all so cut up by wagons and camps. Henry found my knife and pencil yesterday. The wagons are going down to the Landing this A.M. and will fetch up the bag Father has sent me. The mail of this morning brought me a pair of spectacles which Cousin Mary sent me, and Father's letter from Baltimore.

In Kearny's Division one can neither get a sick leave nor an excuse from duty for a day even without application to the Division surgeon. The Regimental surgeon or the Brigade surgeon can neither give a sick excuse. But one thing is certain, as long as I can stand I will do my duty, as I did yesterday; but if I am really sick abed, I can't do it, that's certain. The fact is Kearny wants to show his Division off as being the one which has fewest sick or in which the fewest officers resign. He probably wants promotion and he *deserves* it; but this is not the way to set to work. In this Division it is said, "Yes, you can have your resignation accepted, but it must be on the plea of cowardice." But that wouldn't frighten me at all—my own conscience would be satisfactory; but what I rely on is exchange into another Regiment, and I guess Father can do something.

Send me next mail some pencil leads you will find among my traps somewhere. Cousin Mary wrote me a note when she sent the spectacles—a very kind note. The weather is very hot and the perspiration streams from every pore.

The so-called Kearny patch that Dodge mentions in his July 17 entry was a diamond-shaped patch of red flannel that Kearny had devised

for the men in his division to wear, his intent being to discourage straggling. It became a symbol of unit pride, however, and served as inspiration for the corps badges that the Army of the Potomac would adopt during Joe Hooker's time of command. The decision of Dodge's father to take the post of quartermaster in Elias Peissner's new regiment—to be designated the 119th New York—marked the first step in Theodore Dodge's eventual move to that regiment.

July 16th [1862]

We had Brigade drill yesterday at 6, but before we had maneuvered an hour a terrible thunderstorm came up, at which we left the ground at double quick & "To Your Tents Oh Israel" was sounded. The storm ceased before 9 o'clock, and we passed a comfortable enough night. Poor Miller has been ill the last two days with an aggravated form of what troubles me all the time. He is better today.

I must get some medicine in lieu of dandelions, of which we can get none here. I think some good liquor would do me good. I found out yesterday to my disgust that the parcels directed here would not come from Fortress Monroe unless an order be sent from the person they are directed to. The reason is, they don't want to load up their boats with parcels which will never be called for. I sent the order. Of course Father's parcel will not come till two or three days are past. I am Officer of the Day today, and I have organized the camp very creditably, & discipline by reason of some seven punishments reigns supreme. The Field officer of the day and Colonel B. complimented me highly.

July 17th [1862], 6 A.M.

Have just received yours of the 14th from New York. We had a terrible storm last night. Our camp inclines down hill from right to left, and for about two hours, Miller and I sat on a box in our tent with our feet on our beds and a stream of six or seven inches deep running through our tent all the time. The whole camp was inundated to the depth of several inches. It soon subsided however. I was Officer of the Day and consequently had to be round the camp. I took off my shoes and stockings and waded. The thunder was frightful. A tree fell right at the door of our tent, thrown down by the wind—two feet more and it would have crushed Miller and myself to atoms, as we sat in our tent. It was a narrow escape, and when it came down you better believe it made us duck our heads. It completely barred the entrance to the tent.

Lieut. Wood (who has I hear been a tinker's apprentice all his life and who is a rank abolitionist) was yesterday the cause of a cruel tragedy here in camp. He had a negro servant, who fell ill with chills and fever, of which two or three days' care would have cured him. But Wood never went near him or gave him anything to eat for 4 days, until yesterday he was seized by spasms and in that storm, during which Wood left him out on the ground, he died. How little people, who rank as servants at home, know how to treat servants. When I heard he was ill, I immediately had the doctor go to see him and give him some restoratives—but it was too late. The neglect had killed him.

You would be sorry for our poor boys if you could see them in a thunderstorm. You know we lost all our baggage, tents &c at White Oak Swamp, when we were ordered to leave all on the field, & move up at double quick to support Randolph's Battery before the battle. Well, since then our boys have not been able to get tents. Either there are none, or the Quarter Master is not clever enough to get hold of them. It is not hard sleeping out of doors fine nights, in fact I much prefer it to a tent, but when it rains as it did yesterday, our poor boys have to take it right in the open, and when the rain is over lie down wet through and often in the water, to sleep. They come to me and complain. I of course cannot help them and it makes me feel how hard a soldier's life is, in active service. I tell you this makes a man something of a man, all these hardships. "I ought to have a tent," says one to me. "So you ought, my boy, and I would do anything to get you one, but how can I get one for you when there are none here?" But they can't see why they should be left out in the rain without tents.

It is said, and I believe with truth, that in other Divisions they are giving furloughs whilst in this one (Kearny's) a man may be on his death bed and he cannot get a sick leave. It is too bad and yet it is an honor to belong to Kearny's Division; but it is dearly bought. All the officers in this Division wear a piece of red flannel on their caps—the Line officers in front and the Field officers on the top. This is the distinguishing mark.

July 18th [1862]

Again last night the inevitable thunderstorm, but not as severe as the one on the evening before. This morning the air is very close. It is said that during this & the next month our locality is healthy, but that after the beginning of September it is much the contrary. Even now fever prevails. Two or three poor fellows are dying in the regimental hospital.

I wrote Cousin Mary Platt yesterday, thanking her for the spectacles. So you "forgive me even these" do you? You forgive them for "the dangers they have passed." Indeed they were dangers, as the sequel proved, wherein the specs lost their life. It was during a stormy night, when the blanket was pulled over them, & proved too rough for their fragile form. They died not on the battlefield, but yet in their country's cause.

Miller's and my diet is now exclusively vegetable. We live on potatoes, rice, apples, and hard bread with certain condiments, which Henry cooks up in magnificent style. We have not tasted meat for a week. I shall send down to the Landing today to see if my bag has arrived. Our life now is woefully monotonous. There is always some little anxiety from not knowing what will happen next moment, but here we sit and lie all day long—nothing to do, nothing to read, and perspiring to such a degree as to deprive one of all energy.

Sunday July 20th [1862], 1 P.M.

I have just received yours of the 16th, per hand of the Company cook, who has brought the boys some meat for dinner out to our picket. We have 6 Regiments in our Brigade: the 38th, 101st, 40th, 99th N.Y. and the 3rd and 4th Maine, and every sixth day comes our turn to go out on picket. This time we are stationed as a sort of telegraph between two important points, and behind a swamp which the Rebels would scarce essay to cross. We are only some mile or so from camp, and behind the advanced picket. Hence I feel justified in spreading my blanket beneath a maple tree and spending my time mostly in sleeping, reading, and writing to you.

As you see, my letter acknowledges the receipt of the pencil you sent out (a blue everpointed pencil), just the thing, as everything you send me always is. I wrote to Father yesterday acknowledging the receipt of spectacle frames and divers bits of broken glass, both "orbs" being crushed in the post, and at the same time returning them for repair in the case in which Cousin Mary sent hers, which came to hand intact. I read the extract you sent me some time ago (a scrap speaking of the healthiness of the locality of their camp). Now the Rebels seem to have changed their minds, and to vote our "resting place" malarious.

I was glad Father has taken the berth of Quarter Master with Peissner. I hope he will like it and I long to be with him. I received yesterday a note from him informing me of his movements. I received by today's mail a letter from Pinkie of the 7th. Somewhat detained on the road. I hope Genl. Burnside will join us, for I know Collie would like being here a month. I am sure no advance will be made by us until heavy, very heavy reinforcements join us; and the Rebels would be great fools were they to attack us as we could whip them most unmercifully.

Our line is picketed, as I said before, behind a swamp, and in a wood of maple and beech trees, shady and pleasant; tho' the last day or two the weather has been very cool. No noise breaks the almost melancholy stillness, except now and then the boom of artillery, coming seemingly from the river, or the sharp crack of a rifle, probably fired by some novice at picketing, regardless of the 49th Article of War. Of course some excuse is always made by said novice, and as he does not in any great measure "alarm camp or garrison," nothing is said. Many stray shots are fired on picket. In camp it is different: there we are strict, and I am sorry to say that two of my men are now at Head Quarters awaiting a court martial for "willful discharging of fire arms."

Q. M. Bellows has not yet sent to the Landing for the things the Express must 'ere this have brought me, but I hope he will do so today. Life here is getting so monotonous that you must not hope for a lively journal, as you had some time ago when events trod upon each others' heels. How well I know the passage of Milton you quote. How often have I pondered its beauty.

July 22nd [1862]

Absolute lack of news obliges me for a little to discontinue my journal, till something turns up. I have written to Father two or three times and suppose he communicates with you. I should much like to get a furlough to go to New York for a few days, but there is little hope of it, I fear. Write often.

Late July and early August saw upheaval in the 101st New York and in Lieutenant Dodge's circumstances as well. There was a petition

for a change of command aimed at the then-senior officer, Lieutenant Colonel Johnson Brown. At the same time, Brown was plying Lieutenant Dodge with promises of a captaincy and a posting to New York for recruiting duty, in return for his agreement to become regimental adjutant. With apparent reluctance, Dodge took the job— and then welcomed the appointment of Lieutenant Colonel Nelson A. Gesner, from the 40th New York, to command the regiment. Dodge's concern that Phil Kearny would be moved up to corps command did not materialize. Kearny remained at the head of his division during the next (and his last) campaign.

July 23rd [1862]

I saw Col. Brown: he will send on the recommendations at once and list of vacancies. He will nominate me, and tho' I shall be Capt. of Company G, yet my Commission will not date back to Buckham's resignation, but that of the senior 1st Lieutenant will do so. However, except in getting $20 per month back pay since that time, there will be little difference. Brown means to do the right thing by me, but whether it is "blarney" or a desire to secure Father's services for the Regiment (I think the latter), he does not seem to wish to let me go.

Camp Kearny July 24, 1862

Our life here has grown so monotonous that it is impossible to find anything worth journalizing so I must content myself with writing you an occasional letter.

Yesterday A.M. at 7, we formed in line and marched down to a large plain near the river, for review. Genl. McClellan, who had the day before reviewed Sumner's Corps, was to review ours. We drew up in close column in order of battle— Kearny's Division on the right, Hooker's in the centre, and Sedgwick's on the left. When we had got our relative positions we deployed into line by Battalions, i.e. each Battalion formed line of battle on its own ground. Out of each Brigade of six

Regiments one was on picket, and one left behind to guard camp, so that only two thirds of the Corps was out.

On the right of each Brigade was the Brigade band. Genl. McClellan and Staff, as soon as the parade was formed (which for some 15 or 20,000 men took 2 or 3 hours) came down from Head Quarters and received a salute of 13 guns from Hooker's artillery. He then rode down to the right, taking a line so as to pass in front and rear of each Regiment. As he passed, colors saluted, and when he passed from one Brigade to another, the band of the one he left behind ceased playing and the next band began. Thus he rode thro' the whole Corps. He then took up his stand at the colors, and we passed in review in column by division (i.e. division of 2 Companies, 5 to each Regiment, not general Division). In passing our Regiment he said to Kearny, who of course rode by his side, "A fine Regiment this, what is it?"

Genl. McClellan's pictures look very like him. He is very stout looking in the face and a fine man. The difference between the appearance of the Staff here and in Europe is wonderful. Instead of the gold and glitter of uniforms and horse trappings which you see there, here it is with everyone alike the simple blue coat with shoulder straps, nothing showy, scarcely handsome. But for service, we have shown it does just about as well.

Camp Kearny July 29th [1862]

I wrote you about the change of commander—Lieut. Col. Gesner, 40th New York, now commanding the 101st, is in every way an officer fit to discipline a Regiment to the highest pitch.

Things have gone "up stairs" fast during the two days he has had command. Lieut. Col. Brown feels that his nose is broken, but he wisely holds his tongue. Genl. Birney heard about our petition, which was also signed by the Major. He condemns the petition but approves the motive that started it. The change of Company officers is a step in the right direction made by him. He said to the Major this A.M., "Keep quiet and all will go right: Gesner Col., you Lieut. Col. and one of your Captains, Major, would make a good Regiment of the 101st. Your material is second to none in the service. A Board of Examiners shall be appointed and we'll see." This will be done and Brown will disappear.

We are hard at work drilling and organizing our forces here. Our Division drills 3 or 4 hours daily and strict discipline is enforced. The past campaign affected the perfection of the discipline very materially. Reveillé is at 4 1/2 A.M.; from 9 A.M. to 6 P.M. we do nothing, it being so hot (frequently 100° and more in the shade). Miller and I have got a nice large tent and an awning of leaves in front, under which a table and benches. Here we spend our day.

August 1st [1862]

Genl. Kearny is a Major General. He received his promotion this A.M. He will, it is said, have a Corps under Burnside; & we shall lose our General and the eclat of being in his Division. This will indeed be a loss and our bit of red flannel will have to be banished. We go on picket tomorrow. The pickets have been advanced 1 1/2 miles so that they are now 3 1/2 miles in front of our line. As soon as I get my leave of absence for recruiting, I shall be off like a shot. I shall have a "pal," or brother officer, and ten men, one from each Company. I expect it will cost me some little money, but I am very willing to spend it to get North again.

August 3rd [1862]

The order to send officers on recruiting service has not yet arrived at Head Quarters of the Brigade, but probably will in a short time. As soon as it does, the Colonel will name me and,

I hope, Miller as the officers to be sent. I shall make up to Brown to effect this object, and altho' this is somewhat Jesuitical—*pour quoi non*? I think I have something Jesuitical in my system. Did I get it at Trilemont?

I received a letter from George Jackson this morning, saying that my Commission as Capt. would be sent me as soon as a list of vacancies and promotions reached Albany. This is already done. Won't Brother George be glad to hear of my promotion? So they are going to draft in New York State, eh, after the 15th inst.? That will soon fill us up; much as I want to see the new Regiments filled up, there is no doubt but what the old Regiments ought to be filled up first.

We were out on picket yesterday; our lines were advanced some mile or so. Some 6,000 men have crossed the river. I wonder if this means a move. There have been rumors of a "skedaddle," but I don't credit them. Lieut. Brown, the Quarter Master, offered to bet me $60 48 hours ago that before this we should be away from here on a retreat. It was a safe bet, but I did not take it, as I don't bet.

Camp Kearny August 4th [1862]

Things go on in so monotonous a manner here that I cannot scrape together any news which would afford you any interest, hence my long silence. I have trusted to Father to tell you of my welfare. It is possible (scarcely probable I fear) that I may be sent home on recruiting service. How much I desire this you can imagine, and how hard I shall work to bring it about.

We are always having terrible accidents from careless use of firearms. A poor fellow of Capt. McCarty's Company shot his arm the other day, by accident, so it had to be amputated below the elbow. I was Officer of the Day and as the surgeon had not help enough I was present at the operation, and lent all the aid my little skill could afford. Poor fellow, when the

71

chloroform passed off he cried like a child in grief for having lost it. One pities a poor fellow who is so unfortunate.

We go on picket every 6 days, not very hard work that; and as Secesh [sessionists] are some distance off we are not troubled much. The march out and back is the chief inconvenience. We picketed last some 3 miles in advance of where we camp, and beyond the protecting swamp. I don't think any immediate move can be in contemplation.

CHAPTER FOUR

To the Plains of Manassas

August 11 to September 1, 1862

While the argument about what to do with McClellan's Army of the Potomac dragged on, General Lee took the offensive against the threat of John Pope's Army of Virginia. Stonewall Jackson was sent north from Richmond with orders to "suppress" Pope, and defeated Pope's advance at Cedar Mountain on August 9. From General-in-Chief Halleck now came orders to McClellan to evacuate the Peninsula and combine his army with Pope's. The moment Lee detected this movement, he marched north with the rest of his army to deal with Pope before the Federals could combine forces against him. He succeeded, with scant hours to spare. Only a limited number of McClellan's troops (including Kearny's division, with the 101st New York) had reached Pope at Manassas before Lee brought his foe to battle on August 29 and 30, and defeated him in what Northerners called the Second Battle of Bull Run. After a sharp fight at Chantilly on September 1, the Federals completed their retreat into the Washington fortifications.

What Theodore Dodge termed his "journalizing" was sharply limited during this campaign by the press of his duties as adjutant of the 101st and by a steadily worsening bout with typhoid fever. The best he could manage were bare-bones entries in a pocket diary. In the fighting on August 29, Dodge was slightly wounded, and at Chantilly on September 1, badly wounded. Between his wounds and the typhoid, Lieutenant Dodge would be out of action for almost three months. While spending part of his recuperation at home in New York, he dictated a narrative of the campaign for his journal, basing his account on the entries in his pocket diary.

The following journal entries, for August 11–14, record the confusion of preparations for the evacuation of the Peninsula. Dodge still has a hope of going north to recruit for his regiment, a hope that does not materialize. Indeed, the 101st New York will go into battle at Second Bull Run with but 168 men in its ranks.

Camp Kearny Aug. 11th [1862], noon

I would have written you yesterday, but as Adjutant I had to make out so many reports that I could not. Today we had an order to march at 3 P.M.—have got all ready. The whole Army is on the move, probably to Fortress Monroe. As all cannot go by transports, we (of course Kearny does all *the work*) have to march, and shall have, I believe, to go over Bottom's Bridge, right in the teeth of the Rebels unless they have recently vacated. There is a rumor (which of course I don't believe) that Pope has been driven back on Washington by Jackson. Anyhow, Jackson is the most extraordinary man! Kearny is the only man I would like to fight under against him, with equal forces. More anon.

August 12th [1862], 7 A.M.

After all was packed up and ready to start, we got orders countermanding the first to march. So we slept last night under lofty pine trees. Our harvest moon is so beautiful that this is really greater luxury than those who have never tried it can imagine. Unless it rains, I always prefer taking my blanket and throwing myself down under a tree in the open air. I guess we shall move today. I wish we were going in transports. A march of 90 miles to Fortress Monroe, in hot weather, is not an agreeable prospect.

The very morning (yesterday) this order came, Col. Gesner was going to send in my name to be sent on recruiting service, as I am almost too ill to do my duty here.

I received your letter of the 9th last night. I want to go to Peissner's Regiment.

Noon—

It is probable we may stay here 3 or 4 days. This morning Colonel Gesner sent my name, Lieut. Wood's, and ten men, for recruiting service. In 3 or 4 days it would have probably come back and, unless disapproved, which (as General Orders No. 88 give instructions to send in names) I don't think possible, I should then come North. With such a chance before me, the prospect of a retreat, such as that from Fair Oaks, is not pleasant, though no one shall ever be able to say I hesitated or failed to do my duty under any and all circumstances. This delay of 3 or 4 days makes me think the whole Army will go by water, which before was not the intention.

If you go to Copake, you might as well bring to New York a good coat for me and some clean linen, as, if I come to New York, I should need them, being now in rags.

August 13th [1862], 6 A.M.

All things are packed in the wagons, but still we have no orders to move. Tents are struck, but we don't know when we shall start. It is most annoying. I suppose we shall *march* after all, over Bottom's Bridge. Genl. Kearny has petitioned Genl. McClellan to be allowed to bring up the rear. I suppose he will do it, as usual.

It is wonderful now how things have changed. At Fair Oaks, towards the end of June, if anyone had told me we were not going to Richmond, I should have laughed in his face. *Now we are retreating from the Peninsula!* Well, 'tis best no doubt, for the little row of mounds behind each Regiment shows that this place is by no means healthy, and the worst months are to come. But we have proved that we are better men than the Rebels in every engagement. We are retreating before overwhelming forces & fearful disease.

Noon—

I was expecting a letter from Father today, but no mail came. None has gone out either and I am afraid that you will not receive this for some time to come. I expect that when we get to Yorktown or Fortress Monroe, or wheresoever we are going, I shall be started off recruiting. The 101st is on outpost duty, picketing for the whole Division.

As Adjutant I remain in camp, and when the Brigade moves, I move with it. They say we shall move tonight. I think we shall either have a hard fight of it, as we did in our last retreat, or else no fight at all. If the Rebels are in great force, the first will occur; if not, they will not attack us at all. I mistook in saying we should have to go over Bottom's Bridge—it will be over some ferry or other. If we have pontoons enough we can cross the Chickahominy anywhere; but if not we shall have to go pretty well up the river to get across.

On a reconnaissance the other day, Kearny received a ball through his left sleeve, which of course hangs armless by his side. He looked at it and laughed, saying, "Well, that is a good joke on that bullet." Today he threatened to resign if McClellan did not let him bring up the rear. You know he and [John] Sedgwick fought about this the last retreat. Sedgwick won the day but passed Kearny at White Oak Swamp which we held and left last of any Division.

Ever since midnight of last night, the wagons have been packed and the mules harnessed to them ready to start.

August 14th [1862], 6 A.M.

I saw an officer of the Signal Corps yesterday evening, who told me the order we received to march on the 11th was not to march to the rear, but to Richmond. Now we are ready to march at a minute's notice, with wagons packed and 8 days' rations on hand. Things are getting so quieted down that I begin to fancy we shall not march after all.

George Dodge, in copying his brother's wartime journal, inserted this notation as preface to the narrative of the Second Bull Run campaign: "Theodore's dictation to Mother, while convalescing from Chantilly wound, to make up the leaves of his diary which ill health prevented his sending in usual form, beginning about August." The route Kearny's division followed down the Peninsula to Yorktown was a circuitous one, to guard against reports (false, as it turned out) of a pursuing enemy column.

For several days before we left Harrison's Landing, there were rumors that some great movement was about to take place, and two days before we actually moved, orders came to cut the tents (there being a lack of small shelter tents) up into small tents for the men to carry on their knapsacks, and to be ready to march at a minute's notice.

At 9 o'clock Aug. 14 the 101st was ordered out on picket to relieve 4 Regiments and do picket duty for the whole Division. (The Adjutant does not go on picket.) By the way, I have forgotten to inform you that, on account of some blunder of Lamont, the Adjutant of the Regiment, Genl. Birney ordered a new Adjutant to be appointed. Lieut. Col. Gesner of the 40th New York had been appointed Col. of the 101st and as he desired my appointment to the Adjutancy, I exchanged places with Lamont, and I remained behind with the doctors and hospital in an entirely deserted camp, as the Regiment had gone out in light marching order, all ready and expecting to be recalled only to follow the column in its march. During the day I met a member of the Signal Corps who assured me that, curious as it may seem, orders had come the day before to McClellan to march on to Richmond to act in conjunction with the gunboats, of which there were six lying in the river, and that these orders were countermanded by another dispatch boat in two or three hours afterward.

I've alluded to Col. Gesner, who took the place of Brown, the valiant tailor of Syracuse. A man more fit for his place than Gesner you could not find. He is a young man, not more than six and twenty, small, delicately built, frank, open, almost handsome face, very light blue eyes and light hair, slight mustache the only beard he wore, frank and affable in address, but of great energy and decision of character. A sincere friend, but a man before whom a delinquent, whatever his rank, would quail. He was very kind to me, and often during the latter part of my campaign, when I was so ill that I could not stand, he would spread his own blanket on the ground and cover me up with a hand as gentle as a woman's, relieving me from all duty and doing himself all that was required of me. During our march from Harrison's Landing my contraband (probably tired of the wear) fell out, with my blanket, and was no more to be seen. Always from that time, Col. G. insisted upon sharing his blanket with me so that thereafter we always slept together. My position under such circumstances was the most pleasant I could have chosen in the Regiment.

We expected to have marched on the 15th, but we did not march till the 16th, so that the Regiment came in from picket as usual. On the evening of the 15th, we got orders to be ready to march at 3 o'clock A.M., and in effect did start at that hour, turning our backs upon Richmond. The first day we marched to Jordan's Ford over the Chickahominy; Kearny as usual had insisted on being allowed to do the most fatiguing marching which should be on hand, & accordingly, whilst the rest of the Army took a straight road to Williamsburg, crossing the river on the pontoon bridge, a distance of only 24 miles, we were doomed, hot as it was and hard as we had been worked, to take a circuitous route of 85 miles.

About 3 o'clock P.M. on the first day's march, just as the Brigade was coming to a halt, the 101st was ordered 2 miles back. This, as you may believe, rather ruffled our tempers. We went back, expecting to have at least a little fight, but what was our annoyance upon having arrived at the appointed place to find old Kearny sitting under a tree, who very coolly told us to "about face" and march back again. The cause of this sudden escapade was that some of the pontoon train had stuck in the mud and as Rebel cavalry were hovering about, Kearny feared their capture. You may be sure, as much as we idolized Kearny, we none of us felt very sweet-tempered at this increase, by 4 miles, of our march, which made *us* that day over twenty miles. On the road we were continually passing fields of green corn, and it was really curious to see with what rapidity the boys would light a fire and roast the ears when we halted to rest.

Jordan's Ford takes its name from the farm adjoining, owned by a man of that name. We halted after the first day's march at this man's farm and Mr. Jordan politely invited all the officers of the Division to take their supper and breakfast at his house. General Kearny, however, disapproving of this, we were fain to control ourselves foraging on the good man's sweet potatoes and green corn. Apples were also abundant on the way, and I kept a scout running about to the various orchards to bring to the Colonel & myself whatever he could find which was choice and good. Before we left the Landing I had tried all in my power to find a horse, but having failed I was obliged to march on foot as before.

On August 17th we marched about seventeen miles, from Jordan's Ford over the Chickahominy—a mean little stream at this point about as broad as the dining room, tho' further down it is quite a river. We halted about 4 o'clock near a country residence of the Rebel General Lee. The corn from the corn fields soon disappeared, for as the order against foraging had not yet been issued, the men took the ripe ears for eating and the stalks to build little shelter tents for the night. The Colonel, Major & myself managed after a long search to find a spring where we regaled ourselves with a bath, which, as you can well imagine, after our hot and dusty march was mighty refreshing. The Colonel, Major, Capts. Allen, McCarty and myself messed together, and I had detailed two cooks and a man to forage for the mess; so that where anything was to be got we got it. Our three servants managed very soon to pick up, besides the edibles, 2 horses and a mule, so when any extraordinary supply was found, enough was laid by for future need. Of course these quadrupeds were not thoroughbreds, and it needed all the desperation which long marching produces to induce our servants to mount them. Such was the concatenation of ills which horseflesh is heir to and which had fallen to their lot.

The 18th we broke up as usual about 4 A.M. and marched about the same number of miles as the preceding day, halting in a large open field for the night. The weather all along was intensely hot and the roads one cloud of dust. On the 19th, after a long and tedious march, we reached Williamsburg at 3 o'clock P.M., and then our Regiment had about 1 1/2 miles to march back again to go out on picket. On the 20th we retraced our steps to Williamsburg, passed thro' the town with colors flying, and after about 20 miles' march over the dirtiest roads you can imagine, we reached Yorktown and encamped half a mile outside the town.

On the 21st I had a splendid bath in York River, but as the water was salt, could not get off the grime and dirt of the march. It was, however, invigorating, and when I went on, there were along the beach as many as 5 or 6,000 of our weary and worn men bathing. Such a sight I never before beheld. We were in doubt whether we were going to march to Fortress Monroe or not, and I managed here to purchase a horse for $10!! One of the boys had picked him up on picket at Williamsburg and I bought him. He was an old red horse with a bob tail, and tho' so old considerable of a trotter. But I was doomed not to have any good of him as we had got to the end of our march.

About 10 o'clock A.M. we received orders to march to the wharf to embark, and about 3 P.M. we managed to get our men aboard the transport "Coatzacoalcos." In the evening we started northwards. There were, contrary to the regulations for transports, no provisions for the officers on board except salt and junk, crackers and coffee. The ship officers had a good table. I was cunning enough to slip a fee into the hand of the 2nd steward and point out my stateroom, so that I managed to get a bite off their table. The transport we were on was formerly a Hudson River steamer.

This narrative, covering the period August 22–28, carries Birney's brigade of Kearny's division to its junction with Pope's Army of Virginia in the vicinity of the old Bull Run battlefield of 1861. The reference to the capture by Rebel cavalry of General Pope's papers near Catlett's Station is, of course, something Dodge only learned after the campaign closed, when he was composing his narrative. In the margin next to the anecdote about devouring vast amounts of fruit in Alexandria, Dodge later wrote, "Big fish story!"

On the afternoon of the 22nd we arrived at Aquia Creek, and were informed by a messenger from shore that were to go on to Alexandria, which we reached the next day (the 23rd) at about 10 o'clock A.M. As soon as I could leave the boat, I ran into the town and purchased a pair of boots, as mine were entirely worn out. Our Brigade marched up to the Railway, and towards evening we moved off—a train for each regiment. I found time enough to buy three pairs of stockings and two pairs of drawers; one pair of the stockings I gave to the Colonel, and a pair of the drawers to Capt. McCarty, as I pitied their miserable plight, for by this time we all looked like a pack of beggars. I also found time, as we marched along, to run into a fruiteners, where I devoured with much avidity 1 watermelon, 1 musk melon, both of gigantic proportions, a dozen and a half of peaches, and some apples and pears. I then called in our servants and loaded them with about six times the quantity I had myself disposed of, which came in mighty well for days to come.

About 7 o'clock we got upon our train, which consisted of coal cars and cattle ditto. Your humble servant, not finding a seat in the cars, rode for 30 miles sitting on the end (which is about six inches broad) of one coal car and resting his feet on the end of the car in front, and holding on to the brake wheel for support. The Major sat opposite to me. At last we found out that a passenger car was attached to the train, in which Genl. Kearny rode, and we betook ourselves thither.

On the 24th we were set down, about 8 o'clock A.M., near a place on the Alexandria Railroad, where there had been a cavalry raid by the Rebels, who had carried off some of Genl. Pope's private papers, destroyed some property, and made some prisoners. We had orders to protect several wagon trains in the locality. In the afternoon, just as we had received orders to join our Brigade, which had gone on by rail some miles beyond us, a most terrible shower came up, which wetted us to the skin in a moment, and rendered the road almost impassable. The horses for our Brigade had not come up, so that neither Staff nor Field officers were any of them mounted. Though the distance was short, it was the most terrible march I ever had. I was almost too ill to move, and, wet and weary as I was, the bad roads tried my powers of endurance more severely than they were ever tried before. At last we reached our Brigade after having crossed a stream up to above our waists. I lay down by a fire, wet, weary, and so ill as scarcely to sleep a wink all night.

Next morning (25th) early, the 101st and the 4th Maine were ordered to proceed some 6 miles up the Railway and camp there as a van guard. This we did, marching in column protected by a line of skirmishers in front. We halted at a beautiful place, which we had reached without encountering any opposition; we threw out our pickets, sent out scouting parties, stacked arms and rested. Our staff of servants had procured a suckling pig, off which we dined several days. I however could eat nothing, as my illness had now taken away all appetite. In the afternoon we were ordered to retire, which we did a mile on the Alexandria side of Manassas Station, when we camped near a deserted farmhouse. Our Colonel and Major had managed to procure horses and one of our scouting parties brought in a fine artillery horse for me which they had found at a farm, the owner of which had told a seemingly patched-up story as to its ownership.

26th. Marching all day.

27th. Left camp and marched along the Centreville Road to Greenwich where our Brigade camped and the 101st was sent out on picket.

28th. This morning broke up and marched on to Manassas Junction to drive the Rebels from that point. The same day we marched back to Centreville, where the Brigade camped and contrary to all law and precedent the 101st was again sent out on picket.

Dodge labeled the following section of his narrative, "a few items of my own personal experience in the occurrences" of the first day of Second Bull Run, during which the 101st New York was heavily engaged. The divisions of Kearny and Hooker made up Heintzelman's Third Corps, and the charge Dodge describes was one of a series of assaults made that day against Jackson's corps, positioned behind the embankment of an unfinished railroad. Colonel Gesner, in his report of the action, noted that Adjutant Dodge "was of great service to me."

[Friday August 29, 1862]

On the 29th we marched on the road to Gainesville about 5 or 6 miles, and at 9 o'clock we arrived at the ground destined to be the scene of the day's battle. At 10 o'clock we marched into the woods in line, but our Brigade, proceeding a little farther than the orders warranted, marched right into a masked battery, the fire from which lost us 2 officers and some twenty men. We immediately moved by the left flank through

the woods, to get out of the way of the battery and then received orders to retire about half a mile. 'Twas now about
noon. At 2 o'clock we moved forward again to support Randolph's Battery, and lay for an hour and half under a very
heavy fire of shell. At 3 1/2 we moved 1/4 mile by the left
flank and then lay on our arms.

About 5 1/2 three Regiments of Sickles' Brigade came
skedaddling out of the woods in disgraceful style, the Rebels
having driven them back. This was the more surprising, as the
reputation of Sickles' Brigade is well established for bravery
and good conduct. Of course there was a generous rivalry between Sickles' Brigade, which is the flower of Genl. Hooker's
Division, and Birney's Brigade, which is the best of Kearny's,
and when we saw these three Regiments coming out of the
woods in such disorder, a groan, half sorrowful and half deri-
sive, rose from our ranks. At the same moment came dashing
up to our Brigade one of Kearny's aides waving his hat and
shouting: "40th and 101st, let's see what *we* can do." The two
Regiments sprang to their feet and at a double quick crossed
the clearing and entered the woods opposite.

The country here is undulating and woody, with here and
there a clearing. The woods have generally a thick underbrush, through which one can see some 50 yards. I was again
mounted, having taken the company sergeant's horse. The
underbrush however prevented the use of the horses, which
accordingly were left in the rear. Proceeding thro' the woods
1/4 mile, we came to a little line of breastworks where we met
Genl. Kearny. His simple words, "Now boys, do your duty!"
made our blood thrill and steeled our courage. We passed
thro' an opening in the breastworks and formed in line, the
40th on the right.

We marched in line some 1/2 mile through the woods
when we were met by a heavy volley of musketry. Unheeding
this, we advanced some 50 yards farther on—the men eagerly

and perhaps anxiously inspecting the priming of their pieces for a desperate encounter. This brought us to within 30 yards of the enemy, who held an old Railway cutting some 15 feet deep, with precipitous sides, in which they could shelter themselves while loading, simply showing their heads when firing. Our men had about 100 rounds apiece. First volleys seldom do much execution, and as few had hitherto fallen, the men, as soon as the order to halt and commence firing was given, began their work in deadly earnest. After 3/4 of an hour's firing (which as they said in the rear was more brisk & continuous than any which had been heard thro' the day), our cartridges were nearly exhausted, and as the enemy, so well entrenched in their well-chosen rifle pit, showed no sign of giving way, we resorted to cold steel to drive them out.

The two Colonels having communicated with each other and everything being prepared for a general charge, we sprang forward with a yell which made the woods ring again, and plunged into the cutting. Instead of finding foemen worthy of our steel in the cutting, we saw the whole of them running for dear life on the other side. We drove them 3/4 of a mile through the woods, until we reached a clearing, on the opposite side of which were the Rebel reserves. Our boys were so eager in the chase, that some of them actually crossed the clearing and ran right into the Rebels. Only two of this number got back.

At this moment the enemy brought up a heavy force on our left flank and as we had lost already well nigh half our men, we were constrained, much against our will, to retire. Our Colonel retreated, holding up his sword as a kind of barrier to prevent the men from running, but ne'er a spirit for running was in the men, except towards the foe. One little old fellow, about 60 years old, named McLawire, came to me with the tears running from his eyes saying, "Adjutant, for God's sake, don't let us go back. Let's rather stop here and die." Not receiving reinforcements however, we fell back in good order to the line of breastworks of which I spoke, where we stopped under a heavy fire of shell till about 8 or 9 o'clock P.M., when, leaving a picket behind, we retired to our camp.

I forgot to tell you that the Rebels had planted two or three howitzers at the end of the Railway cutting through which we had to pass some hundred yards up, with which they opened upon us vigorously on our retreat. Foolish as it was thus to expose my life uselessly, I was so excited that I stood during the whole firing looking down an opening in the underbrush. It was a strange fascination but I found myself almost unable to leave the place. While we were lying behind the breastworks, a spent howitzer ball grazed my right arm, laming it considerably and paralyzing it for the time. I had to wear it in a sling for several days after.

Lieut. Col. Brown had been attached to the 40th in place of Lieut. Col. Gesner. Altho' Brown is an ass he is no coward. Genl. Kearny asked him afterwards how many men the 40th had lost, and Brown answered, "About fifty," which was much less than the actual loss. "Pooh," says the General. "Why that is not so much as they lost at the Battle of Williamsburg," evidently disappointed. We took into the fight 180 muskets and 16 or 17 officers. Of these we lost 90 men and 9 officers. When the official report was made to Genl. Kearny he was appeased.

On the second day of Second Bull Run, Kearny's division held the right of the Federal position (and was not, as Dodge states here, under Burnside). The battle turned that afternoon on a massive Confederate flank attack under Longstreet. Phil Kearny's glowing tribute to the 101st, recorded pridefully by Dodge, was repeated by Kearny in his report of the battle written August 31, the day before he was killed at Chantilly.

[Saturday August 30, 1862]

The Rebels, having vainly endeavored to break through our lines on Friday where Burnside (under whom we were) was stationed, kept up a slight fire during the [next] morning at the same point, and meantime swung their forces round, opposite to McDowell, who was on the left of us. Our Brigade was held in reserve all day, and exposed only to a fire of shell. Suddenly, towards evening we heard a heavy fire on our left, which got farther and farther to our rear and it was not long before we got orders to retreat. The enemy had broken through McDowell's lines at first onset, & had outflanked us on the same ground as at Bull Run. We fell back steadily half a mile or so, when our Division halted to check the enemy, advancing in great force. It would have done you good to see our Brigade maneuver, better than ever on parade. Kearny was moving about rapidly from point to point, stationing different Regiments in proper places. He soon pitched on the 101st and led us at a double quick almost half a mile off on the extreme left, to hold a piece of woods. It was near dusk. We remained there till 10 o'clock P.M.

Then we got out as well as we could, leaving a small picket to keep up appearances (who were all taken prisoners). We rejoined the column and marched all night, crossing Bull Run and Cat Run Creeks, in water over our waists, toward Centreville, which we had left so short a time before. We did not feel in very high spirits as you can imagine. I had the evening before taken the company sergeant's horse, and was tolerably mounted. We halted some distance from Centreville and camped.

[Sunday August 31, 1862]

Next day we moved on towards the town. During the march Kearny rode up from the rear of the Division. The 101st was second in order of march. Each Regiment gave him

3 cheers as he passed. When we had saluted him like the rest, he stopped and said: "101st, you are a brave lot of men and have proved yourself as efficient as any Regiment I ever had under my command. I thank you for your valorous conduct!" Then turning to the Division he waved his hat and cried out, "Three cheers for the 101st," and, himself leading, the Division gave us 3 rousing cheers. That we felt proud just then you can imagine.

Stonewall Jackson's attempt to outflank Pope's retreating army was blocked at Chantilly, a savage, confusing clash fought in a blinding rainstorm. It cost the Federals the lives of two major generals, Isaac Stevens and Phil Kearny. Theodore Dodge took a bullet in his left thigh and was carried from the field and from there to Washington. The 101st New York lost 124 men in the campaign, leaving it a shell of a regiment, soon to disappear from the rolls of the army.

[Monday September 1, 1862]

We lay at Centreville over Sunday night and not till 5 P.M. next day did we break up to pursue our march to the rear. This was Monday September 1st and we little expected to have a fight. We marched some hour and a half or two hours, when all of a sudden a terrible fire was heard on our left, and we learned that Genl. [Jesse] Reno was engaging the Rebels, who had attacked our left flank.

Kearny was ordered to relieve Reno. Birney's Brigade was the first up, and the 101st was sent in before all other Regiments to the fight. It was raining in torrents and, after a march of nearly a mile through the woods, we came to a cornfield, where we relieved some Regiment of Reno's Division. We went into this fight with over 250 men (many stragglers having come in). We were in some three quarters of an hour, and when the Regiment came out, we had 5 officers and 30 men left.

The Lieut. Col., the Major, and I had dismounted and were on foot. Our men fired kneeling, and with great precision, at the line of Rebels who were stationed across the open field on the edge of a wood. The way the poor fellows fell was terrible, but not a groan or cry could you hear. Presently the Major came over to me and said, "The 40th [New York] is getting mixed up with us." I replied that probably they had come to relieve us, which proved to be the case, and immediately after, I was wounded. Two boys whose pieces were so wet they could not fire, carried me to the rear.

CHAPTER FIVE

Marking Time in the Eleventh Corps

November 21 to December 14, 1862

*O*nly *in November 1862 was Theodore Dodge sufficiently recovered from his Chantilly wound and his typhoid fever to return to duty. During his recuperation, recognizing the declining fortunes of his regiment—the 101st New York's survivors were fated to be assigned to the 37th New York in December—he had resigned his commission in favor of a new posting. His father, quartermaster of the newly organized 119th New York, was instrumental in getting Theodore the position of regimental adjutant. The 119th New York, commanded by Colonel Elias Peissner, was attached to Franz Sigel's Eleventh Corps, Army of the Potomac.*

The Eleventh Corps was, in fact, the renamed First Corps of the Army of Virginia, and before that, John Charles Frémont's Mountain Department, and it was an outfit with a checkered military history. The Eleventh had a decidedly German flavor, which caused it to be slurred by the rest of the army as "the Dutchmen." Young Dodge, fluent in German, was a natural choice for regimental adjutant, although he notes here that he found his duties more challenging than they had been in the 101st. At the time he joined the regiment, the Eleventh's posting was as a "corps of observation" along the Orange & Alexandria Railroad west of Washington.

Centreville Nov. 21st, 1862

I got a pass this morning at Genl. [S. D.] Sturgis's (Military Governor of Alexandria) to pass the guards at Fairfax Court House. So I reduced my carpet bag to a size convenient to strap on my saddle, made a roll of blankets to strap on before me, and having provided myself with some biscuit and bologna sausage, which were deposited in my saddle bags, I set forth on my journey to the Regiment. I met a party on the way, whose destination was the same as mine and we travelled on together. Arrived at Fairfax Court House, I made my way to Sigel's A. A. G. who told me that 119th New York was at Centreville, so I set off for that place where I had so often been before and, after a ride from Alexandria of 25 miles, arrived safely.

November 23rd 1862

We have got a chance to send a letter right thro' to New York by the hands of two round fat Brewers and one thin lank Brewer, so I avail myself of the opportunity to write a word to you. I dare say you have already heard of my arrival at Head Quarters and of my having found everything satisfactory, tho' I must say the 119th is not as easy a Regiment to manage as was the 101st. There are Germans who don't understand English, Frenchmen ditto, Swedes and Spaniards who don't understand anything, and Italians who are worse than all the rest together.

Lieut. Col. [John T.] Lockman was trying to make 4 men, a Swede, a Spaniard & 2 Germans, understand that they would be held responsible for some meat stolen from the Quarter Master's Department, while they were on guard there, and such a scene of translating and incomprehensibility you never saw. Then there has as yet been scarcely any discipline at all, but this will soon come by my constant exertion. I have already made one or two friends in the Regiment—Lieut. Col. Lockman for one. He is a man about 25 or 27, medium height, with a good tempered face and very affable manners. He was married at 11 o'clock of the morning he left for the war. Don't it seem queer? But he told me that his wife wished to have the right to nurse and tend him should he be sick or wounded, and so they were married.

It is pretty cold here now, and as we are in an exposed position we get the wind pretty well about the ears, but we manage nevertheless to keep warm. I find my Canada jacket very comfortable. It is nice having Father with the Regiment. The Lieut. Colonel, he, and I sit together all the time we are not busy. We have a capital mess—almost as good as St. Nicholas' [hotel] fare—the very best I ever saw in camp. It costs only $5 per week.

November 14th 1862

Had target practice this A.M. Six men hit the target at 150 yards—favorable for action that, eh? We were to commence at 9 o'clock, but by Col. Peissner's botching were not able to begin till 11. I don't think much of Col. P. I detailed one of the German Captains as Officer of the Day and he said he would not act—he was going out. I told him he would be reported if he refused, but he replied, he "didn't care, he wasn't going on, for it wasn't his turn." However he thought better of it and did go on. This is my first dispute with any of the officers.

This P.M. Father and I rode over to Chantilly battle ground. We found the place where the 101st fought, and where I was wounded, and picked up an old kettle on which I had sat down, while waiting to be carried to the rear. He took it to a house hard by and gave it to the inmates to keep, telling them he would give them a dollar for it when he had a chance to get it again. The ride there and back was very pleasant. Father and I have changed horses, by which I make a very good bargain. His horse is worth much more than mine, tho' I had quite a good animal when in Washington. I wished to buy one or two horses which pleased me more than mine, but I was limited to price and could not afford a better one than I got. Now however by the exchange, I get a much better animal than I expected.

25th November 1862

Col. Peissner and I rode out after breakfast to Fairfax Court House to see Genl. Sigel about sending Lieut. Lewis home on sick leave; poor fellow, he is anything but strong. We got him leave to go to Washington for 48 hours, from whence we hope he may be able to get home.

Genl. Sigel is a little man, not more than 5 ft. 5 and was anything but military in his appearance this morning. He was dressed in a nondescript coat, several sizes too large for him, lined with fur—tho' the day was warm and he in a warm room besides. A coat in fact somewhere between a Hussar's jacket and a "Noah's Ark"; his feet were encased in shoes also lined with fur, and several sizes too large for him, and his legs clad in not-to-be-mentionables-to-ears-polite, very much worn and very much awry. In the corner were a pair of boots which looked large enough for the General to hide in, decorated with very gay spurs. He wears his hair very much over his forehead, which does not improve his appearance. Has not good features except his eye, which is sharp and expressive. I should judge that he spoke English with only tolerable facility but in this I may be mistaken, as our conversation was entirely in German. He is almost entirely surrounded by foreigners, tho' I do not know as he is prejudiced against natives. It seems very curious to speak German to everybody here. It is like a German settlement. In fact when I see a soldier I involuntarily speak German to him.

The grey mare is a beauty. Today is the first time I have ridden her far. She is very plucky and not afraid of anything. "Vouldn't shy if she vas to pass a vagon load of monkeys with their tails singed off." She is a nice jumper too. I ran her a stretch today of 1/2 mile and find her very fast.

November 27th 1862

Col. Peissner and I went out this A.M. in company with Genl. Carl Schurz, our Division commander, and some of his Staff, among whom were three or four who wished to have some racing. They had good horses and we had quite a little steeple chase. I ran the grey mare a few hundred yards against the winner but got badly beaten. I did not try the steeple chase, for tho' I do a little running in a quiet way, I had not got shaken into my saddle since my illness. The grey mare jumps well—a little wild, needs more checking than urging, and breaks into a wild gallop after jumping, but I am getting her well in hand. I am riding her on the curb to bring her neck into a better curve. She is a fast trotter as well as runner, will lay her ears back and do her mile in three minutes.

They had a very good breed of running horses here in Virginia—small horses, nervous and lightly built. One of the aides had a very bad spill by the girth's breaking. All the Germans here ride on English saddles. What sort of saddles do the English cavalry use, I wonder?

We have a very pleasant Field and Staff mess, and live very well. The great benefit derived from it is the regularity of the meals.

We are on high ground here at Centreville and overlook the country for miles around. Towards the west we see the Bull Run range of hills and Thoroughfare Gap, about a dozen miles from here. The country is naturally beautiful but is now entirely devastated. We had no turkey at Thanksgiving, for they were too dear for soldiers. We were expecting our boxes from Washington, but they did not come either. We had hoped to brew a hot punch but must go without now.

As Adjutant Dodge settled into his position, he began to appraise his new comrades-in-arms. The 119th New York, along with the 58th New York, 75th Pennsylvania, and 26th Wisconsin, made up a rather polyglot brigade under Colonel Wladimir Krzyzanowski, a onetime Polish revolutionary. The divisional commander, Carl Schurz, like corps commander Sigel, was an émigré from the aborted German revolution of 1848. Schurz's division was regarded as the most foreign in the army, eight of its ten regiments being German; the second brigade was led by Alexander Schimmelfennig. Elias Peissner, colonel of the 119th, was said by General

*Schurz to be the natural son of the famously eccentric King Lud-
wig I of Bavaria. But it appears here that the man who really made
things run in the 119th was quartermaster Nathaniel Dodge; in his
journal Theodore, citing "military etiquette," refers to his father
simply as the Quarter Master, or Q. M.*

November 28th 1862

I had a long talk with Genl. Schurz (our Division commander) yesterday. He was our late Minister to Spain and in
the late elections came out as a very eloquent man. He is of
middle size, thin, and wears long hair—one of those men in
character who make very good military men. He is a nice, affable man. He is a great admirer of Kearny and asked me a
great deal about him.

We had our boxes in from Washington today and the
Quarter Master (for so, I call Father now as military etiquette requires) had two or three boxes of liquors and
wines, a present from New York. So this evening we called
together the American element of the Regiment to have a
quiet glass of punch. Songs circulated &c &c and we have
just broken up. We had a dress parade today and the effect
of the arrival (not the Q. M.'s) was evident. The color sergeant and his right hand corporal were as drunk as could
be, as was about every third man in the ranks. I had the two
first reduced to the ranks for their behavior, but it is aston-
ishing how soon men will get drunk in camp when they can
get a chance. They can't be moderate.

Here, as in all Regiments, there is the same admixture of
gentlemen & boors, as Dr. Aymé, our good surgeon, just observed. The Field and Staff belong to the former class and I
find my companions entirely among them. The surgeon is one
of the most lovely of men—about 45 or 50 years old, very
handsome, one of those benevolent and admirable faces
which one delights to look upon.

November 29th 1862

The weather has been for the past few days dull but not cold. This evening it has rained a little. I took a ride with the Q. M. towards Fairfax Court House, some 3 or 4 miles. This A.M. Judge Van Colt of New York, whose son (a Lieutenant in the Regiment) is sick here of typhoid and is scarcely expected to live, came on. His son however is too far gone to recognize him. How sad such a thing makes us. Lieut. Van Colt was a universal favorite. He was ill before I came, so I have never seen him.

Oh! the stupidity of Germans! Sometimes I get raving over their stupidity & impenetrability to common sense. Among the line officers there are not more than three or four real gentlemen, and they are Americans.

The Lieut. Col. and I, who tent together, give up our quarters tonight to Judge Van Colt and Judge Jonda, who came with him. The doctor is to spend the night with Lieut. Van Colt, and I occupy his bed in the Q. M.'s tent. There are no signs of moving from here as yet, nor are we in the immediate presence of the enemy, so that we go to bed, and rise undisturbed. If however we are to make winter quarters here, they will be cold ones, as it is very much exposed to winds, being on the north east side of the hill upon which Centreville is situated. The Q. M. just tells me, that Judge Van Colt and his friend wish me to go to the Chantilly battle ground with them tomorrow.

November 30th 1862

Rode out this morning with the Colonel and Judge Jonda, with the intention of going to Chantilly battlefield. Tried a cross cut thro' the woods and lost our way; after some wandering came out near a house which we recognized as being close to our camp. Had however a very pleasant ride, tho' we missed our object. How hard it is to find one's way thro' a wood on horseback—one has to turn so often to avoid the trees and intervening obstacles that the direction is very soon lost.

Judge Jonda left for home at 10 A.M. today. At dinner Judge Van Colt made a very queer remark, viz. "That he would not give much for a man who couldn't eat, sleep and enjoy himself under affliction." He seems to enjoy himself very well, considering that his son lies deadly ill. In the afternoon Lieut. Col. Lockman, Judge Van Colt and myself, again set forth and rode over to Chantilly—this time finding our way.

Col. Peissner proposes making a squad of all the mounted officers in the Regiment, and going out on a scouting party after some "Bushwhackers" near Bull Run. I wish we could. Our Major (Harvey Baldwin) is, I suppose you know, detached on Genl. Sigel's Staff as Assistant Inspector General. I saw him the other day. He is a nice young fellow—a small handsome man, delicate in build and looks & showing the same refinement outwardly that he does mentally. He is fond of horses and always handsomely mounted. His is a nice position on Genl. Sigel's Staff—very little to do—and has quarters in a house.

Among our line officers there are only two or three with whom I associate much. One, Lieut. Odell, who reminds me much of Charley Dewey, was acting Q. M. for some time and spends much of his time now in the Q. M.'s tent. This tent is the common resort of evenings for Field & Staff—the Q. M.'s attractions causing a great influx. We sit and read, while the Q. M. writes and reads too.

December 1st 1862

The Q. M. went to Washington this A.M. in a wagon, which belongs to the Regiment—half buggy, half dog cart—bought in a moment of frenzy by a youthful Lieut., and which was taken off his hands by the Colonel. The "conveyance" partakes in a measure of the state of mind of its owner at the moment of purchase—that is, rather *rackety*, & as from here to Washington is a succession of stony hills of by no means the mildest, we don't know whether he has got safely to the end of his journey or not. We expect him home tomorrow afternoon.

I got my portmanteau from Washington a few days ago. As we do not expect to move about much now, it being so late in the season and we have been in the Reserve, I hope I shall be able to carry it with me. We took a ride round about the camp and town in the afternoon, and stopping at General Schimmelfennig's quarters had a very nice glass of *kümmel* (I suppose that is the way of spelling it). It is a liqueur tasting of aniseed. Afterwards we were constrained to stop at a sutler's by Col. Schwann of the 26th Penn. to take a glass of lager beer.

December 2nd 1862

At midnight we got an order "to be ready to march at an hour's notice," which may mean something or nothing; so we are all holding ourselves in readiness, i.e. have done everything towards breaking camp except packing up beds and striking tents. I rather think we shall move.

Today poor Lieut. Van Colt died. He suddenly got an attack of diphtheria from extreme exhaustion and died of suffocation before help could be given. This afternoon Judge Van C. took the body to Washington on his way North. There was a funeral escort with muffled drums, 6 pall bearers and all the officers & half the men followed as mourners. We escorted the ambulance which bore the coffin beyond the pickets between here and Fairfax Court House, and as it moved away, we fired three volleys in memory of the first officer of the 119th who has passed from amongst us.

December 3rd 1862

The Quarter Master came back early this morning and brought me a copy of "Les miserables," Victor Hugo's new work. I am reading it with great interest. All were glad to see him—he is the favorite of the Regiment. I rode out this morning all alone, and so halted on the way now and then to jump some fences. I ran my mare at one rather big one when she balked and pitched me right over her head. I came down soft however.

Today we had the first Battalion drill which we have had since my arrival—the men drill better than I expected but they do not execute the movements with precision enough yet. Capt. Batterson, the second senior Captain, sent in his resignation today on account of ill health. He is troubled with some complaint which becomes troublesome when there is a chance of making a move in direction of the enemy. He is a vulgar bar-room hero, of whom we shall be glad to get rid.

December 4th 1862

We dined early today and directly after I had mounted guard (at 12 M.), the Col., Capt. Willis, Lieut. Odell & myself went out to Chantilly to a prize drill, where 5 Regiments contested. A cavalcade was to start from Genl. Stahel's Head Quarters, and we joined it. It was composed of some 40 or 50 officers, who were headed by Genls. Sigel, Von Steinwehr, Schimmelfennig & Krzyzanowski. We rode to a large plain in the vicinity, where the drill came off with great éclat. The 29th N.Y. I think took the prize. They executed all their movements at double quick, and with great precision and beauty.

I was anxious to see whether Fanny would stand fire; and as there was much firing of blank cartridges, I was able to test her coolness under fire. I found her very steady, which pleased me much, as the Q. M. thought she would not stand fire. On the way back we supped at a Mrs. Robertson's, a secessionist's, off chicken and wild rabbit. I hope it was not poisoned.

December 6th 1862

A day of fearful N.W. wind, which blows the snow about like dust; a day cold wind withal, which does not allow the sun to thaw even the surface of the snow. Thermometer down to 15°. Our tents really almost blew down, and do what we will to stop up air holes and keep a roaring fire, we cannot keep anything like warm. We have to dress warmly, else we should freeze. We found a stable in the village for our poor horses, which was a mercy, as they would almost have perished in the cold. One of Col. Lockman's boys stays with the horses.

My boy Henry has not come yet. I do not know whether he will or not now, it is so late. You have no idea how uncomfortable our mess tent is now—no stove nor any means of heating it, & the last two days we have been obliged to jump about during meal times to keep warm. Of course, in this extreme cold we do little work except writing &c. However we send out pickets every day of from 60 to 250 men. We have very severe picket duty here, our men frequently being obliged to go on after a rest of only 20 hours.

December 7, 1862

Another day just like yesterday—only more so. It is really a painful duty to go out even for a minute, the wind is so sharp & biting—very little like Sunday is it here. No one seems to know or care what day it is & even I did not remember it was Sunday till near noon. We generally have a little private service in the Quarter Master's tent—the Lieut. Col., Chaplain, Dr. & I. Most of the officers of the Regiment would prefer to have no religion at all; have voted against any chaplain, 19 votes against 6.

Some clothing, much needed by our men, came today. Poor fellows! Some have had no stockings this awful weather. It seems to me the troops are poorly provided, tho' to be sure, there is always this sort of thing in active service.

Dear Mother, I have got to complain of your Husband, the Q. M. He actually took those stamps you sent me the other day for himself. You must write & reprove him. There is no news at all except every now & then we are driven out into the cold by a smoky chimney. But we are all well & merry—what more can be desired?

(Note from the Q. M.) "The Adjutant is a sponge. He drinks my whiskey, eats my rations, begs my horses, borrows my money, burns my candles, uses my tent, sleeps under my blankets & yet grudges me 10 stamps—which I had to give him back."

The movement Dodge describes here was to the south, toward the Rappahannock and the Army of the Potomac, where Burnside was confronting the Confederate army across the river at Fredericksburg. The Eleventh Corps was slated for the army's reserve, but the marching orders did not promise its arrival in time to support the start of Burnside's operations on December 11. The harassing Rebel cavalry was Wade Hampton's, of J .E. B. Stuart's cavalry corps. The sound of battle Dodge reports on December 13 was Burnside's blundering assault on Lee's impregnable position at Fredericksburg. "Why is it we are always defeated?" Dodge asked.

December 10th 1862

We received orders in the middle of the night to move at 8 A.M., which accordingly we did. We joined the column on the Fairfax Station Road. Of course we left many things behind. Only 3 tents out of the six belonging to the Field & Staff could go in the wagons, & no tents at all for any others. All superfluous goods have been sent to Fairfax Court House during the night. We are only allowed 6 wagons to a Regiment and they are disposed as follows. One to the Field & Staff, one to the Company officers, one to hospital, two to Commissariat &

one to Quarter Master's stores, such as blankets &c. However I managed to get my things aboard. The inevitable buggy followed all, with rations.

I had my first set down from the Colonel in the morning. The Companies did not march forward fast enough when I wished to form Battalions—the fault of Company officers, not mine. So the Colonel in a great fury went off with 3 Companies, declaring he would not wait for the rest. However, he thought better of it & did not go far, for when I marched forward with the rest, he was waiting for us at a turning about 200 yards off. He certainly made more of a spectacle of himself than of me.

I had *such* trouble getting my mare shod yesterday—she had cast a shoe, and as it was generally known that we were to move, all the forges were busy with other horses. At last I bought a pair of shoes and went to a battery close by, where they had leisure but no shoes & they did the job for me.

At 3 P.M. we camped 5 miles beyond Fairfax Court House, & having wagons with us put up tents and camp cots and slept well.

December 11th 1862

Started up from our sleep at 3 A.M. to get wagons ready packed for marching. We were to have moved at 8, but did not get off till 9. When we had got fairly started and had forded a brook 3 times (which was a *bad* start for a cold morning), we marched about 5 or 6 miles, when we halted, it was said for the night. We took dinner, i.e. those of us who had any to take. I had a piece of bread & gingerbread which the Q. M. had received as a present and shared with me.

Orders now came for us to move on, and as we had a sharp hill to ascend some mile or so ahead, they wished to get the wagons up it before morning, when the roads would be frozen and slippery. So off we went, crossed the Occoquan at

Wolf's Run shoals, ascended the beyond, and then enjoyed a most superb view of the valley beneath. The country about here is really most beautiful—rolling & woody. Two miles beyond brought us in the twilight to our camping place, where the Field and Staff encamped in the wood & the Regiment at the edge of the same. We (the Field & Staff) always go together. There are the Colonel, Lieut. Col., Dr. Aymé, Q. M. and self; and sometimes Lieuts. Odell or Schwerin or Capt. Lockman (the Lieut. Col.'s brother) drop in and camp around the same fire.

December 12, 1862

Of course we have to get on here by hook or by crook on the march. As to eating—bread, sometimes soft but oftener hard, & coffee constitute chiefly our fare. Salt pork eaten raw or fried on a stick over the fire, is another article of diet, and is not so bad either to a hungry soul. We gave this morning two days' rations to the men & set off towards Dumfries. Before we had gone far, we got views of Stuart's cavalry, which was hovering round. We marched slowly forward, which made the men very tired, for fast marching (3 miles an hour) is not so tiresome as marching & halting & standing about. The Rebels had blockaded the Turnpike & as the obstructions would have taken 3 or 4 hours to remove, we marched by the side roads, which were very deep & the trains ahead of us belonging to the 1st Brigade stuck fast frequently, which made our progress very slow.

Some of our men foraged a pig during a halt, & having cut him up, presented me with a leg. We will have it boiled for dinner when we halt next. We heard on the road, at a farm house, that there were 1,500 of Stuart's cavalry who had been there but an hour or two previously, but decamped before our column came up. They had captured 8 sutlers & their train on their way to Dumfries.

At 6 P.M. we arrived at Dumfries, very tired & hungry. We set the negroes at work to get supper, & just as we were consoling ourselves in the prospect of hot coffee, the Chaplain unluckily walked round the fire (for we and the cooks were all at one fire) and knocked over the pot in which it was boiling. Poor Chaplain, he got his fill of blame for his misadventure. However a quarter of an hour's patience repaired the loss, and we supped off bread and pork & coffee. We then lay down to sleep. I carry 4 blankets and 2 India rubber ditto on my horse, rolled up & strapped to my saddle before & behind; so I sleep warm. The Q. M. has not yet got here with his trains, but will probably be here tomorrow morning.

December 13, 1862

The Q. M. arrived early this morning, having spent the night with the Q. M. of the 26th New York. We were expecting to march at noon, or as soon as the wagons came up. However it grew too late before they actually got to our camp, that order came not to move tonight. So we put up tents and once more had a table laid for a meal combining dinner & tea. The Q. M., though tired, was in good spirits. We all went early to bed.

During the day we had been treated to the sound of the battle which Burnside is fighting on the south side of the Rappahannock. The cannonading is continuous. I hope Burnside may be successful.

December 14th [1862]

During the night orders came to march at 6 A.M., and to reduce our baggage from 6 to 2 wagons. All superfluous things to be left behind till they can be sent for. So almost all we have with us, is blankets and food. A ration of whiskey was served to the men last night and in consequence, as is always the case, many were beastly drunk, among others the teamsters, so this morning the Q. M. had lots of trouble in getting things started. However by 6 1/4 we did start, which was more than we expected to do. Our horses have had oats, but not a bit of hay, & in consequence are not as strong as they might be. We let them graze whenever we halt near a field, but they don't get enough.

At 10 A.M. (now) we have marched some 3 or 4 miles, and are to march to Stafford Court House, some 6 miles from here. Dumfries, which we passed through this morning, is a village of one street, with three brick buildings, a rare thing in the South. Some 50 houses may be in the place. Halted at 1 o'clock for dinner. The men made coffee and ate their rations. We had some sandwiches of raw salt pork & bread. While we were waiting, Genl. Sigel & Staff came by. We heard that Burnside attempted to cross the river at Fredericksburg, & was repulsed with fearful loss. He has called for Sigel and we are hastening to reinforce him. So at last we are to have some fighting, it would seem.

Why is it we are always defeated? I cannot understand it, for the Rebels *do not* fight better than we do. They are *certainly better led* & have I believe more heart in the cause. But we ought certainly to beat them by force of numbers. It is curious however, with 500,000 men, they should always at given points oppose to us superior numbers, while we have 1,000,000 men. All this is strategy. Why did Burnside give them a month to fortify themselves? Why did he not bombard the city weeks ago?

We marched on to Aquia, when we halted for the night. The rations were all gone & the men had the choice of marching 3 miles to Stafford Court House where they could get rations, or of camping where they were. Fatigue was more potent than hunger, and we camped. I made my supper off coffee and the leg of pork foraged for me the other day but never a cracker or bit of bread had I. After supper we went to bed, but we could not keep our fire going, for the smoke would not rise (which presages rain) and almost suffocated us. However it was warm and I slept comfortably. It had been very warm all day long, the sun being almost as powerful as in summer. The country we passed thro' is beautiful even now at this season of the year, & with the desolating track of war over it; but during the summer & in times of peace it must be a paradise. It is a rolling, undulating country, beautifully wooded with beech & pine, presenting always a lovely prospect.

CHAPTER SIX

A Winter of Discontent

December 15, 1862, to January 24, 1863

Veterans of the Army of the Potomac would look back on the six weeks following Fredericksburg as the nadir of their wartime service. December 13 (as it turned out) was the costliest single day in the army's four years of fighting, and Burnside's incompetence was evident to even the lowliest rear-rank private. Furthermore, army administration was breaking down, and morale plummeted. The final straw for many was Burnside's attempt at renewing the campaign in January 1863—the infamous Mud March.

The Eleventh Corps missed the Fredericksburg debacle, and was in reserve during the Mud March, so Theodore Dodge's journal does not reflect the worst of the army's troubles in these weeks. Yet in these pages Dodge often catches the army's mood. In his own sphere, the way he believed the 119th New York was administered offended his sense of order and his respect for military discipline. In this period, as usual, camp rumors flourished. Dodge's speculations on General Nathaniel Banks is an example. In reality, Banks, last in charge of the Washington defenses, was then on his way to take command of the Department of the Gulf.

December 15, 1862

You cannot imagine the horrible state of the roads here; no one can know how bad roads *can* get, unless one has seen them after an army has passed over them. The men have to march on either side, and even at that they *wade* in the mud. Progress therefore is very slow. We left our camp at 8 A.M. and at noon arrived at Stafford Court House, where we halted for a couple of hours to draw rations & cook our coffee. There we met the Q. M., who came on with the Regiment for the rest of the day. We also for the first time received rations for the officers, to be put to their credit. Of course the rations consisted of hard tack & coffee, but even this was acceptable. We have camped half a mile this side of the Rappahannock, near the Aquia Creek and Fredericksburg Railroad.

Heavy firing is going on along all the lines. The papers will tell you of all that happens before you get this, but defeat seems to be the result!

December 16, 1862

We got to within half a mile of Falmouth last night, the Q. M. for a wonder with us, his wagons however behind. We lost our way three or four times trying to follow the Brigade, as we had Regiments behind for the 2 or 3 miles of the march. However we at last camped on the side of a hill, & lay down to our rest, after a supper of crackers & two or three spoonfuls of coffee, cooked in two tin cups. During the night a high wind arose which all but blew our clothes off our backs and our blankets away.

Towards morning (we were to march at 6 o'clock) came on a heavy shower, which made the water run above and below us. This continued till 8 A.M. and in the midst of all Col. Peissner, who thought we were to move in the rain and darkness (he has never been on campaign before) kept sticking his head out of his blanket & calling "Adjutant!" to send me here and there. He is forever doing something unnecessary, which he calls "obeying orders," i.e. we had orders to march at 6 A.M. But as it was so dark and rainy, the reveillé was not sounded from Head Quarters as usual. But Col. P. must have it all down in the 119th, and so we stood there, all ready to march, the laughing stock of the Brigade. We lay in camp all day, firing going on occasionally along the lines.

In the P.M. we got verbal orders to be ready at a moment's notice & we supposed we were to be led to attack somewhere. However the plans were changed, in War Council by Burnside, Sigel & others, & instead of marching, orders were sent to send the wagons for 4 days' rations. These were distributed this evening. We pitched our tents & passed the night quite comfortably.

December 17, 1862

Today we are marching back to Stafford Court House, which we left two days ago. What it means no one knows. It really seems as if we are playing at soldiers. We lounge about all day with no definite purpose, & take part in no movements in the Army. It is rumored that Lee & Burnside had an interview at Fredericksburg. If so, what could it have been for? It is said Lee left in an angry mood. Some say we are going down to join Banks at Harrison's Landing, where he was said to be at last accounts. I scarce believe it, but think we are sent to oppose some raid of Jackson's or something of that kind. We have had heavy frosts, which make the roads somewhat better than they were the other day. Still they are anything but good, and the straggling, despite our short marches, is awful.

I fear my journal is dreadfully common-place, but you have no idea of the difficulty of keeping it. Really there is no moment of the day, while marching, when I have real leisure, & when in camp there is nothing of interest. However, as you want it, I will do my best. We received a mail this evening after arriving at Stafford Court House, and in it a letter from George, which gave us unusual pleasure, as all his letters do. What he says is true, "No one can ride except on an English saddle."

This marching is very hard work for a horse at this season of the year, on account of the load they have to carry. Three or four blankets, saddle bags full of rations & necessaries, 2 feeds of corn or oats, and the man in heavy winter garments, making a heavy load which is apt to make their backs sore & ruin them very soon. We have camped in a pine wood, where Franklin's old Division used to be. We found huts half destroyed, but better than bare ground. We make them a foundation & pitch wall tents over them. The trains we left at Dumfries were here when we arrived, & as those we were allowed are also here, our full compliment of 6 trains is complete.

The Q. M. is also here. He hopes to get into Washington some day soon. It is said we shall stay here some days or even weeks. We have hard living: for example, for a week we have had nothing but hard tack and salt pork. So it goes: no sleep—no food—plenty of hard work! Yet "who would not be a soldier?"

Stafford Court House, December 18, 1862

A week more and Christmas will be here; Xmas fraught with so little of the gaiety which will greet its arrival in the North, or indeed anywhere out of the limits of an army in the field. You will have to celebrate & enjoy for us, and allow us to participate with you by post. Actually another Xmas is at hand. It scarcely seems as if it could be so. Yet to think about it, it seems a long time since last year at this time. When I was North last, it seemed as if the year had been short; but so many events have been crowded into it, that it seems long. This is the second Xmas I shall have passed in camp.

We are sitting in our wall tent after tea, the Q. M. writing, the Colonel ditto, the Dr. and Chaplain opposite to me on the Lieut. Col.'s camp bed, reading. We are pretty comfortable considering the cold, having got some boards on the floor and there being a blazing fire in the stove. Colonel, Lieut. Colonel, Q. M. and I sleep in the tent on account of the stove, tho' the tent belongs to Lieut. Col. and myself. Two camp cots are in it now and a table, which at night is removed to make room for two more cots. The two "permanencies" are the Colonel's and Lieut. Colonel's, the two "temporaries" are the Quarter Master's & mine. Chaplain and Dr. occupy another tent, while the one put up for the Colonel, and abandoned for this one with the stove, is taken possession of by the Adjutant's table & desk, and occupied by Sergt. Major Mengel and my clerk.

By the way, I don't know as I ever told you about the Sergt. Major. He is a fine looking, strong fellow about 24 years of age, and intelligent. He is a German. The first time he saw me he was in the Adjutant's Department, and he said to Berger, the clerk, who was writing there: "I have seen the Adjutant somewhere." Afterwards he asked me if I had ever been in Berlin and I found out that he and I had been to school together there. He has a wonderful memory, which often serves me a good purpose.

Major Baldwin came over from Head Quarters this morning. He is a nice little fellow. Col. P. had an inspection this morning—a failure as usual. Lieut. Col. Lockman has just been ordered as Brigade Officer of the Day to Head Quarters. He will have 5 days' hard work. What a difference there is between our old 101st and the 119th!! In the first, discipline and order, in the other, nothing but folly in management and consequently a Regiment in a sad condition. Could we have the Lieut. Col. command for a month, things would be in a different condition.

What folly and imprudence was shown by Burnside in his attack on the Rebel position beyond Fredericksburg! The columns had to march up a slope of half a mile, and during the whole of their progress were swept down by a storm of grape, canister & musketry. Not a million of men could have carried the position!

The following journal entry is unusual in that the normally optimistic Dodge erupts in an outburst of pessimism, even going to the extreme of confessing that all his enthusiasm for the war "is gone." Certainly, he was accurate in believing that most in the army shared his opinion. And his longing for the deposed General McClellan was also a widely shared sentiment.

Stafford Court House, December 19, 1862

Slept very cold last night, my feet being like two lumps of ice. Could not keep warm anyhow, and made myself quite lame by drawing myself into a heap to try to keep warm. We had an inspection in the afternoon by Major Baldwin; the whole Brigade was turned out, Genl. Burnside wishing to know how many men he could rely upon in the Corps in case of need.

It is said here that it was an express and direct order to Genl. Burnside from Genl. Halleck to attack Fredericksburg in front, while Genl. Burnside's plan was entirely different. If so, Genl. H. ought to be removed. We hear of Banks now and then, but no one knows where he is. Sometimes at Suffolk, sometimes at Norfolk, joining the troops there. As to us, no one knows what we are to do. Sometimes we are said to be about to make an attack on the right, sometimes on the left; then again we are to retreat. It is always mismanagement and defeat. All my enthusiasm for the war is gone. We fight for no set purpose except to please politicians. Our best Generals are set aside to make way for men whose plans, however noble a force they have, always end in defeat. I often feel we might just as well be at home. Either let us adopt such a course as will ruin the Rebel cause, or let them go in peace. Almost everyone in the Army is of the same opinion. Take us into action and we fight like heroes, because it is our individual nature to desire to exterminate individual Rebels; but not because each man has the encouragement of obtaining the desired end of conquering a peace.

I still fully believe, if McClellan had been left in command, all would have been well and so do all who ever served under him. The poor boys who were led up to that fearful hill beyond Fredericksburg think so too. A squad of some 100 or more wounded were lying near our camp at Falmouth. I talked with them and they said "McClellan would not have led us there—he knew better."

Dodge was right to credit the rumor of an enemy raid in the army's rear. It was one of several such strikes in this period by Stuart's cav-

alry, this one led by Wade Hampton. The various other rumors listed in these entries were just that. The Prince Felix Salm-Salm mentioned in the December 21 entry, former Prussian cavalryman, was married to the former "Miss Leclerq," actress and circus rider. In the December 28 entry, Lieutenant Dodge meets the princess, and is dazzled.

December 20th 1862

Slept colder last night than the night before even, and the night itself was colder. However as soon as one gets breakfast one is warmed up again. We have got our mess in order again; for breakfast this morning we had stewed kidneys, hash and beefsteak. Now this sounds well for camp, don't it? For dinner, curry, boiled pork and beans; good too. For tea we shall have cold beef; good again. The only thing is, it is all beef. No other meat can be procured, except salt pork, and between the two you can well understand how a man can get tired. But this is better than most soldiers have. I have been desiring several days to change my underclothing, but it is so cold that I never get to it. My hands too get so badly chapped that they give me much inconvenience.

We have just heard that 39 of our teams have been captured, and there is a rumor that the Rebels are at Brentsville, between here and Washington. I am inclined to credit it, for, as I tell you I have no faith in our leaders. We shall probably move tomorrow. I am glad to see that Government has begun to dismiss officers who fail in their duty. We have so much trash in the way of officers from our mode of recruiting that many need to be dismissed. A list is now published at Head Quarters of Army of Potomac which gave items as follows:

"A. B., Lieut. Colonel, dismissed for cowardice," &c &c. Among others old Brown of the 101st, our intriguing old Lieut. Colonel. By the way, I have got a little nigger, Johnny Bush by name, stands 3 ft. 3 in. in his stockings (when he has any), strong & healthy, black as a crow, as sharp as a chisel,

11 years old. If you want him and will pay his passage, I'll send him to you. He understands horses & will ride anything, and would make the best little tiger in London. What say you?

December 21, 1862

To go back to the beginning of the last 24 hours. I arranged my bed in a new fashion last night, and managed to sleep tolerably warm; but a camp cot is something very different to a double post bedstead. It doubtless has its advantages: it rolls up in a bag 1 ft. 10 ins. long and weighs only 10 1/2 pounds; but it certainly requires practice to sleep comfortably upon it in cold weather. First, it entirely prevents one from drawing one's self into a heap. One must be straight. Next, unless you are clever at "tucking yourself in," the cold assails you most unmercifully in the flank, and you know to be attacked in the flank is the most dangerous of all misadventures. Now, if one is apt to change his position in the night from right to left, or vice versa, or from lying on one side to lying on his back (these being the only positions one can indulge in), he has to proceed with the greatest caution, for if he should happen to give a "jerk" or be at all precipitate in his movements, an inlet for the icy air is at once made. It has to be done by a gradual process.

First make up your mind as to whether it is best to undertake the change at all, and if you decide in the affirmative, begin by turning your head one "point" (we will suppose there are 32 points in the circle), then you follow the same with your shoulders, then body, then hips, and so on to the nether extremities. You then repeat the process, one point at a time, till the desired change is made, taking care not to begin a fresh movement with the head till that with the feet is completed. As to having a nightmare or bad dreams, these are entirely inadmissible, as they would necessitate making up the bed several times during the night.

This is one of the comforts of camp life. Everybody says, "I hope you won't go into winter quarters—something must be done first." I should like them to be in our places a few weeks. I tell you it is getting late in the season to keep up this campaign. It is so cold that not the slightest sign of thawing is seen during the day; the roads remain hard and brittle, and at night the thermometer regularly falls to 10º or 12º.

Rumors are of course more prevalent in camp than "on charge." I give you now and then one to shew you what we have to occupy our minds. Today Harper's Ferry is said to have been taken by a cavalry raid. Three Regiments—in all 1,000 men—were the garrison, who (says Genl. Slocum) were Marylanders, and would all run at the sight of a horseman. 2nd. Genl. Sigel has been called to the command of the Army of the Potomac. 3rd. The Cabinet has resigned *en masse*. These are the rumors of the day.

Took a ride with the Q. M. this P.M. Went out 2 or 3 miles toward Falmouth. Saw a farmer at a house who had lost an arm in the Secesh Army. Later, rode with Colonel to see Major Baldwin at Genl. Sigel's Head Quarters. The Major is a great hand to want to "trade" everything he has. He wanted to trade coats with me, but I didn't see it; then spurs, then horses; result the same. We then rode out to see Prince Salm-Salm, Col. of 8th New York Volunteers, whom we found a blasé, played-out, gentlemanly man; really combining both these qualities. He expects the Princess S.S. to spend Xmas. Lord, how delicious a petticoat will look! The Q. M. is just lecturing on the war to Lieut. Schwerin and the Dr.; he is called the patriarch of Brigade, is the Q. M., and he lectures accordingly.

December 22, 1862

Today we have heard through the newspapers of the indignation of the North at the slaughter in the mad storming of Fredericksburg batteries, and it does not at all astonish us. We received a letter also from Mother, in which she speaks in high language on the topic. Today's rumor is that Genl. Banks has taken Fort Darling on the James River, & that has caused the retreat of the Rebels from Fredericksburg. Also that Genl. McClellan has taken Halleck's place, Burnside resigned, and Sigel is to take command of the Army of the Potomac. Of course we never know what to believe and what to reject.

Capt. Willis was sent to Washington today, to bring some India rubber blankets sent from New York State for our Regt.; and to transact some other business. The suitable person to have sent was of course the Q. M., but as we do not know when we may move, Genl. Schurz said he could not be spared. We all envied Capt. Willis, for each of us would like to have gone.

We had a singular piece of good luck today for this barren country. Our mess scouts succeeded in getting some milk, some butter, & some fresh bread. Those who have not been deprived of these articles during a fortnight's hard marching, and have lived during that time on hard tack, can scarce imagine what luxury they were.

This evening at supper we had a merry time. We started betting on some of the events of the war—all of us betting, including the Q. M., from one to twelve bottles of champagne. The Q. M. says he don't consider betting *in camp* wrong, as it keeps from laziness & consequent wickedness. I wish we could get the champagne here at Xmas.

In his report to his superiors, dated December 17 and released to the press, Burnside accepted full blame for Fredericksburg. The fact that his superiors, he wrote, "left the whole management in my hands, without giving me orders, makes me the more responsible." In a marginal note next to his account of the less-than-merry Christmas observances, Dodge laid blame on the War Department, which "with

its usual sagacity" forbade the return of the sutlers to the camps,
"and in consequence the Army had no Xmas dinner." For much of
this period, General Sigel was absent in Washington and the
Eleventh Corps was commanded by the Hungarian-born Julius Sta-
hel, yet another émigré from Europe's revolutionary upheavals of
1848. Dodge's first impression of him was not favorable.

December 23, 1862

Today we have Burnside's report exonerating the President from all blame in the matter of the late battle. In my opinion it is a weak document, unworthy of any man who pro-
fesses to be competent to command the Army of the Potomac.
Just what I foretold has come to pass: McClellan, who was
slowly on his way to Richmond by way of Warrenton, was removed and Burnside put in his place. I was sure it would end
in some botch or another. Burnside's first idea was a blunder.
He expected to get halfway between Fredericksburg and
Richmond before he met the Rebels, and force them to fight at
a disadvantage by cutting off the Fredericksburg & Richmond
Railroad, and consequently their supplies. Instead of that, the
Rebels got to Fredericksburg first; then instead of shelling
them out of the town at once, he gave them 16 hours' respite.
Three weeks after, when he had given them time to erect
strong fortifications, he attacks them, and is of course beaten.
Had McClellan been left in his place as commander in chief, I
believe Richmond would have been taken almost a year ago.
But of course what is destined to be, is. I feel as if nothing but
our reputation for good fighting were left us.

Our horses have been very short of forage lately; plenty
of oats but no hay. Today however some hay came, and the
horses greedily devoured it, leaving the oats untasted. This
is a hard life for horses, when on marches there is scarce
anything to eat. In camp therefore we have to feed them up,
so that they frequently get from 16 to 20 quarts of oats a day.

Of course alternately stuffing and starving does them no good.

This A.M. the Colonel and I rode out together, and stopped in to see Colonel Von Gilsa, commandant of the 1st Brigade of Stahel's Division. He has his wife with him and has had during all this war. Madame is a rather good looking woman of 26 or 27, and says she likes camp life. She certainly looked very nice in this wilderness of men. Our only women are laundresses, rather amphibious creatures and not worth looking at, even in camp. We saw Genl. Stahel too—a misanthropic looking man.

There is a great lack of whiskey in camp; nobody has any, and everybody is going the rounds begging for it. Tobacco has also run short, and all the sutlers have gone to Washington for supplies for Xmas.

December 24th 1862

Christmas Eve has come again, and here we are in camp still. No sign of festivity seen anywhere, and it might be any other day in the year for ought you could see in any change in camp routine. We have not been able to get even the extra issue of flour and dried apples expected for the men; and the whiskey promised us is not yet forthcoming. I heartily wish we could get a little something to celebrate on, but there seems to be no chance of it.

The Colonel, Lieut. Colonel, Quarter Master, Lieut. Orleman and I all rode out this P.M. to see if we could not forage something for tomorrow; but all we succeeded in getting was some apples. We heard of some pigeons, but we could not see any. We also saw some chickens, but the owner would not part with any as he wanted them to breed from. Major Baldwin has got one bottle of champagne, and the Colonel another, and we are going to club and see what we can do in the way of drinking health to our friends. Some of the men this evening have manufactured Xmas trees. One of them is illuminated with 3 bits of tallow candle, and is hung all over with hard biscuit. Another is decorated with bits of salt pork. The Brigade drums are going about serenading this evening (there are some 30 in all), and such a din you never heard. The men of our Company are singing a German *Te Deum* just outside my tent, which is pleasant to hear.

December 25, 1862

I have really no spirit to write on Xmas day, so little like Xmas is it to me. This A.M. Lieut. Col. Lockman and I were out again to see if we could find anything in the way of fowl for dinner. We rode a long way round the country and at last found a fine farm, one of the more flourishing I have seen in Virginia, the road to which was entirely blocked up by fallen trees (probably the cause of its prosperity). There were 5 or 6 turkeys, hens, guinea hens, and other farmyard animals, presided over by a testy old woman, who refused to part with any for our Xmas dinner, for love or money, and who was backed up by a safeguard of two men from Sykes' Regulars. The old crone was inexorable, and we had to feast in imagination on the fowls.

However the cooks of the mess managed better than we expected. They gave us a piece of salt beef and potatoes, besides a cracker pudding and rice ditto, and a dessert of apples. All this was enriched by a bottle of champagne, which the Colonel had nourished up in his trunk to be drunk after our first fight; but as that don't seem to be forthcoming, we made merry over it. So you see we ate heartily and did not starve after all.

In the P.M. some of us rode out in search of a drink of whiskey, the scarcity of which has made us all feel very *dry*. We met Major Baldwin and under his guidance (he is a lucky fellow at procuring the "O-be-joyful") found a bottle of "tug-for," half of which we drank and took the rest to the Q. M. Capt. Willis has returned from Washington where he has been after India rubber blankets. He has done his business well.

December 26, 1862

Turned out the Battalion today at 9 o'clock A.M., and marched some 2 miles toward Falmouth, where we found a fine drill ground and drilled till 1 P.M. I have come to the conclusion that none of the officers of this Regiment know anything about drilling. Some of them make perfect asses of themselves. I acted as Major.

A new Lieut. (Southworth by name) came today and began his duties. Yesterday at dress parade, 4 noncommissioned officers' names were read out for promotion at the proposal of Gov. Morgan, there being vacancies in the Regiment; and they are to act as 2nd Lieuts. I have thereby lost my Sergt. Major, but he will be well replaced; he is a nice fellow and I am glad he has got a Commission.

December 27, 1862

I changed quarters today to the tent which the Col. first put up for himself, but which he left when the Lieut. Col. put up our tent. The Col., Lt. Col. and I have hitherto been in one tent, which obliged me every day to take down my cot, I being the junior officer. As this was inconvenient, I have put my cot into the Adjutancy, hanging a screen to shelter it from the public gaze. I am now very comfortable. Dr. Aymé has given me a stove which formerly belonged to the junior assistant surgeon, Dr. Stadler, who has left us very mysteriously, no one knowing his whereabouts. However, I always stay with the Q. M. during the day. He tents with the Dr. and Chaplain. His tent is always the most frequented in camp. We mess there now, as we were not able to bring along our mess tent on the march from Centreville.

Today is the first for several weeks that I have not taken a ride, but I have been so busy all day that I have not thought of going out. It is seldom my mare gets a rest. I dare say it will do her good. It takes a *good* horse to do all the work for an Adjutant, week after week. I wish I could afford to buy another. If I can get one cheap, I think I shall try for one and feed it up against the spring. (Note by the Q. M. *No he won't.* The Govt. owes him $300 & so he feels rich just now.) There are always lots of good horses on sale about camp, owing to deaths, or resigning officers wishing to get rid of their stock. Also horses run down by hard work, which feeding and care will make as good as ever.

The Confederate cavalry raid noted here was led by Jeb Stuart in person, and was a gaudy adventure. Stuart penetrated to within fifteen miles of Washington before returning to camp after extensive captures that included nine Yankee sutlers' wagons. The derelict pay system Dodge speaks of was scandalous and one of the reasons for sagging morale in the army. For soldiers with dependents it could mean true hardship. Aquia Landing, mentioned by Dodge on December 29, was the Army of the Potomac's supply base. The supply line ran by water from Alexandria to Aquia, and from there to the camps by a section of the Richmond, Fredericksburg & Potomac Railroad. Falmouth, on the north bank of the Rappahannock diagonally across from Fredericksburg, served as army headquarters.

December 28, 1862
Slept very well for the first time in my new quarters, altho' they were somewhat damp, owing to there being no fire in them since they were put up. After a stove has been in a tent a few days it dries up the ground and makes it much more comfortable.

The Col. and I rode out this A.M. and on our way met Prince Salm-Salm (Col. of the 8th New York) walking with his wife, who has come to visit him. She is quite a pretty woman and looked doubly lovely in our eyes who have not seen a woman for a long time. In my opinion Prince Salm-Salm is at the present moment the happiest and most lucky man in the Army of the Potomac. I tell you it made my mouth water to see a man walking around with a pretty woman among these desolations.

Here in camp we are something like the Californians in the first year of the settlement. There was only one woman in San Francisco, when it had got to be quite a large place. When she passed along the streets the men would run out of their houses and cry, "There goes the woman! There goes the woman!" very much like "Mad Bull."

Genl. Schimmelfennig, commanding the 1st Brigade of our Division (Schurz's) has been out to Dumfries, 12 miles north of this, to repulse a raid of Stuart's cavalry. He left yesterday, and as since 3 A.M. today no news has been heard of him, the 75th Pennsylvania and 26th Wisconsin, two Regiments of our Brigade, were sent out towards Dumfries to reinforce him this afternoon. Genl. Schurz and Lieut. Col. Meysenburg, the A. A. Genl. of Sigel's Corps, went out too. About 4 P.M. Col. Peissner, who was at dinner with Colonel Krzyzanowski (our Brigade commander, who has just returned from Washington, where he has been for 3 weeks past) delectating off macaroni soup, tongue, turkey, mince pies, &c, &c, was summoned in hot haste to Genl. Stahel, who commands the Corps during Genl. Sigel's absence, & ordered to be ready to march at a moment's notice. So we commenced preparations. We were to have gone to Aquia. At 7 o'clock the Col. went over to see Genl. Krzyzanowski, and came back laughing, saying we might make ourselves comfortable again, which we accordingly did. It seems that Schimmelfennig had a fight today at Dumfries (we heard the cannonading) and drove the Rebels back. All the officers, except Lieut. Col. Lockman and Capt. L. (his brother), who were old officers of the 9th N. Y. Militia, were in high glee and eager for a "recontre" with the foe. But we tell them that after they have been in one or two fights they will not be so anxious for another. The 75th and 26th are on their way back, having had nothing but their march.

Our Chaplain, Charlier, has gone to Washington to meet his brother, who came from New York to see him. A Chaplain, you see, can always get a pass, having so few regimental duties to perform.

We are making out muster rolls for payment, a duty which falls to our share every two months. We are mustered 6 times a year but not paid more than 3 times. The Government owes many men in the Regiment 6 months' pay; they owe me $300 odd. We are all very hard up nowadays, and sometimes scarce know how to scrape together enough to keep up with the mess. We are going to have a general break-up on the 1st provisimo—discharge all niggers and give up the mess, as it costs more than it comes to.

December 29, 1862

Capt. Graham, one of our Captains who has been on sick leave, returned today. He is a German Jew in every action and word; not a pleasant addition to our list of officers. With him came Lieut. Peissner, the Colonel's brother, a *nicish* little fellow—the very miniature of a man. He got a fever at Centreville just before we left and is now but just able to come on.

The Q. M. and Col. took a ride this A.M. to Aquia Landing; they say it is a beautiful ride, and that it looks like home when you get there. It is only 8 miles from here and I think I shall ride down there some day.

I have been very busy today examining pay rolls. No one knows how to make them out & they run to me every minute

131

for information. We have the dullest set of officers you ever saw, and more than this they won't learn. I am making out the monthly report, which, of course, I consolidate from the Company reports, and sometimes I have to send a report back 6 or 7 times before I can get it correct. This is one of the minor evils.

Owing to the march of the 26th and 75th yesterday, we had to furnish a picket for today (while we only came off picket yesterday), and also a fatigue party, so that our camp is almost deserted. We do not do picket here as we used to in Kearny's Division. There, a Regiment used to march out at once; here we have only a certain number of men detailed from each Regiment. This last is much more irksome, as picket comes on oftener, and then the men are not always commanded by their own officers, which renders the duty less precise. Our Brigade has only 200 men to furnish daily, which after all is not very hard.

December 30th 1862

I have got all the pay rolls finished, by dint of pushing, and we are all ready for muster tomorrow or whenever the mustering officer comes. Generally the Colonel of each Regiment musters his own command, but this time no orders to this effect have been given. It is to be hoped that they will send our Paymaster out soon, for some of the men have owing them from date of enlistment last May and June. The trouble is, money is scarce. There are no "greenbacks" on hand. They cannot be got out fast enough.

Lieut. Boas, a querulous, dirty old man, with the bad habit of sticking his face close up to yours whenever he is talking to you, resigned today—having been ill for some time past and not being able to get "sick leave" (for none are now granted unless the surgeon gives certificates that the applicant is in danger of permanent disability or his life). The Lieut. has resigned to the great joy of all. The resignations, six in number, since I have been in the Regiment, have all been for the best, and are beginning to clear out some of the rubbish.

One of our darkies, Dick by name, got thrown from a horse today and broke his collar bone. The Dr. set it, but just like a negro, he groaned and groaned till he made everybody angry, and until the Q. M. went to his tent and told him to "stop" (very much in the manner he told me when my finger was cut off when I was a child), "that he wasn't going to die, and that he needn't try to make believe he was either." Whereupon Dick stopped, to the relief of all and to his own good. He will be removed to Washington in ten days or a fortnight. The Dr. had to have the bandages and apparatus for setting the collar bone made, and a very pretty one it was too. I am getting to be, by frequent practice, somewhat an amateur in operations, and I am thinking something of studying surgery.

The Q. M., Capt. Willis and I rode out this A.M. to Mr. Lawrence Cliff's, the place Lieut. Col. Lockman and I found the other day when hunting for an Xmas dinner. We tried to get them to sell us something, but even the Q. M.'s logic was to no avail—the gruff old Secesh woman would not part with a thing. This farm is the most cheerful picture of country life I have yet seen in Virginia—12 or 14 head of cattle browsing upon the corn stalks in a field hard by, a flock of turkeys wandering about, with barn yard fowls and guinea hens, the pigs basking and grunting in the farm yard, and the hens cackling, and children playing about the yard, and the negroes working here and there about the premises. I asked a bright little boy "Whose son he was." "Mr. Rose's," said he. "So you are not Mr. Cliff's boy?" "Oh, no." "Where is your Father?" "In town," i.e. Richmond. Poor boy—he had been given in charge of Mr. Cliff while his Father went to fight in the Rebel service.

The Col. was on the point of buying a new horse today, but as the owner wanted *cash*, he could not. The horse was young, and a good animal for the price ($80) altho' considerably worked.

It has begun to rain slightly this evening, I fear the prelude to the rainy season. It has been remarkably mild almost all this month. The farmers say there has never been known such a season before. The roads will probably get bad again.

Tonight the mail brought the "News of the Churches" directed in Mrs. G.'s hand. Lieutenant Colonel Lockman, on seeing it, said "Punch," thinking it was "Punch." Thereupon the Quarter Master and I thought we would ask you (George) to send us Punch every week. It would relieve our monotonous life oftentimes. Will you send it?

December 31st 1862

Four or five hours more and we shall write 1863! I feel as if it were the end of the year, and just low enough to enact the part of the grey-bearded old year. I have been trying to write a business letter & failed, and I fear what I now attempt will be intolerably stupid.

We were mustered today by Capt. Lockman of our Regiment—Lieut. Col. and Capt. Lockman (his brother) were appointed to muster the Brigade. It was a hard day's work, as the day has been cold and windy. We sent our pay rolls in to Major Campbell, our Paymaster, by private hand, and hope to be the first on the list for payment. He wrote today saying he hoped to be with us early next week.

Our Chaplain went into Washington a couple of days ago, and got mustered out of service, and in again as Captain of the 157th N.Y., his brother, a professor in New York, having procured him the Commission. This evening he came back and brought his brother with him to see camp. We are sorry and glad to lose him, as he is too "nagging" to be the best of companions, tho' a nice fellow enough.

The Q. M. and I took a ride this P.M. off towards Falmouth. We took a road which I had partly explored, and after a long detour it brought us out near Mr. Cliff's farm, which I have before mentioned. It was a curious road, in some places showing signs of considerable travel, and again completely lost in the woods and so concealed by fallen leaves as to make it difficult to follow it. There have been many troops in this vicinity and of course the country is all cut up with roads leading in every direction to and from the camps.

We received a warlike letter from Mother this evening and also one from George, of the 12th inst. The Q. M. will write soon, but has not been able to through all this marching and counter-marching for the last 3 weeks. A ration of whiskey and an extra ration of sugar has been served out today, of which to make the New Year grog. The men have most of them already partaken of the luxury, and are now making it manifest by songs and cheers—a little too noisily to suit my ideas of discipline—but not the Germans'.

In obedience to the custom of going calling on New Year's Day, Adjutant Dodge and his colonel made the rounds in the Eleventh Corps. It was said that their brigade commander, Colonel Wladimir Krzyzanowski, put up for brigadier general in November 1862, failed to be confirmed by the Senate because no one in that body could pronounce his name. In fact, of the six brigades in the Eleventh Corps, only Nathaniel C. McLean held brigadier's rank appropriate to the position. As with most diarists and journal writers, Dodge included in his first-day-of-the-year entry an overview of affairs, and he left no doubt who he wanted in command of the army. Nor did he leave any doubt of his opinion (January 2) of the effects of the Emancipation Proclamation. The Seymour mentioned in the January 3 entry is Horatio Seymour, Democratic governor of New York.

January 1st 1863

I did not sit up to drink the New Year in last night, but I nevertheless saw '62 change into '63. We all went to bed early, but were awakened at 12 o'clock by three vehement cheers in front of the Col.'s tent—the most appropriate place, as the men thought. Some captain had kept his Company up and cheered the New Year as it came in. At the same time there began the most outrageous discharge of firearms—many men, as I suppose, had let their allowance of grog get the better of them, and were venting their superfluous *spirits* in utter disregard of all military rule. It actually went so far that whole volleys were fired by the excited Dutch soldiery before it was stopped. A provost guard was patrolling around the camp in order to arrest the delinquents, but I believe they did not succeed. I caught one man, whom I bound to a tree with his accouterments, which effectually quenched his mirth. Gradually the excitement subsided, and quiet was restored.

This A.M. the Col. and all the officers went over to Col. Krzyzanowski's to wish him "Many happy returns of the day," for which piece of politeness we were rewarded with some hot punch brewed out of such wretched whiskey that I got a severe headache from it. However the intention was hospitable—but it was my habit of using *good* liquor when I use any that made it disagree with me. *That* could not be put down to Col. K.'s account. This same Col. K. is a crockery dealer at home; & while he is off to the wars, Madame K. keeps up said business. She comes out here occasionally, at which times she is Madame La Générale; at home however she is Mistress Crockery. I have never had the happiness of seeing her. Of my immediate Brigade commander I will not speak, having the Articles of War in my memory, but I may state that he has the reputation of being an old bear.

Later in the day the Col. and I rode out to make a few calls. These were to Major Baldwin, Genl. Stahel (who received us courteously; he at present commands the Corps in absence of Genl. Sigel), to Col. Von Gilsa, whose wife is in the camp, and to Genl. McLean, who is absent in Washington. There was however a beautiful band playing in front of his quarters. Col. Krzyzanowski had another dinner today, to which our 3 field officers were invited. As usual they had all which goes to constitute a good dinner—Col. K. is a great hand at getting good things out here.

In the P.M. the Quarter Master and I rode out to Aquia Creek—some 8 miles from here. It did me good again to see a large body of water. We have thought a great deal about you today and wished you many a happy New Year. By the next return of this day, I hope we may all be in more prosperous circumstances and this wretched war be brought to a close.

By the way, I may as well tell you how the Army feels about the conduct of this war. *Everyone is longing for McClellan.* They say now, "Let us go into action and a few get killed and then the rest retreat." This is just the feeling they have about Burnside, no confidence in his ability at all. But every heart is so turned toward McClellan that his being put in command of the U.S. Army would *this* moment more than double the force of the troops. They will go *anywhere* under him, but with reluctance under any other leader; and any day I believe McClellan could lead us up & take those Fredericksburg batteries, considered now impregnable.

January 2nd 1863

The Q. M. got a pass to Washington to get India rubber blankets, and started after an early dinner from here. The Lieut. Col. and I accompanied him as far as Aquia Landing. You would be astonished to see the road there. It was quite hot during the day, which made everything except the woods appear summerlike. The road was flat and hard, covered with a thin layer of dust, as good as you could find in summer, and had it not been for the fallen leaves and dry corn stalks in the field, one would have supposed it a June day. Indeed no one has ever seen such weather at this season of the year. Since October 20th (when I arrived in Virginia) there have been but 3 or 4 *days* of cold weather, & now there has been no rain for 2 or 3 weeks. Consequently we are daily expecting a change, and when it does come I fear it will be severe. Two days of rain would make the roads, now so good, quite impassable, and perhaps this is what prevents forward movements. Should we get bad roads behind us, it would play the mischief.

We today got the Proclamation, "All slaves shall be and are hereafter free." Will it have much effect I wonder? I fancy not. I tell you plainly I do not believe the people of the North susceptible to unity to a degree which will be required to put down the Rebellion. Could we have unity of purpose as the South has, we could easily accomplish all we desire. Now you see by the Proclamation that we are fighting, not for the Union but for the *nigger*. I however am *not* fighting for the nigger. I fight because having once gone into it, I will not back out.

This evening we got a chess board belonging to one of the line officers, and have had a nice game or two. The Col. came in and joined us. He plays a superior game—it is one of his fortes. Afterwards we played Fox and Geese, which is very scientific in its simplicity.

January 3rd 1863

It is very lonely without the Q. M., and all look forward to his return with eagerness. We hope also that he will bring back many things, such as "O-be-joyful" and other camp luxuries. He will try and bring out a case of champagne. We all made some bets a month ago in champagne, which we hope to see paid.

Today we went out to a drill ground some 2 miles from here, where we had a good drill till 2 P.M. The men did much better today than I ever saw them do before. All the mistakes which are made are entirely through the stupidity of some of the officers. We had sent out 3 Companies to Head Quarters this A.M. for fatigue duty, and consequently I consolidated the 7 remaining Companies into six. There were only 250 men out, which shows the low ebb of the Regiment. It has never been in action, and yet only 485 men appear for duty on the morning report. They say we are going to be filled out with drafted men, but I don't believe Seymour will draft at all.

Ever since I have been in camp, I have been growing in flesh. When I came to camp I weighed 135 lbs., now I weigh 155—a clear gain of 20 lbs. They laugh at me and say I am getting "obese." The good Dr. told me so in his queer way a few days ago, which sounded like "a beast," and since, it has been quite a by-word. I however am not muscularly as strong as I used to be. We live very regularly of course in camp, when not on the march, and eat a great deal of flour which I suppose is fattening. The Dr. thinks too that riding has a tendency to make one fleshy.

We have been playing chess again this evening. The Col. gives Queen, or 2 Castles, and beats everyone then. He is really a fine player.

January 4th 1863

Sunday is never Sunday in camp, and today has appeared less like Sunday than ever, by reason of the Q. M.'s absence. Our quarters (I mean Field and Staff) seem almost deserted without him. He is about the "live man" of the camp, as Uncle Isaac calls him, and his tent is our usual resort. I got a letter from him today dated at Willard's, thro' the Q. M. of the 38th New York, in which he says he will be down on Tuesday morning's boat, and as he orders 2 teams to the Landing, we hope he will bring some good things along.

Today a great event has transpired. We have been able to smuggle in 2 boxes of whiskey. You must know that liquor is contraband, and not allowed to be brought into camp. Lately a box directed to Genl. Burnside was opened, and liquor being found in it, it was confiscated. However a few days ago Major Baldwin informed us of a chance to get some thro' as "Medical Stores." Of course we immediately confided the money to his care to secure the desired "drugs." Today, when we rode up to see him, he told us they had arrived. This will set us up for a long time to come.

In the Grand Division organization of the army under Burnside, Franz Sigel commanded the two-corps Reserve, consisting of his Eleventh Corps and Henry W. Slocum's Twelfth Corps. At this writing, Sigel was in Washington for a court of inquiry investigating Irvin McDowell's conduct at Second Bull Run. Sigel would barely have time to exercise his elevated command before Joe Hooker disbanded the Grand Divisions. Thus reduced to corps command, Sigel would resign in a huff. Adolph Von Steinwehr and Carl Schurz led the Eleventh's "German" divisions; Julian Stahel would in due course be assigned the cavalry defending Washington. Battalion drill (January 6), in the Civil War, meant drill by regiment, at which the 119th's German captains, in Dodge's view, were perfect "Schäfsköpfe" (sheep's heads).

January 5th 1863

The Colonel proposed to me this A.M. that we should ride over to Falmouth, which proposal I eagerly embraced. At 10 we had our horses saddled and rode over to the Head Quarters of Genl. Stahel. Genl. Stahel has command of the 11th Army Corps now that Genl. Sigel is absent in Washington on the Courts of Inquiry proceeding there. Genl. Sigel is to command a Grand Division consisting of ours & Slocum's Corps, and will be made a Major General. We got a pass therefore. Altho' refused at the Adjutant General's office, we got one on personally applying to Genl. Stahel.

We set off at 11 o'clock and took a beautiful road through the woods, which we followed for about 2 miles, and which brought us out on the Telegraph Road to Fredericksburg. After about 12 miles' riding we arrived at Falmouth, when we found our way to Genl. Von Steinwehr's quarters, which are some mile or so out of town. As the Col. wished to make him a visit, we dismounted at his door (he is quartered in a nice country house) just as he was about to sit down to dinner. He insisted on our sitting down to dinner with him, which after our long ride was too good an offer to be refused. We accordingly sat down with him and his aides at a nicely spread table. Genl. Von Steinwehr is the oldest Brig. Genl. in the 11th Army Corps, and commands the 2nd Division, Genl. Stahel having hitherto had the command of the 1st & Genl. Schurz of the 3rd.

Genl. Stahel is considered the better officer of the two, and was accordingly appointed to the command of the Corps. I think Genl. Schurz would have been the best man to promote. The General received us most kindly; he is a fine looking man, small build, but with a noble head and a magnificent sword cut from the forehead across the right eye and cheek. He probably got this in the Revolution of 1848 in Germany.

After dinner we went over to the 134th New York, which was raised in and about Schenectady, where the Colonel has many friends, and among whom I found some acquaintances. We then started on our way back. Passing thro' Falmouth we stopped at a baker's and got 12 loaves of bread (an article we cannot get here) and as we had an orderly with us and good sized saddle bags, we were able to carry it to camp. Falmouth is on the north side of the Rappahannock about 1/4 of a mile above Fredericksburg, which is on the south side. It may have contained in peaceful times some 2,000 or 3,000 inhabitants. The river is much smaller than I imagined it to be—not wider now than the Thames at Maidenhead, and fordable but for the many deep holes in its bed. Our pickets occupy this side and the Rebel pickets the other, so that they are not more than 300 yards apart. It is an understood thing that there is to be no picket firing, so that officers pass freely along the river road, and the men sit carelessly down at their posts.

Fredericksburg seems to be a considerable town, and looks beautifully from the high banks on this side. We saw many Rebel soldiers, on the opposite side, clad in our uniforms, which they had picked up on the battlefield probably. Coming home we followed the Telegraph Road most of the distance but found it very muddy.

There is a rumor that we are going from here. The Dr. made a requisition for some hospital tents, but they were refused by the Medical Director on the ground that we were about to move.

January 6th 1863

We turned out for Battalion drill this A.M., and just like our Colonel, he must go out on a ground near Genl. Schurz' Head Quarters, imagining that because the men drilled well last time they would this. Col. Krzyzanowski and several Staff officers were looking on & of course the Battalion drilled very poorly, at which the Col. swore at them, and of course the men drilled worse, so that on the whole we became quite a laughing stock. Some of the Captains are perfect *Schäfsköpfe*.

There is a Board of Examiners at Corps Head Quarters, especially for Colonels to send their inefficient officers to, in order to get rid of them. Col. P. is afraid to send in any name, while our next neighbor, Col. Jacobs of the 26th Wisconsin, sent his Lieut. Col.'s, because he wished to get rid of him. Col. P. don't dare even to send up a 2nd Lieut. Well, I hope the Regiment will improve in time.

At all events I am not sorry now that I came here, since the 101st has so shamefully been mustered out of service and the officers have all lost their Commissions. It is a burning shame that a Regiment which had been reduced down to a hundred men by hard fighting and severe service, should be consolidated with the 37th New York, and the officers who have risked their lives on so many bloody fields should lose their places in the Army as a reward of their bravery!!

The Q. M. came back this evening and brought a great many things with him. His return was greeted by all of us with great enthusiasm. He had many letters from the P.O., parcels from Express, brandy and whiskey for officers, and champagne and turkeys for tomorrow's dinner, which is to take the place of the Xmas and New Year's feasts. I got a huge pair of saddle bags for the march, which I asked him to purchase for me, among which was "Somebody's Luggage."

He also brought my old servant Henry. He is the least of a negro I ever saw put up in a black skin. There is no "yah, yah" laugh about him, the universal mark of the nig. here. He is quite an acquisition. I have been without a servant ever since I came out here, using the Q. M.'s. We opened our first bottle of champagne this evening, and enjoyed it much.

January 8th 1863

The principal event yesterday was the turkey and champagne dinner. Of course these luxuries overshadowed everything else. 1/2 doz. bottles came out of the baskets & disappeared in toasts to one and another, far and near. But as usual with great dinners it had its drawbacks, or at least so I fancied, as I for one wished I had dined off pork and beans.

The Q. M. has become the happy possessor of a barrel of apples. Yesterday, while they were loading down at the Landing, a man offered him a cigar, which he accepted. The man then begged the favor of having some barrels carried to Stafford Court House as his (Q. M.'s) wagons were not heavily loaded and he could not procure transportation. Being in a manner caught by the cigar, he consented, and lo! when the wagons were unloaded at camp (the man had taken out his barrels as they passed through the village) a barrel of apples was found, which had been left by the man! We seized upon the apples as a gift of Providence.

Major Baldwin went today to Washington and will perhaps get leave for a while, as he is not well and we are afraid will be down with camp fever. We have only had 4 deaths from this complaint since we came here.

January 11th 1863

I have not written for several days on account of a bilious attack, which has confined me to my tent since the 8th inst., and which has indisposed me for writing. As for that matter nothing having transpired, my not writing has been no loss.

Night before last Col. Schimmelfennig proposed to Col. Peissner to accompany him on an expedition, which he was about to undertake with 800 infantry and 200 cavalry and some artillery towards Catlett's Station, to find out if any Rebels were in the vicinity. They started with the party at 11 P.M., the Colonel taking Lieut. Orleman as his Adjutant, as I was too ill to go. After 24 hours passed in the saddle, they returned last night in a drenching rain, and as the expedition had no very particular results, rather disappointed. I am glad I was unable to go, as I am not in favor of long tramps to no purpose. The cavalry, during the 24 hours, traveled at least 70 miles, tho' of course the infantry went only part of the distance.

Among the Regiments who went was the 157th N.Y., the one in which Charlier, our quondam Chaplain, now Captain, is commissioned. It was his *maiden* tramp and he thought it glorious. He came over to see us today. He is getting on nicely, but says there is a vast difference between our Field and Staff and the Line of the 157th. Today the Q. M.

took out my mare to give her some exercise (as I have not been out for several days) and he is so pleased with her he declares he will have her back.

January 12th 1863

The 26th Wisconsin, which was camped just behind us and cramped us greatly as to space, moved a couple of days since, giving us room to extend our camp to double its original space. So we staked out the whole space into company streets, and set the men to moving and building huts. We may move any day, or we may stop here a month; but huts are greatly needed by the men at this season of the year, as they have only common shelter tents (*tentes d'abri*). So trees are being felled in every direction to furnish material for building; pine logs with the crevices filled in with clay make the best log house. The Q. M. had a very nice house built and fixed his tent on top of it for a roof today, and I changed quarters at the same time, and am to have a hut built tomorrow.

Today the Colonel got a box from home by Lieut. Lewis, who has been home on sick leave, and has just returned. Everything one could think of was in it, and among other things a parcel done up and labeled "For the Field and Staff. For their amusement in leisure moments." When opened it was found to contain a dancing monkey on a pole, the like of which every child in this country buys for 5 cents. A second one was sent to the Colonel in the same way.

January 14th 1863

Father is sitting at my side writing a letter to Mrs. Peissner to thank her in the name of the Field and Staff for several little niceties she sent us in the Colonel's box.

I feel almost well today and think I shall not again relapse. We have just had dinner. Major Baldwin has returned from Washington quite rid of his jaundice. A grand dinner off Mrs. P.'s box, *boeuf à la mode*, lima beans and accompanying vegetables, rice pudding, and for dessert, dates, prunes, candies, Xmas cake, and crackers and wedding cake. Champagne, and as liqueurs *aqua vitoe aromatica*, a most delicious cordial, sent to the Colonel lately by a club of which he is a member. Now don't this speak well for camp? Of course I could not join in at all.

We have just got our camp in nice order: Field and Staff in the centre; right and left wings of Regiment flanking in Company streets; avenue of fir trees leading up to a grand hospital tent which the Colonel put up today as his Head Quarters. Flags pendant on either side of entrance, and everything O.K.—when all of a sudden a rumor becomes prevalent that we are to move. A combination of events lead to this rumor. Genl. Sigel has returned from solemn conclave at Washington, and has twice been in confabulation with Genl. Burnside since he returned—Staffs, or slaves as we call them, of both assisting. Genl. Schurz came from the same city yesterday in seeming haste, and at once commenced with Genl. Sigel; orderlies are flying round, and orders to turn in this and turn out that, are brought to the several Regiments.

The Major, who generally knows more than most of Sigel's Staff, confirms the rumor. He thinks that Sigel has "roving orders" of the Stonewall Jackson character, and is about to maneuver with his Grand Division. If we go anywhere, we shall probably go towards Warrenton or Fairfax. But as yet, I am unbelieving; and until we get orders to send our sick away, I shall not give credit to the rumor.

We have just received orders to be ready to march at a few hours' notice, and although some of the officers (the Colonel and those who have not yet been in action) want to be off, the Lieut. Col., Q. M. and I are in the dumps. "To be ready" however does not mean that we are actually to move, and I hope we may not.

January 15th 1863

Genl. Schurz visited Col. Peissner today and he does not think we shall move for two or three days, if at all. The Q. M. thinks we may not move at all, from signs in the Q. M. Department of the Corps, which is generally a pretty good oracle. We have heard also that the whole Army of the Potomac has the same orders that we have, and this makes me think that we are simply under the same kind of marching orders the Army was while in winter quarters last year.

There has a most terrible order been issued today from the Q. M. Department. It seems that hay is getting scarce and they are reducing the quantity of hay, per horse per day, from 14 lbs. to 7 lbs. This, with 12 lbs. of corn, is not enough for horses so much used as those in the Army. The orders say the teamsters are to cut leaves and limbs of the maple, elm, and other soft (?) trees, which furnish a good substitute for hay. Where I wonder are we to get these in a section of country which only produces fir and pine. Rather a precarious footing our poor horses will stand on. The order furthermore says that the teams are to be kept in the best possible condition, which I suppose is to be the result of the reduction of forage. The glanders is getting common among the horses here. Today all the horses of one Regiment were shot to prevent the spread of the disease. Animals are dying off faster than Uncle Sam can supply them. The consumption of mules and horses is terrible. Out of the 30 or 40 mules and horses in this Regiment, there are at least 2 or 3 die every week.

The Lieut. Col. and I rode out this afternoon, and taking the road to the Landing we met two gentlemen who had come on from New York to see Lieut. Meade, who was sick and who had left yesterday. They had the journey for nothing, and were glad we met them so near the Landing as to save them the 6 Virginia miles' journey up to camp.

17 January 1863

We received a large mail yesterday, some hundred or more letters and a corresponding lot of papers, & in it your letters of the 9th and 12th inst. Your appeal to me not to eat and drink so much met with a hearty laugh. The truth is, you *will* have a journal, and as there is literally nothing to write about, I must write about the dinner. Your well-fed denizens of the St. Nicholas have no sympathy for us poor coffee-and-cracker sufferers. You are so encompassed with the good things of this life that the mere mention of the mediocrities of this camp palls on your senses.

Col. and I took a ride over to Head Quarters to accompany Dr. Aymé, who, poor man, has been detailed to the Corps hospital at Aquia Creek, and feels almost distracted about it. In fact he is such an impractical man, that he cannot get on except among friends, and he hates to leave us. We are exceedingly sorry to lose the good Dr., who by gentleness and real merit has won the hearts of us all.

While we were over at Head Quarters and were trying to find Dr. Brueninghausen's room, in the house where Genl. Sigel is quartered, we opened the door of a room where was a lady. Happily the Col. knew her—a Mrs. (Major) Lyons, and we were invited in and had a long and pleasant chat with her.

The weather is cold again. After 2 days of soft south wind and great mildness accompanied by rain, it has turned cold. Last night the thermometer was quite low, as low as 20°. However it continues fine, a winter such as no one about here ever remembers. I fear the bad weather is brewing, and just as it comes on, with our general luck we shall be obliged to move forward, after watching listlessly the Fredericksburg fortifications thro' the past month of marvelous fine weather and roads, and opportunities for maneuvering.

These machinations for high command of the Eleventh Corps would come to naught under the Hooker regime. Dodge's hopes that among the various promotions might be his own, to be brigade adjutant, were also dashed.

January 19th 1863

We were all certain last night that we were to move early this morning, inasmuch as an order had been sent for a fatigue party, which was to march with arms and accouterments and 3 days' cooked rations and shelter tents. We supposed it was a party to act as pioneers on the march, but it turned out a party sent to Aquia Landing to build hospitals. I was up at 3 A.M. to get them off and a fine time I had of it, as the men had a great repugnance to rooting up their tents when there was a chance of their coming back to them. It was so dark too that one couldn't get hold of the men, so that it was full a half hour after time before I got them started.

Our Corps seems to be under such orders because the powers that be are still undetermined what to do with us. Some imagine that our Grand Rescue Division are to cross the river some miles above here and try to flank the Rebel position; others, that we are going into winter quarters anyhow. I have no faith in anything that we are about to do, nor do I believe anybody has.

I don't remember whether I wrote you that Major Baldwin has got to be Assistant Adjutant General of the Corps. He is a competent officer and a good man for the place. He was recommended by Genl. Sigel to Genl. Stahel, and in case of Stahel's confirmation as Corps commander, he will be mustered Corps Adjutant, who is usually a U.S. officer. The Major is in high glee over it, as it gives him the rank of Lieut. Colonel, and is altogether a most desirable position. If however Genl.

Schurz should get the Corps, he may not get the position. All these Division commanders are trying for the position of Major General, viz. Genl. Von Steinwehr, Genl. Stahel, and Genl. Schurz. The one who is first confirmed by the Senate will command the 11th Army Corps. Stahel is now commanding as senior Brig. General.

These entries for January 21–24 describe the Eleventh Corps' role in the notorious Mud March. Poor Burnside— anguished over his December failure at Fredericksburg, his leadership undermined by his own generals—sought desperately to refurbish his record by a movement up the Rappahannock to force a crossing of the river and outflank Lee's defenses at Fredericksburg. On the evening of day one a nor'easter struck, and in short order the Army of the Potomac was literally stuck in the mud. Theodore Dodge's description vividly recreates the moment. His regiment was fortunate to make its march before the storm came, and its posting left him a stationary, if soggy, observer of the army's misfortune.

Camp near Berea, 4 miles N.W. of Falmouth
January 21st 1863

At last, after our numerous scares of being under orders to march at a moment's notice, we received day before yesterday orders to move "at 7 A.M. tomorrow. Further particulars will be sent," said the order, and we accordingly went to bed at 9 P.M., ready to start at any moment to carry out the provisions of any further orders that might arrive. About an hour after I had gone to sleep, an order did arrive, giving the order of march and directing our Brigade to fall in behind the 1st Brigade, which would pass our camp about 8 A.M.

This gave us a clue as to the direction in which we were to march, viz. towards Falmouth. We thought we should go to

Brooke's Station, and that the Corps would be stationed along the line of communications between Aquia Creek Landing and Burnside's Army. We were partly right. Just as we were breakfasting at 6 1/4 o'clock A.M. yesterday (20th), Lt. Stoldt, the Acting Assistant Adjutant General of our Brigade, came over with orders not to wait for the 1st Brigade but to fall into line and march at once. So, we hurried our things together and got off at 7 o'clock.

We took the road towards Falmouth, and came over the road which Stahel's Division had taken for Aquia Creek Landing and Brooke's Station; and further we found that we were destined for Hartwood Church. This point we reached about 3 P.M. and our present position about 5. The roads were good and we had a very prosperous march. Berea is on the direct road from Warrenton to Falmouth, 4 miles from the latter and consists of a fine farm house and accompanying buildings. Near this house we met Burnside's Army passing on to Banks's Ford, 4 miles from here, where a pontoon bridge is to be thrown across and the Army to pass the river. They expected to have done this last night but the wind was so high and the rain in such torrents that it was not possible. We got a little supper and then retired for the night about 8 o'clock.

The Q. M. had brought his trains along the good road at a fast pace, getting here almost as soon as we did, so that we were able to put up two tents—one for the Colonel and Lieutenant Col., and one for the Q. M. and myself. We tried to make a fire in the tent, but the stove would not draw on account of the wind, and the smoke nearly drove us wild; so we at length gave it up as a bad job, and took refuge in our cots. Towards morning, I woke up and found the wind had loosened the pins of the tent, and that it was on the point of falling. So I determined to get up and fix it. I groped about for my specs, which having found, I was trying in the dark to distinguish between the Q. M.'s boots and mine, when a sudden gust of wind raised the unfortunate tent from over our heads, and carried it several yards to leeward of its original position, when it suddenly collapsed, leaving us at the mercy of the elements. "Quarter Master!" shouted I to the cot opposite. No answer. "Quarter Master!" "What's the matter?" said he, coolly uncovering his head which had to that moment been buried in blankets. When he saw the desolation around him and the wild waving branches of the tree above him, he was filled with astonishment. It was a mercy the tent pole did not fall upon him. We roused teamsters & servants and finally got the tent pitched again. It was now nearly 6 o'clock, so we concluded to stay up and make a fire, which we accordingly did. Now (towards noon) the wind has gradually abated and there is a chance for getting fixed.

Batteries and troops are pouring on towards the river incessantly. We have just got notice that we shall stop here some time, so before night we hope to be all right again.

January 22nd 1863

Much to our surprise & gratification, a mail came this morning bringing us three letters from you. One which had been delayed since the 6th, one of the 16th and one of the 17th inst. We did not expect a mail so soon after our arrival here, and were in high glee to find our postal communications again established. We were very sorry to hear that your chilly, damp weather and east wind was afoot again and commencing his annoying attacks on your throat. What an inveterate throttler he is to be sure! He never seizes you anywhere else, but always straight at your throat. I hope, dear Mother, that his grip may be less powerful this time than his last attack.

We seem to be here to guard the communications between Aquia Landing and Burnside's Army. Stahel's Division is posted at the former place and along the R. R. to Brooke's Station, from whence to Falmouth I believe Von Steinwehr guards the R. R.; from Falmouth to Burnside his own Division along the Warrenton Turnpike. At all events, we have the post nearest the main Army, tho' if the weather should now prove so bad as to oblige us to go into winter quarters I should much prefer Aquia Landing; for a more desolate place you never saw than the one we are now occupying, rendered doubly so by rain and wind. Troops are continually passing on to the river below, and really when I see the poor wretched fellows tramping through the ankle deep mud, and remember from many sad experiences how hard such marching is, I feel as if our position were to be envied.

You have no idea of how soon the roads turn from good to bad here in Virginia. A clayey soil is hard and the very best for marching on in favorable weather, but let it rain but an hour and troops and wagons march over the road, and the mud is worse than anyone who has not been in Virginia can conceive of. The wagon train passing down to the river got stuck last night and could not move for many hours. If Burnside gets far away from the R. R. there will be the devil to pay, for the wagon trains can scarce move over the roads. You watch a train a little while and you will see horses dropping dead from sheer exhaustion every now and then. A four-horse team cannot possibly drag more than 1,000 lbs. over these roads and scarcely that.

Trains are a very different thing to manage here from what they are in Europe, where the roads are good. A turnpike here is what would be a shocking bad country lane in England. The rain ceased about 10 this evening, but the wind has not yet entirely subsided. These N. E. storms generally last 36 hours at least.

January 23, 1863

As expected, so it has come to pass. The batteries, which moved down to Banks's Ford 3 days ago, are now moving back again. It seems that Mud is really King. He sets down his foot and says, "Ye shall not pass," and lo and behold we cannot. But Mud wields more despotic sway these last two days than ever I saw him wield before. The horses sank into mud up to their bellies, and it is said down near the river you sometimes have to put sticks under the mules' necks to prevent their being engulfed in the very slough of despond. How inspirited and confident the men feel in their leaders you can well imagine. The Genl. Commanding announces to the Army of the Potomac "that they are about to meet the enemy face to face once more," says General Order No. 7, January 20th. "Go back from where you came," says order of today.

This Corps will probably wait till the Grand Divisions of Hooker and Franklin have once more waded their weary way through the mud to their old positions near Falmouth; then we shall do the same. At all events we shall have drier roads by that time, I hope. How it happens that Burnside did not make calculations upon the possibility of its raining whilst he made his move, I cannot imagine. It would seem that plans ought not to be made which rest on the favor of the elements.

The Q. M. and I pitched a new tent yesterday, and gave the one which blew from over us on the 21st to the Commissary Sergt. Owing to a scarcity of tents, the Q. M. and I have our Departments together. It is rather crowded on account of his having one clerk and I having the Sergt. Major and another clerk in the tent most of the time, but we get along tolerably well. The weather is still very damp, and as we have no flooring to our tent, cold feet are prevalent. This is however one of the minor evils. We have got out of wood today, on account of most of the rails round the farms here have been taken to corduroy the roads, and we cut down an immense oak tree close by our tents. It was a tree several hundred years old probably, & very large. We got a corporal of Co. K, who is a woodman by trade, to cut it down, and we watched with great interest to see whether he would fell it clear of the Colonel's tent and ours, which he succeeded in doing. The old tree fell with a terrible crash and thousands of branches flew up into the air like spray from a waterfall.

The other night, when the tent blew over, it broke my camp cot, and I have to set it up every night now with the greatest care, and lie still on my back all night for fear of its giving way and my coming down on to the ground. It is one of those complicated cots that pack up very small and is exceedingly difficult to mend. We have been wishing to ride down to the river these past two days, but the mud is so deep it is much too serious an undertaking.

Berea Church, January 24th 1863

A singular circumstance occurred today. The pontoons, the horses to which had been used in bringing the artillery up from the river along these excruciating roads, were being dragged up by Regiments, about 50 to each pontoon, fire engine style. This, though hard work, rather pleases the boys, & they were cheering as they came to good bits of road and running races with each other. We sat in our tents watching them on the road, about 150 yards off, when the Lieut. Col. proposed to go nearer and see what Regiments were there. As we reached the road the Lieut. Col. spoke to a young Lieutenant, who was trudging along through the mud. He turned out to be Willie Hyslop, whose family we know so well and whom we had thus singularly met. He got leave of his Colonel to come over to our tent & stay for dinner. We found him a very intelligent fellow and had a pleasant talk with him.

We asked him what the troops in his Division thought of this move. He said they quoted the proclamation, "If the Almighty is willing," and had come to the conclusion that the Almighty was not willing; that they all thoroughly laughed at Burnside, & were of the opinion that if McClellan was known to have been reinstated, not only would such cheers go up from the Army of the Potomac as were never heard, but that they would march with such a will and confidence upon Fredericksburg, either to storm the heights or to outflank the town, as would inevitably insure success. Col. P. is an inveterate opponent of McClellan, and was pumping Hyslop for his opinion, when he got the above, which *rather* took him down.

Poor Hyslop has been in active service since June '61, and is now only Lieutenant, never having been home at all. It is curious how different the chances of promotion are in different Regiments. Here is Hyslop, for example, who has been 2 years in the service, has been in almost every battle, and has served well and faithfully, and has only risen one step in all that time. Then take George Pomeroy, who has, in much less time, risen from Lieut. to Lieut. Col., and is now paymaster in the Regular Army. Some of the very best of the old Regiments are slowest in promotions.

CHAPTER SEVEN

Hooker Takes Command

January 25 to February 28, 1863

On January 25, 1863, President Lincoln removed Ambrose Burnside from command of the Army of the Potomac and put in his place "Fighting Joe" Hooker. Like most of his fellow soldiers, Lieutenant Dodge was relieved to be rid of Burnside, and although he still longed for McClellan's return, he seemed willing to give Hooker his due. Yet he wondered if that general was really capable of handling 150,000 men, and concluded, "I fear not."

To await the spring campaigning season the army took up winter quarters in the vicinity of Falmouth. Dodge thought the scene reminiscent of Valley Forge. Meanwhile, to general surprise, "Fighting Joe" Hooker turned out to be better named "Administrative Joe." Producing a barrage of reforms and initiatives, he shook up the army and boosted morale manyfold, and Regimental Adjutant Dodge was put to the test to keep up with the new commanding general. Dodge also devoted himself, in these weeks, to trying to overcome the lackadaisical ways of the 119th.

In the margin of his January 26 comments on the Fitz John Porter court-martial—Porter had been cashiered for misconduct at Second Bull Run—Dodge wrote, "All this was later disproved." Indeed, in 1878 Porter's case was reheard and the verdict overturned.

January 25th 1863

One of the first things the Q. M. generally does when we come to a new camp, where there is a chance of staying several days, is to send one of his boys to scour the country surrounding for milk, which is a great luxury. We generally manage to obtain it. When we first came down here, a farm in close proximity to where we camped supplied us, but Col. Mahler of the 75th Penn. established his Head Quarters there, and, as the woman told us, the gentlemen drank so much milk, she has none for us. Yesterday we granted a safeguard to the farm of a Mr. Miles, some mile or so from here, and today the Q. M. and I thought we would ride over there and see if the people would not sell us some milk, in return for our protection, but it turned out that they had none, or at least said so. Coming home by a somewhat roundabout road, we came across a small farm, the house scarce more than a hovel, at which we stopped, noticing two cows in a pen by the yard. The owner, Burton by name, was at first a little gruff, but the Q. M. came a little blarney over him and at last got him to sell us some milk. We promised him too some sugar and coffee in exchange for the milk, which he greatly preferred to money, and this afternoon we sent him several pounds of each.

This afternoon the Q. M. rode out, in fact on this very errand, to carry Mr. Burton his stores, & with Harry Hunter, his clerk, in case he should forage anything. He rode much further than he intended, and in fact got way down to the river, where he saw the Rebel pickets on the other side, and some cavalrymen. I believe these are the first live Rebels the Q. M. has seen, and he was greatly elated. In the meantime Col. Peissner and I went riding out with Genl. Schurz, whom the newspapers of today confirm as Major General. He is a good officer and deserves it, though if he gets the Corps my arrangement with Major Baldwin goes up in a balloon.

January 26, 1863

We moved camp today to a better and drier location, some 300 yards from our old place. The soil here is clayey and soon becomes penetrated with water when it rains, making it so soft and damp as to be not only very inconvenient, but unhealthy. We were down in a hollow before, but are now situated on pretty high ground, our tents (those of Field and Staff, I mean) in an orchard belonging to a farm close by us. We have also a stable for our horses, which is a great boon, as the poor animals have generally to weather all storms out of doors. It took but a short time to move the Q. M.'s tent; in less than an hour we were as comfortable in our new quarters as we had been in our old.

Today one of our teamsters, Greenwood by name, born under the sound of bow bells, picked up a cavalry horse with an awfully sore back, which I fancy was the cause of its being left behind. It is a fine young horse—6 years old, black, and very well built, and will make a most excellent saddle horse when its back gets well, which will be probably in a month or so. He may be reclaimed, but I should fancy not.

This afternoon, as we were changing camp, an aide of Genl. Schurz rode up and told us that the enemy had attacked our pickets some 2 or 3 miles off, and that we were to hold ourselves in readiness to march at an instant's notice. Col. Krzyzanowski and Col. Mahler, the senior Col. of the Brigade, were out in a reconnoitering party, and Col. P. as next in seniority took command of the Brigade. I acted *pro tem* as Assistant Adjutant General, and rode round to see that the Regiments were held in readiness. But the glory of Col. P. was short-lived. Col. K. came back in about half an hour. Nothing came of the attack, which was I fancy only a clash between scouting parties of cavalry.

I have been reading today a rèsumé of the Porter Court Martial by Joseph Holt, Judge Advocate General, U.S.A., and have come to the conclusion that if the evidence adduced be really true, the man ought to be shot instead of cashiered; for it would seem that the Battle of Manassas was lost entirely through his refusal to obey orders and attack the enemy, by reason of which McDowell was driven back and the battle lost. He seems all along to have done his best to make Pope lose battles out of personal motives. Under McClellan, Fitz John Porter was a brave and valuable officer, but political spite was stronger in his breast than his sense of military duty when under Pope.

January 28th 1863

Outside it is snowing fast, not a cold snow, but a wet snow, and the ground is covered with slush. Every now and then someone comes in, a disagreeability, as everybody diffuses an uncomfortable moisture. The stove is behaving splendidly this morning and emits an agreeable warmth throughout the tent. Comfort to us would probably be most uncomfortable to you, accustomed to warm houses; but I can tell you we appreciate a tent after having been outside on our several duties. It is a comfort that we are not on a march today. I guess winter has finally set in.

They say Hooker, who, as you have heard 'ere this, is in command of the Army of the Potomac, is in favor of winter quarters. I hope so. What think you of this same appointment of Hooker? "Fighting Joe" Hooker he is called, and I believe, in fact I know, justly; but is he capable of handling 150,000 men? I fear not, any more than Burnside. Sumner and Franklin, who commanded, each, one of the four Grand Divisions, and good Generals they are too, have also been relieved, to get McClellan influence out of the Army, I guess. What ill or good it will do, is more than anyone can predict, but "when a man is hauling a heavy load up hill, he has no time to stop and swop jackasses" (old Abe dixit), and if he have a team of six jackasses, it is still less advisable to stop and swop single ones, in my humble opinion.

Don't it show the lies of the papers up to the world to see one day, "A great battle is being fought beyond the Rappahannock and Hooker is mortally wounded," and the next day an announcement that not a shot has been fired, that the Army has not crossed. Evidently the whole thing was concocted beforehand. This from the *Herald*.

I intended to write to George on his birthday, but Father filled the letter up full and closed it before I got a chance. We received in today's mail Mother's letter of the 21st enclosing

Mrs. G.'s. How long it takes to hear from England that they have heard about certain events here.

Among the officers' amusements described here, Colonel Peissner presented the French version of Punchinello, from the old Italian pantomime best known as Punch and Judy. In his turn, the quartermaster's clerk offered a shadow-boxing contest between the famous pugilists Tom Sayers and John C. Heenan, to "universal merriment." The following day, in sharp contrast, Dodge and his father witnessed firsthand the desolating effects of the war on Virginia's civilians. The month's end inspection of his regiment was occasion for Adjutant Dodge to wish Colonel Peissner had more of the martinet about him.

January 29th 1863

We have not yet moved from Berea Church, nor does it appear likely that we shall do so for a month to come. Winter has decidedly set in. Looking out from our tent upon the camp, one is greatly reminded of the pictures of Valley Forge. Everything is covered with snow and during the sunny part of the day the eyes are almost blinded with the glare of white expanse around. Last night it stormed and blew hard as it had done during the day, the wind being cold at night and damp in the daytime. The snow was so penetrating that we were sitting in a perfect shower bath in our tent, and were prevented from writing or reading, so frequent were the huge drops falling on our paper or books. It was altogether a most wretched day. Towards evening, however, it began to freeze, which obviated the greatest part of the difficulty and inconvenience, the wet. It blew great guns during the night, and had it not been for the pins having frozen into the ground, I have no doubt but what the tent would have been blown down again. I lay awake several times thinking with consternation of such a possibility. I was thankful when morning came without our being unhoused.

Today the sun shown pleasantly all day: a more beautiful day overhead you never saw; but the snow melting fast under the influence of the sun, and the wet, clayey, sticky soil underneath made it almost impossible to move about out of doors. Nothing of note occurred during the day, except perhaps a ride over to the 157th N.Y., a mile or two from here, to see Capt., late Chaplain, Charlier, and to exercise our horses. These objects were both accomplished, particularly the latter. Two or three times I sank up to my stirrups in mud and snow, and the horses could scarcely get on. However the animals need exercise greatly this weather. One great trouble with them is that they have to stand all day in the wet and mud, which is very apt to give them the "scratches."

After supper the Colonel and Lieut. Colonel generally come to our tent a little while, and we four sit round the table and converse, the Q. M. and Colonel generally getting into some argument or other. Tonight the question arose as to what we were to do, having run entirely out of envelopes. The Q. M. suggested folding in the old style, and Col. P. showed us several ways of folding paper. Thereupon we degenerated into making paper boxes and paper bellows, and paper nicknacks of all kinds, from which intellectual occupation we verged into making night caps and rabbits out of pocket handkerchiefs; and the Col. gave us a Polichinelle exhibition with the handkerchiefs on his fingers. This gave rise to shadows on the wall, and Harry, the Q. M.'s clerk, came in and gave Sayers and Heenan on the wall, producing universal merriment. We broke up in a high state of laughter at our silly devices to kill time.

The men are singing in camp some of their German songs, and the drummer boys, the wretched little villains, are doing ditto by some not very choice but popular street ditties. There is one boy among them that has a most beautiful boy's alto, and when he sings plaintively it is most pleasant to hear him. There is something peculiarly attractive about a boy's voice when it is good, that always takes my fancy amazingly.

It is probable now that Schurz will get the Corps, and that Stahel will be chief of cavalry of the Grand Division. Whether Major Baldwin will get a detached position as U.S. officer or not, we cannot tell. They are consolidating Regiments too, and I should not be much surprised if ours came in for it, and there goes for mustering surplus officers out of service.

Berea Church, January 30th 1863

We today have had a specimen of Virginia bread. The Q. M. took some flour over to Mr. Burton's, a man who furnishes us with milk, and he promised to have us some bread baked. It was sent home in time for tea this evening, & we were congratulating ourselves on the prospect of once more enjoying bread & butter, but our hopes were dashed. Instead of the well raised loaf of firm wheaten bread, there was a round flat cake about half an inch thick, looking like an India rubber valve of considerable size. When we broke the cake, behold a tough, doughy substance, such as no one of us ever remembered seeing in a baker's shop, and with no flavor at all. We had a hearty laugh at our Virginia bread, though we had been cheated by it out of good materials which could have been used to better purpose.

Never were war's desolations brought more forcefully to my mind than today. Father and I sallied forth to try to find some boards to floor our tent with. Some distance off the main road, we saw an apparently deserted shanty. We rode towards it, intending to strip it of its boards, a thing done to all deserted buildings when the Army is about. On approaching however we spied a poor weak old man of seventy or more wandering disconsolately through the little yard, and as we came nearer he looked frightened, as if he thought we were intending to do him some harm. We asked him if he could let us have some boards, when he began to complain that the soldiers had carried off everything he had in and about his house; that he had not a mouthful left to keep him from starvation. They had taken his stove, his axe & tools, his wood and furniture, every plate and cup and saucer, knife, fork and spoon, in fact all the poor old man had, and he was afraid to go to the General to complain.

This is by no means a rare instance of the destitution which prevails, for I believe there are many on this contested territory who die literally of starvation. The Burtons, and they are comparatively well off, tell me they have been living for a long time on Indian corn crushed between stones, as the miller has been arrested as a spy, and his mill demolished. We lately sent them some of our stores, pork, beans, rice, coffee &c, &c and you cannot imagine how grateful they were.

There are two young women there, one a widow with a little child—her husband was shot in the Rebel ranks—and they knit socks to sell to the Army to get clothing for themselves. Where they get clothing however is more than I can tell, for they are as it were, entirely cut off from the outside world. They can get nothing in Falmouth and there is no other town within our lines, and no one is allowed to bring anything from Washington. We bought some socks of them, very nicely knit. Half the people one meets hereabouts are dressed in the cast off garments of our soldiers, which plainly shews they can get nothing else.

We are anxiously awaiting the Paymaster, as several Regiments have been paid off. Major Campbell, however, who is to pay us, is a slow old coach, and at best we shall be paid only up to the 31st of October.

January 31st [1863]

Col. Peissner is going, tomorrow A.M., to ride over to Stafford Court House, to get a pass signed by Genl. Sigel to go to Washington, and I therefore send this by him, hoping by that means it may reach you somewhat sooner.

Quite an amusing incident occurred today. Some time ago a Mrs. Harold wrote to Col. Peissner to ask about her husband, who had once been hospital steward in the Regiment. The Colonel gave the letter to the Sergt. Major to answer and he wrote, "Your husband is no more hospital steward." The good woman was probably a slow reader and when she got to the "no more" and making a pause there, the supposition of her husband's decease flashed upon her. She wrote a most pitiable letter to Col. P., begging to know the manner of her poor husband's death, and what things he had left behind him! For aught we can know, the impulsive young widow may be married again before we can undeceive her and assure her that, tho' her husband is no more hospital steward, he is alive and well. However this may be, we had a hearty laugh over her letter.

This morning we had the customary monthly inspection. With few exceptions the men looked dirty, and as unsoldierlike as possible. The Colonel is very remiss in obliging his officers to attend to their Companies as they ought. The Captains don't make their Sergeants do their duty up to the handle, and consequently the Regiment looks but poorly. I really wish the Colonel was a little more strict. His way of doing business is to ask, "Well, Gentlemen, what do you advise?" instead of, "This is my plan and this must be done!" Our officers' meetings are nothing more than debating societies, of which the Colonel is chairman.

Feeling in want of some exercise this P.M., the Q. M., Lieut. Colonel and I took a gallop of two or three miles on the Warrenton road; and pretty sights we were when we got back to camp. The turnpike has dried up a little, leaving about 6 inches of thin mud upon the surface, so that it is possible to get on, if you ignore mud and the possibility of breaking your horse's legs and your own neck.

The most immediate problem Hooker faced, and the largest in its consequences, was desertion. Men were leaving the army at the rate of 200 and more a day; it was estimated that one in ten on the Army of the Potomac's rolls was a deserter. The paperwork Dodge describes in this entry was no doubt a response to Hooker's order to list the absentees of every regiment and battery, with full descriptions and notes for everyone absent without leave. Local authorities would then be put to the task of tracking the deserters. Dodge's description of a well-run hospital (February 3) must have been an exception (or the result of a recent reform), for appalling hospital conditions comprised a major mark against the Burnside regime. The promised "strict" inspection of the regiment was another reform by Hooker's newly appointed corps of inspector-generals.

Head Quarters 119th New York, February 2nd/63

The Q. M. went off to Falmouth this A.M. at 8, with a train. He was to go on to Aquia Landing per rail, and bring back some Express packages, lying there for the Brigade, to Falmouth, where the teams are to wait for his return, to fetch the parcels to Head Quarters. He has not yet returned (9 P.M.), but I expect him every minute. We hope to get Mother's box and one from Prof. Jackson, containing some prime whiskey and other choice goodies.

We received Special Order No. 22 from Head Quarters, Grand Reserve Division, today, ordering Col. Peissner to proceed without delay to Albany to confer with the Governor of New York about the reorganization of the Regiment. As the

Col. was probably in Washington, I sent it on to him. It may mean that they are going to fill up the Regiment; and it may also mean that we must consolidate our ten Companies into five for joining some other organization. I sincerely hope this last may not be the case.

Lieut. Col. Lockman and I rode over to the 157th N.Y. to give Capt. Charlier a letter which had been sent him. Coming back we passed a farm house, Genl. Schimmelfennig's Head Quarters. The Col. pointed out a grave stone in the middle of a barn yard, trodden down by horses and cows and partly hidden by a compost heap. We succeeded in deciphering, "Henry Marquess, Born   Died 1821"

> "Remember, man, as you pass by,
> "As you are now, so once was I,
> "As I am now so you must be,
> "Prepare for death and follow me."

Survivors certainly had not shewn great respect for Mr. Marquess' warning.

We received today a telegram from Col. P. from Washington, "The Paymaster is coming out tomorrow. Send an ambulance to the Station for him." This was indeed good news and you may be sure the ambulance will await his arrival. When the men heard of it there was one universal cheer.

I have just completed a most complicated and voluminous report, which has kept the Sergeant Major, my clerk and myself hard at work all day, and I feel tired from holding my pen. So excuse any more journal.

February 3rd/63

The Q. M. did not get back until nearly noon today. It only shews the impracticability of the system that he was sent at all. He proposed to our Alsatian Jew Brigade Q. M., Capt.

Worms, to send the Q. M. Sergeant, a hard-working man, in his stead. But no, no one but the Q. M. himself would do, altho' he had hard work enough here, and had to be absent two days. After all, there were but nine paltry packages, which a drummer boy might have attended to. Capt. Worms said he had brought out all the packages, altho' he had not secured in his late visit to Washington one in twenty of them. The Q. M. (having to stay all night) stopped with Dr. Aymé at the 11th Corps hospital, at Aquia Landing. He says this hospital is one of the most beautiful sights. There are 800 hospital tents, laid out in streets over half a mile long, all fitted up with stoves and every convenience, and accommodating 11,000 patients. It forms a settlement half a mile square. The worthy Dr. was overjoyed at seeing him. He was poorly off there in comparison to what he was here, for he never knows how to help himself. This afternoon we got a special order relieving him of further duty at the hospital, so we shall soon have him back here again.

It has been a real cold day, freezing and blowing hard without a moment's interval. Lieut. Col. and I rode out today, but almost perished before we got to camp. It would have been a splendid day for a march.

February 4th/63

Today, Greenwood, one of our teamsters, coming back from Falmouth, caught a fine horse nearly 17 hands high, fine build, some 7 years old, carries his head beautifully. Of course the Q. M. took charge of him, and rode him this P.M. He however is too large for the saddle, especially for one of the Q. M.'s stature, not fast, but easy nevertheless. He would make a fine carriage horse.

We are to have an inspection tomorrow, by Major Hartung, an officer appointed by the Corps commander. I believe it will be very strict.

The march described here took the 119th New York from its Mud March posting to the winter quarters it would occupy near Stafford Courthouse. The purpose of the imposed inspections (February 12) was to brace up the regiments by promising furloughs for those that met the new high standards. For this reason, and no doubt thanks to Adjutant Dodge's persistent efforts, the 119th at last began to display "a manifest improvement" in its performance.

February 7th/63

At about 9 P.M. on the 4th, an orderly came from Brigade Head Quarters, with an order to the Quarter Master to draw 5 days' rations at once. This was unusual, as the 5th was the regular day for drawing rations, and on questioning the orderly, we heard that marching orders were at Head Quarters. A telegraphic dispatch had come from General Hooker. The Q. M. at once roused the commissary Sergt. and his men, and sent the teams after the rations. They came back at about 3 A.M. and we distributed them to the Companies. About midnight came the marching orders, and we sent them round to the various commanding officers. Our Regiment was to start at 7 A.M. with the wagon train, which we were to guard, the remaining Regiments and batteries to follow in the rear. Guarding a train is by no means an agreeable duty, as it turned out, but each Regiment has to do it in turn.

We were all ready at 7 A.M., having breakfasted at 5, but we had very hard work striking our tents, as the ground was frozen so hard that we could not get the pins out. After we got ready they kept us waiting about an hour, in a freezing snow storm, as is usual; but we did in effect start at about 8 A.M. We took up our line of march towards Stafford Court House, and having all day to make six miles, we at length halted at Potomac Run, in a hole of a valley which seemed just made for us to be bagged in if we should be attacked. Everything was huddled up in this valley—teams, artillery, & Regiments.

It snowed all day, and we had a very disagreeable march, cold and wet. At last however we got a tent up, and made ourselves tolerably comfortable. The Lieut. Col., Quarter Master and I, all that was left of the Field and Staff, occupied the tent together, and having found some boards at a saw mill close by, we passed a very good night. We had plenty of blankets and a stove, seeing the teams were with us, and we kept the sentry inside instead of outside our tent to keep the fire up.

During the night we got orders to move with the train at 6:30 A.M. the next day, the 6th. We did not start tho' till nearly 9 A.M., and then the bridge over Potomac Creek that the pioneers had built the night before, had swept away, and we were obliged to build another, which we did in about an hour, and very nicely too, covering it all with boards. Over the run there was a very steep hill, which the wagons and artillery found it very difficult to get up, only managing it by doubling teams. Our Regiment crossed as soon as we had built the bridge, and went up the hill, where we halted until the train got all up. The Lieut. Col. took 5 Companies ahead with him, to march with the first part of the train, and left me behind with 5 Companies more, to distribute them along the rest of the train according to discretion. This I did, but so bad was the hill (and an incessant rain and the ruts made by the wagons rendering it worse and worse each hour) it was actually 1:30 P.M. before the last team came along, and I with two Companies as rear guard, got started. The Quarter Master, with our 119th teams, was last in order and I marched along with him.

Whilst we were waiting at the top of the hill, we went into a small log house near the road, where lived an old woman, three daughters and a son. Two of the daughters were quite pretty, and I got them to cook some coffee for us. Two or three of the officers and I sat in there out of the rain for some hours.

As soon as the Quarter Master came along, we cheered him with a cup of coffee, and then set off. Such a trudge as we had! Every 200 yards some team or other would get stuck, and we would have to get it out. Once we tried for an hour and a half before we got a team out of a hole. We got to Stafford at nightfall, having left 3 teams behind, and found the Regiment already in quarters in a pine wood. Our whole Division is close together, about two miles south of Stafford.

Today (the 7th) we changed tents; the Q. M. and I took a large 17 ft. square tent for our joint Departments, and have fixed ourselves up pleasantly. This is a very nice camp, and we have got orders to fix ourselves, as we shall stay here for some time. We also got a mail, which pleased us greatly.

February 8th 1863

Good Dr. Aymé came back again last evening in an ambulance. He had been relieved of duty the first of the month, and like the good Dr., had followed us on to Berea Church, just in time to find that we had left that place; so by way of mending the matter he goes to Falmouth, and there heard we had come on here, whither he managed to get, after a week's tramp in pursuit of us. He was glad to get back to what he calls home, and we were glad to have him here. We put him in the tent which the Q. M. and I had just left, but he makes our tent his sitting room.

Indeed our tent is the common rendezvous of all, now we have so large a one, and every evening we have a dozen or more visitors. We have not yet been able to floor it on account of the scarcity of boards, but today I have sent out a party of men to cut pine logs which, split in the middle & smoothed off, will make a very solid and dry floor. Carpenter, the Q. M.'s Sergeant, is going to lay it.

We have had no forage of any description whatever since we came here, & the poor horses are obliged to live on the dry grass of the fields, where we turn them out. With all this they are expected to do the same amount of work which they do when they get their regular allowance. It really goes "against the grain" to mount or drive the poor things under such circumstances. My mare's back is shewing the effects of mounting at six in the morning & not getting down till 10 at night.

We are just having a fireplace built in our tent. We put one of our conical stoves, which are furnished the hospitals, in it, and it warms the place nicely. A fellow named Dunn, a mason by trade who does a great many odd jobs for the Q. M., is building it, and takes his pay in tobacco and whiskey, which the men prefer to money.

February 10th 1863

The mail communication is partially interrupted at Aquia Creek by the embarkation of the 9th Army Corps, which is to go South, I believe. The 9th is Burnside's command, you know. Today we have finished our floor, and it is remarkably comfortable, tho' very rough. The tent is doubly warm with it laid. The Q. M., I am sorry to say, is a little under the weather. He has taken cold on the bare ground in the tent, which is frozen 9 or 10 inches deep, and, naturally became very damp when the fire was kindled. I hope a couple of days will see him all right. He does not write today, not feeling in the mood.

The unlucky Paymaster has not yet arrived. It is now 3 weeks since it was reported that he was certainly on the way to pay us off. Mr. Funk (our old sutler), naturally much interested in his appearance, for the liquidation of many claims against the men, has been here all the time awaiting him, and it is laughable to hear the expressions of the men towards him, when he comes into camp. He (Funk) has been prophesying the Paymaster so long that the bare mention of him provokes laughter and ridicule. I hear that a paper of charges has been

The Union retreat to the James on June 29, 1862, during the Seven Days' Battles, sketched by Arthur Lumley. Theodore Dodge wrote of this scene: "On the West Point Railway a train of 25 cars were burning; near it a huge pile of the knapsacks of a whole regiment blazing and crackling; everywhere tents & boxes of stores on fire." (Library of Congress)

Combat artist Alfred Waud pictured men of Kearny's Division,
in which Dodge's 101st New York
served, fighting off a Rebel attack
in the woods near Glendale on
June 30, during the Seven Days.
"The grape and canister flew in
torrents in our direction," Dodge
wrote, "but none harmed me
or my Company." (Library of
Congress)

After the Seven Days, the Army of the Potomac retreated to Harrison's Landing on the James, where it sweltered through the summer of 1862. Artist Waud labeled his drawing of a sutler's establishment, which served as a haven for Theodore Dodge and his Third Corps comrades, "Skedaddlers' Hall." (Library of Congress)

"We rejoined the column and marched all night, crossing Bull Run," Dodge wrote on August 30, 1862, of the Federal rout of Second Manassas. "We did not feel in very high spirits. . . ." Rufus Zogbaum pictured the scene as the beaten army crossed Bull Run that night. Two days later, Dodge's favorite general, Philip Kearny, was killed at Chantilly, as sketched at right by Alan Redwood, and Dodge himself went down with a serious wound in the same battle. (Above and right: *Battles and Leaders of the Civil War*)

Chancellorsville was the baptism of fire for Dodge's new regiment, the 119th New York of the Eleventh Corps, and for both regiment and corps it was a disaster. Top left, Edwin Forbes shows Stonewall Jackson's battle line storming out of the woods against the Eleventh Corps' flank. Below left, a lone officer tries to halt the stampeded Yankees, as drawn by Alan Redwood. (Top: Century Collection; Bottom: *Battles and Leaders of the Civil War*)

In the chaotic scene below, Alfred Waud pictures Couch's Second Corps moving up in support of the Eleventh Corps "disgracefully running away." Waud's list of the routed regiments he could identify does not include the 119th New York, confirming Dodge's claim that at least the 119th "stood well against great odds" before it too retreated, "slowly though not in good order." (Library of Congress)

Alan Redwood's drawing titled "At close quarters on the first day of Gettysburg" could easily describe the setting in which Theodore Dodge fell wounded and was left on the field to be captured when his regiment retreated. The photograph of Dodge, probably taken at an army reunion, shows him well embarked on his postwar career as a military historian. (Top: *Battles and Leaders of the Civil War*; Photo: U.S. Army Military History Institute)

made out against Major Campbell (the Paymaster) by the 75th Penn. (a Regiment in our Brigade also paid by him). At all events he deserves a court martial, but I should have thought it more desirable to wait till after we are paid, before we try to get rid of him.

Now that Hooker is in command the old severity about reports is coming back, which was prevalent in the old Army of the Potomac on the Peninsula. Multifarious and voluminous reports have to be made out and Adjutants are very busy. Luckily I have a most excellent Sergt. Major, Fisher by name. He speaks and writes German and English with equal facility, & understands his business perfectly. My old clerk (Berger) has fallen ill, poor fellow, and is in the hospital with typhoid. He is in a sad case. Lieut. Lewis, the Colonel's brother in law, who was home a short time since on sick leave is, I am afraid, relapsing. He has all the premonitory symptoms of the fever, and as he has so lately had leave of absence that it would not be granted again, he will probably be obliged to resign, or will die. I thank God I am now so hale and hearty.

Lieut. Coleman, a nice fellow, was today detached from the Regiment to the Brigade topographical corps. He is a good engineer, I hear. He is the second detached from the 119th. If you can get a chance, send me the book on topographical engineering I had at home.

February 11th 1863

There is positively nothing to write about. It has been mild all day and this evening is raining. The Q. M. is much better today and having taken to rhubarb and dieting is in a likely way to be as well as ever tomorrow. He sends all manner of kind greetings. I am reading the 3rd volume of Carlyle's *Frederick the Great*, & am getting interested in it, and think more of Carlyle every page I read. The few battles described in this volume are magnificently real.

February 12th 1863

We have had an inspection today by Major Hartung of the 74th Pennsylvania Volunteers, whose Regiment took the prize at the prize drill at Chantilly last December. He was to have inspected us before we left Berea Church, and arrangements were made for inspection the day we left there. He is a rough and ready fellow and as ungainly a man as you will see, but a thorough soldier. He however cut things short and made the inspection light for us.

I have been very busy today. You remember my writing you of a very voluminous report I had made out about a week ago. Well, after making it out and sending it to Head Quarters, today it came back with some blank forms, and had all to be copied over again upon same. I had two good writers detailed and set them to work, and this evening I have again got it finished. This is just a sample of how things are done. Instead of giving out the blanks in the first place, they wait till the reports are sent in, and then send the blanks for them to be copied upon.

An order has been printed in the *Washington Chronicle*, which we received this evening, from the War Department, ordering, among many others, Lieut. Lewis of our Regiment and Adjutant Felton of the 74th Penna. Volunteers to appear before a Board of Investigation, to answer charges for having failed to report at the Convalescent Camp as ordered, when on passage through Washington. There were on the order some 80 or 100 names, all for trivial offenses while passing through the city: such as failing to report under arrest by the provost guard for traveling without a pass, when ordered to do so. The worst was for drunkenness in the streets. In Lieut. Lewis' case nothing probably will come out of it, but some of them will no doubt be severely handled. Several of the men mentioned I know.

Forage is so scarce that our horses and mules have actually taken to eating off each other's tails. Within a week at least a dozen such cases have come to my knowledge, and I am going to have my mare's tail tied in a knot for fear of it. Today the Adjutant of the 26th Wisconsin, of our Brigade, who owns the finest horse in the Corps, came round with his horse's tail (a regular fine long tail) eaten off to the bone by some other animal. How do you think they can live with such privations? We have had hay for them today for the first time in more than a fortnight.

Camp on Queen's Farm, Stafford Court House
February 15, 1863

The above is the exact location of our camp. It was not till yesterday that I found out. You may remember of my writing you about the colonel & myself having visited a house where there was an ex-Confederate soldier who had lost an arm, and where we bought some apples. That was Queen's Farm. We are about 1/4 of a mile south of this house and within the limits of the farm. Genl. Von Steinwehr has his Head Quarters at the house, and a gay flag flaunts from its roof, which, as the house is on a high hillock, is visible from all the country round.

We have just received a letter from you dated the 5th inst., which has been to the 114th N.Y.V., as the 9th was not plainly written. You must take special pains to write 119th plainly, else the letter will be apt to get astray. Some time ago Prof. Jackson wrote to Col. Peissner, 119th, Willard's Hotel, Washington, but the letter came straight to the Regiment, nor do I wonder, as the number of letters for the Army is perfectly enormous. There is probably an average of 80 to 100 letters and papers for each Regiment every day, and as there are 2,000 Regiments in the field, you may fancy the work of the General Post Office.

There has been an order just issued for 4 hours' drill each day, which of course must be carried out; but there can be nothing done but drill in the manual of arms, in the Company streets. As to Battalion drill, which is ordered every afternoon, one might as well attempt to polka in a swamp. All we can do is to have an odd dress parade now and then.

A detail has today been made to build stables for our poor horses. They are being got up under the superintendence of Sergt. Jackson, a Kennebec woodsman of our Regiment, in grand style, 50 feet long and wide enough for 2 horses, tail to tail, with an alley between. These stables are to be inspected day after tomorrow, by which time they must be finished. We keep 20 or 30 men all the time busy on them. Sergt. Jackson today felled a big tree, by the Q. M.'s Department, which was 4 feet in diameter. It was a grand sight to see it fall. It will furnish wood for a long time.

It has rained a greater part of the day, being however clear at times. In one of these intervals we held the customary Sunday inspection, Lieut. Col. Lockman and I visiting each Company. There is a manifest improvement in the Regiment of late, specially in one thing. When I came, it took full half an hour to form a Battalion in line. Now we do it in 5 minutes. This I flatter myself is owing to my persistent punishing of the orderly Sergeants, than whom no one has more influence over the Company. If a Captain has a good orderly, the Company will be good; and the reverse is equally true. The Lieut. Col. gives me credit for the improvement. As to our Line officers, but one or two of them takes any interest whatever in their duties.

It has been a very warm day, but the wind is now rising and the sky clearing. There are two most singular clouds, just such clouds as I can imagine an untutored mind ascribing to the supernatural and being frightened about—two huge shadows scarcely seeming to have the aspect of clouds at all.

The Paymaster is actually here! He has paid off the 134th N.Y., and will pay us day after tomorrow. I said I should not believe his being here till I had the money in my pocket, but as Lieut. Lewis leaves for Washington tomorrow, and he has actually paid him and he has shown me the greenbacks, I take heart of hope.

Grand reviews were a feature of the McClellan era, and Joe Hooker resumed them as a morale booster. Lieutenant Dodge thought General Hooker played his part well enough, although not up to the standards of his idols, McClellan and Phil Kearny. Dodge had good reason to be amazed at his receipt of his Uncle Isaac Jackson's plainly marked box of O-be-joyful and other pleasures. Hooker had ordered the inspection of all such deliveries to soldiers to cut down not only smuggled liquor but the sending of civilian clothes to the desertion-minded. In this case, Dodge believed, compassion had triumphed.

February 16, 1863

Today we have had a review (or as officials in this Brigade say, a parade) by Genl. Hooker. We got notice about 11 o'clock to be ready for "parade" at noon, and we accordingly were ready—Companies being equalized. We marched out soon after to a swamp which is called the "Brigade Parade," where we marched & countermarched for about an hour and a half before the Brigade was decently formed. (I should like to see it in action.) We then stacked arms, and lounged about till 3 o'clock, when Genl. Hooker arrived and inspected the 1st Division on their parade ground, a fine large field, which for a wonder is hard & dry. The day was beautiful; it had been cold till about 2 o'clock, when a pleasant sunshine broke out, making a fit day for a grand review. After the 1st Division had been inspected, we marched over to their ground and were drawn up in line. Arms were presented as Genl. Hooker rode by. He took his place at the colors and we passed in review before him. This done, we marched back to camp.

I was very much fatigued, for I had not done so much since last September. I did not ride, partly out of pity for my mare's back, and partly that I have not mounted her for so long that she is quite coltish and not staid enough for an Adjutant on review.

We finished our stabling today and a fine building it is. Of course it is for the public horses & mules; the private ones will tomorrow be lodged in a separate building.

"Fighting Joe" Hooker looked very well—much better than when I spoke to him last at Warrenton, when I was in search of the 119th. He was then just recovering from his wound received at Antietam. He was then for some reason as red as a beet, a complexion which in no wise improved his appearance. This has now entirely disappeared. He is not as handsome a man as McClellan, and by no means of as fine a military appearance as poor Kearny was. The Colonel came back tonight and we found him in camp when we returned from review.

February 17th 1863

I have really forgotten whether I told you we had received your nice practical box yesterday. Jimmie Christie went down to Hope Landing, at the Q. M.'s suggestion, to see if any boxes had come; and after searching diligently among the thousands there, spied Uncle Isaac's barrel and your box. The latter he brought to camp on his horse. Today a team was sent down to the Landing and brought up some 8 or 10 parcels for the Regiment. Uncle Isaac's parcel was directed (which doubtless caused its detention) to "Sergt. Aymé" instead of to "Surgeon Aymé," and on it was a card printed "Wines, Liquors and Cigars," and we were at a loss to make out how it escaped the hands of the Provost Marshal, as it was "contraband." Some good-natured fellow, who had a weakness for the "O-be-joyful" himself, might have had the handling of it and taken compassion on "Sergt. Aymé," or perhaps the very imprudence of the printed card "Wines, Liquors and Cigars" protected it, as Custom House officers sometimes pass contraband goods under similar circumstances.

Anyhow the package was evidently first opened by us, and out of it taken a 3 gallon demijohn of prime whiskey, which was at once deposited in a place of safety under the Quarter Master's bed. Some tea next, of which we have now a fine supply. Then came (a present from Gertrude to me) a splendid box of Brian's Candy, which will furnish a tid bit for many days. Of course this day will be marked on our calendar with a red line.

Among the boxes brought out was one to Harry Hunter, the Q. M.'s clerk. His Mother kindly sent a box of nice fresh butter to the Q. M., and a bottle of catsup (tomato) homemade, both of which are specially nice & acceptable. Harry's Mother sent the Q. M. a pair of knitted stockings by post the other day—she seems specially grateful for his kindness to her boy. Harry also got some Stewart's Candy and lots of cakes. This was a box of goodies such as you would fancy a nice country woman's sending.

Today the Q. M. had carpenters build him a bedstead. From the Brigade surgeon I got a couple of bed ticks filled with straw, all of which makes the best bed in camp. He will sleep like a top now.

February 18, 1863

More wretched weather than we have had this week you cannot imagine. Yesterday and the day before it snowed and today it is raining like Noah's flood. Our stables are not yet completed & in consequence the officers' horses are almost dying in the storm.

All day long we have been waiting for the Paymaster who has for two days been paying off the 75th Pennsylvania Vols., and will pay us next. The old fool (he ought to be hung up as soon as he has paid out all his money) thinks the weather unfavorable, so he stays in his comfortable quarters, when he ought to be over here. He promised to be over here by 10 A.M. and actually sent us the pay rolls to sign, but he has not yet made his appearance.

The Q. M. has taken so greatly to the cap which Fanny knit for him that he wears it all the time. He has been christened by the Lieut. Colonel "Q. M. Ben Lomond McGregor." It is indeed a most comfortable thing. I always wear mine at night. Col. P. brought me the piece of leather and a pair of gloves, which the Q. M. has appropriated as if they were his.

"The shameful neglect of the proper officials at Washington to pay our brave soldiers," wrote a Potomac army soldier that spring, "has been the principal means of causing the wholesale desertion in the army." Certainly the failure of destitute families to receive the allotment checks described here by Dodge drove otherwise dutiful soldiers to desert. And the fumblings of paymasters like Major Campbell, as described here, certainly added to the general discontent in the ranks.

February 19th 1863

The Paymaster came just about dark last night, and in time to take tea with us; after which he and his clerk and another one I furnished him with set to work to make out the "Allotment Checks" for the first 5 Companies. Allotment Checks are checks issued by the Government which can be drawn by any person to whom a certain portion of the soldier's pay is allotted by himself, and which any bank will cash. Most of the men allot to their families and some to savings banks. All these checks should have been made out before the Paymaster came here, but lazy old Campbell did not take the pains to do so, so they stayed up till nearly midnight writing. I went to bed at about 9 with a little headache. It is lucky the Q. M. and I have such a large tent, for else there would have been no place at all for paying off in, or for accommodating the Paymaster & his clerk. As it is they both slept in our tent and are now paying off Company A in it.

Last night when we were thoroughly full, we were astonished by the arrival of a poor woman, wife of one of our sergeants who is now sick in Washington, advised by the surgeon of the Douglas Hospital and several Congressmen to come out to camp and get a "Descriptive List" in order to get his discharge from the service. They had previously written for this Descriptive List and I had sent it, but without allowing time for it to arrive, they must send the poor woman out here after it.

Just fancy on a dark rainy night, mud over her ankles and holes large enough to swallow her every step nearly, did that poor woman trudge up from Brooke's Station here to see Capt. Lloyd. She got here about 8 o'clock P.M., and of course everybody was put to their wits' ends as to how to quarter her for the night. Finally Capt. Lloyd and his Lieut. vacated their tent for her. They then came up to us asking shelter, but we had already two guests and could not keep them. Where they passed the night I don't know. The poor woman got off this morning with her dear bought Descriptive List, and when she gets back to the hospital she will find a duplicate, and that she has had all her fatigue for naught.

I think I have sometime mentioned my old clerk, Sergeant Berger. Poor boy! he died yesterday in the regimental hospital, of typhoid. It was not till after his death that I found out how imprudent he had been. He had been ailing for many weeks and altho' urged by the doctor to come to the hospital and get some medicine, he always refused. The day before we left Berea Church he was taken with fever, but it was too late to get him into the hospital, and he had that weary march of two days on foot. It was too much for him, and tho' put into hospital as soon as we got here he sunk away. He has not a friend in this country—they all live in Berlin. Yesterday before he died he signed his pay roll, but as the Paymaster was so late, it may be a year before his friends can collect his dues from the Government.

When I heard he was like to die, I went to the hospital, & the scene struck me powerfully. In the tent was a space partitioned off where the patients were lying. The first was a man only partly indisposed, eating his supper. Next lay poor Berger in death throes. Next and so close that their clothes touched, another man eating. Next to him a fever patient. The steward and nurses sat by coolly eating their supper, none heeding the grim King who was passing thro' the curtains of the tent. All this in a space only 9 feet square. It was natural and yet curious, and to one who does not know how hardened the mind gets to death in this trade of ours, would seem almost brutal. The contrast struck me forcibly and painfully.

February 20, 1863

Major Campbell paid the Staff last night—me only from October 18th to 31st which amounts to $54, $33 net, a large sum as you see. We hope in March to be paid up to the 28th February which will be 4 months. Our pay has been cut down. I used to get as Adjutant $136 per month; now, only $118.50, and that further reduced by a tax of 3 per cent.

Lieut. Col. Lockman got a furlough last evening and left this morning. He will call on you directly. He is by no means a brilliant fellow, but more of a man than almost any one I know of. I hope you will see his wife; you remember he was married only an hour or so before he left home with his Regiment, with more self-denial than most men are masters of.

February 21, 1863

It has been a beautiful day, warm and mild, but a strong wind has been blowing which has dried up the mud, in a degree, which the snow and rain have made.

Major Campbell & his ourang-outang clerk left this morning before daylight for the Landing in an ambulance, and Funk the sutler went with them. He has been collecting his debts, and will soon return again with a load of good things. He talks of keeping an officers-mess tent, but I don't believe it will work. We were heartily glad to get rid of the Paymaster, for while he was here our tent was too crammed all the time for cleaning or getting things into shape.

Today I have been out riding for the first time since we came to this place, but the roads are so bad one can't enjoy a ride at all—creeping along in mud 6 inches deep every step and the road so full of holes as to prevent either trotting or cantering. Poor Berger was buried yesterday. We got the band of the 33rd Massachusetts, and a Mr. Sarner, who is trying to get the chaplaincy of this Regiment, officiated in German.

Soldier addresses and papers like the one circulated in Krzyzanowski's brigade were numerous in the Army of the Potomac in the dark months following Fredericksburg. Peace Democrats, often called Copperheads, were then actively promoting an end to the fighting by means of an armistice, and these soldiers' addresses, published in the newspapers, were designed to counter their efforts. Dodge explains (February 23) that this one was approved only after its "political tendencies" were toned down. Hooker's furlough system permitted two men per company, and two officers, to go home at a time, and on their return, the next pair were furloughed. Anyone who deserted stopped the process. On the evidence of these entries, compliance in the 119th New York was shaky.

February 22nd 1863

A fearful storm is raging outside. Last night at 10 o'clock the sky was clear and sparkling with stars, but towards morning a strong wind accompanied by snow sprang up, and I believe that there is now nearly a foot of snow on the ground. Heavy gusts of wind carry the falling flakes into every crevice of the tent, and our floor is continually damp. However it is by far worse outside than in, and thank Heaven military laws don't require many men to be astir at a time of such weather as this. I pity the poor fellows out on picket.

Today is Washington's birthday and just now (noon) a salute is fired, at Head Quarters of the 11th Army Corps, of 68 guns, followed by salutes from many of the other quarters. The salute was fired by couplets and very well fired too—regularly as clockwork.

We were to have had a Division review today but the weather has cut that short, and the circular which countermanded it invited all the Colonels and their staffs to Brigade Head Quarters. It was to hear Col. Krzyzanowski make a speech, and to drink some awful whiskey punch. As to the latter, I remembered the New Year's punch in the same place, which gave me such a racking headache, and so I only sipped a sip for courtesy; even that has given me a headache again. Col. K. had a paper drawn up which he wished us all to sign, assuring the President of the firm determination of this Brigade to stand by the Country, to put down the Rebellion, in spite of the traitors who circulate pamphlets &c &c. He has given it to Col. Peissner, who will I suppose have it read at officers' meeting and signed by those who choose to do so; and then it will be sent to the 75th Penn. Col. K. is fishing for a Brigadier Generalship, and this I suspect is a fine new bait.

Capt. Theune, Col. K.'s A. A. Genl., who was wounded at Manassas, has come back to resume his duties. Now there are none but Jews over there. He (Theune) is an arch Jew by his looks. The old Adjutant, Stoldt, was a nice fellow, but now he is only Aide de Camp. Tomorrow the officers on furlough we expect will be back, and the first application which will be made for fresh furlough will be for Q. M., and I feel sure he will get it.

February 23rd 1863

This is the day when the two officers, Capt. Lockman and Lieut. Orleman, ought to have returned from furlough; but they are not here. They probably think that one day, only one day, cannot make any difference; but it is surely a very selfish thing to remain overtime, for it debars others from going. Of 8 enlisted men who went North on the 13th inst. for 10 days, only one, Cooper the butcher, has come back this 23rd. Such is the looseness of the screws somewhere.

The thread you sent by mail came today—many thanks. The snow is deep on the ground, the mud below is deeper still. It is cold, but the cold cannot penetrate through the 10 or 12 inches of snow to harden the ground. The Colonel has been riding, but neither the Q. M. nor I have ventured it; however I think I shall try it tomorrow, for any kind of exercise almost is preferable to sitting all day long in the tent, reading or writing, and yawning the day away.

Lieut. Lewis, who left today, made me a present of his Shakespeare, which I have had in my keeping for several weeks of late, and was loth to part with. I have been reading *Macbeth, King Lear, Coriolanus*, and several other plays over again. It is quite refreshing in contrast with the novels one is all too apt to stuff one's self with in camp.

The address to the President, which Col. Krzyzanowski wished us to sign, was debated upon yesterday evening at an officers' meeting, and was strongly opposed by some of the officers, the Q. M. among others, on the ground of its political tendencies. A resolution was passed to recommit the document to Col. Peissner, who has received it from Col. K., with the desire that he should take it back to Col. K. and ask him to change it. This was successfully done. The Colonel and Q. M., at Col. Krzyzanowski's request, remodeled it and then it was signed by all our officers who were present.

Our drum major, a good man who has invariably done his duty, was quite disappointed the other day when the Paymaster was here. He expected drum major's pay; but it seems that there has been an order abolishing the office he held, and Major Campbell said he could only give him drummer's pay. This was a comedown for the poor fellow; so today I have been round collecting a subscription for him and have got $20 and a promise of $28 more. He will have a nice little sum; he has a wife and six children to support. The Col. is going to make him Sergeant in one of the Companies and detach him to take charge of the drummers and buglers.

Our whole Division and Von Steinwehr's are in close proximity, and altho' there are many objections to the crowding of several Regiments together, there is one thing which is agreeable. There are several bands near us, and in the evenings at Tatoo and after, they enliven us with music. The 33rd Mass. and 73rd Ohio are the contending 2 bands. They however sometimes get playing different tunes together at the same time, which is not agreeable. Our music organizations in the field are not well managed. It is so expensive out here to keep up a decent drum corps.

February 24, 1863

The Col. and I rode out this morning. The roads were very bad—in fact nothing but snow banks, in which the horses plunged about like porpoises; but the Col. was bound to ride fast and it was miraculous the progress we made under the circumstances. It is often as much as one can do to get the horses out of the holes they fall into; several times I have been in so deep that my feet were completely imbedded in the mud. It is a wonder more horses don't break their legs than do.

When we got to Stafford Court House (which was our destination) we went first to the Medical Director to see about Dr. Aymé's leave of absence, and found that Dr. Hamlin, who used to hold that place, had been appointed Inspector General somewhere, and that the new Medical Director had not yet come out from Washington. No papers were to be acted upon until his arrival; so we pled Dr. A.'s leave until it could be attended to. We then went over to Genl. Stahel's Head Quarters to see Major Baldwin, but found him still on furlough in Washington. As we were about to mount our horses to ride homeward, Capt. Meyer of Genl. Sigel's Staff met us & invited us to his tent, where in company with some other officers, we dispatched several bottles of Rhine wine and some doughnuts, together with much political business in which as usual we settled the fate of nations.

The Col. and I afterwards visited an establishment in a log hut calling itself "The New York Pie Bakery," where we exchanged some of the "legal tender" currency for some very nice doughnuts, which I tied up in a clean silk handkerchief I happened to have with me and gave to the orderly to carry. This same orderly is one Jack Kirby, the Colonel's groom—a Paddy, and an excellent ostler. He appears on the Colonel's second horse whenever he rides out, much to his own and the Colonel's glorification. He is very convenient to have about to hold our horses when we dismount, which the Colonel does at every friend's place he passes.

You of course have heard of Joe—alias Thomas Johnson, the Lieut. Col.'s servant now, but really the Quarter Master's. Joe went to Washington on Saturday on a three days' leave, having got paid off by several officers whose service he had been in. Just like a nigger, he came back last night about 9 P.M. with a huge bundle of clothes under his arm, upon which he had spent every cent of money he had!! It was a full suit of nice black, as good as I would buy, and just about as much use out here as a fiddlestick. "Yah, Yah," said Joe, "I ain't gwine to New York widout bein' dressed up well, Yah, Yah." He is determined to go with the Q. M. who, we are all sanguine, will get a furlough when Lieut. Col. L. returns. He (Joe) once came from New York out to camp at Fairfax Court House without paying one cent, and this last time, tho' he had a pass, he got to Washington & back again for nothing.

About the Q. M.'s furlough, the first order was that he should be counted in among the Line officers, and then he would have gone upon the return of Capt. Lockman and Lieut. Orelman (which neither of them have done as yet), but yesterday came another order that one of the Field and Staff could be absent as well as two Line, which counting the Q. M. among Field and Staff keeps him here till Lieut. Col. L. returns, which will be about Sunday or Monday. We got your letter of the 21st in the A.M. mail. Am glad you saw Lieut. Col. The Q. M. is a little under the weather and will not write tonight.

February 25, 1863

Time has again jogged on 24 hours. The year and month are that much older as well as the world and I. Neither much good nor much wisdom has fallen to my lot during that period; part of the time has been slept away, part eaten away, and a much larger part thrown away on official routine. There is really nothing to do, and it is impossible to get away from our camp to another to visit friends with the least degree of comfort. Indeed one almost stultifies.

Lieut. Orleman came back last night and Capt. Lockman this morning, and I am sorry to say neither of them was put under arrest, altho' they had so far outstayed their leave, this not only breaking all rules of discipline but selfishly keeping others from getting leave until they had reported.

We are making out pay rolls for January and February. I hope there will not be such a culpable neglect again in paying off the troops. We shall be mustered on the 28th inst. The Colonel and I again rode up to Head Quarters 11 Corps on official business.

Major Baldwin had come back from Washington; but had gone off to Genl. Hooker's Head Quarters at Falmouth. We saw Dr. Peale, acting Medical Director, and we shall get a hospital tent tomorrow (which belongs to the Regiment but was left behind with sick in it when we left Berea Church) and set it up for officers' meetings, instruction room, &c &c.

The Q. M. is still under the weather. I hope he will be able to get leave, as I think it will do him much good.

26 February 1863

The Q. M. is better this morning. His trouble is an attack of ague (brought on by the dampness) which will pass off in a day or two, the doctor thinks. It is raining hard today, and what with the melting snow and the rain combined, we shall be in a pretty state by tomorrow. I guess this storm, which has now lasted with little intermission for a week, is the "breaking of the winter." It is now near the 1st of March, which is generally the time for recommencing military operations; but winter having begun so late will probably last late into the spring. If we begin to move by the 1st of April we shall be lucky. I never wish to see such another winter; give me summer campaigns. A man can stand marching on dry roads and dry fields to almost any extent. Of the two evils, I should certainly prefer dust to mud, for the one only chokes one, the latter threatens to engulf one.

February 28, 1863

Last night's mail brought the letters you enclosed from Mrs. G. and George. We were perfectly astonished at the news, & nothing better illustrates the distance between us than that George should have had the smallpox and recovered from it, before we discovered that anything was the matter. How noble it was of that dear little lady to tend George all through his illness. Tho' it was but natural for her to do it, I cannot think of it but with gratitude that George should have such a friend.

Today is the last of February, and we are to be mustered at 1 P.M. by Col. Brown of the 157th N.Y.V. Our men are out on picket but will be in camp by 11 or 12 o'clock. We and the 1st Brigade do picket duty by turns, each for a fortnight and our turn is on now. Our Regiment has to furnish pretty much all the men there are for duty every other day. They grumble fearfully about it but have to go "willy nilly." Just now fatigue duty is hard work, as the roads are so very bad they have nearly all to be corduroyed, which keeps a large force at work all the time.

The furloughs are working badly. Of 8 men let out on furlough only two have come back in time; 2 more came back in two days more and are now in arrest; and four have not come at all and so are looked on as deserters. So four other men are cheated out of their chance of a furlough till these stray sheep find their way to the fold. Of the two officers on leave, one came back 24 hours late and the other two days. Col. P. has been obliged to issue a strict order on the subject. We are hoping that Lieut. Colonel Lockman will come back from his leave tomorrow, and then the Q. M. will at once make his application, which will probably take two days to get approved.

King Mud is now more despotic than ever. There is no more fear of attack from the Rebels, or of our picket line being disturbed, than of the French marching up from Mexico. There is a brook nearby which must be crossed to get to Stafford Court House, a mere brook which one can jump across in summer; but now if you wish to get to town you have to swim your horse across. Last evening the Colonel and I rode over to see Genl. Schurz, and found him proposing to ride over to Genl. Sigel's Head Quarters at Stafford Court House, and mighty angry was he at having to swim the brook. The name of the stream is Accakeek Creek, pronouncing which would be a good test as to whether a man had been drinking more than was good for him.

Yesterday the Colonel and I called on Mrs. Jacobs, wife of Col. Jacobs, 26th Wisconsin Vols., who is here to visit her husband, and were treated to a bottle of champagne, a great rarity in camp. One of the Captains has his wife in camp, and an ugly little wretch she is too.

Col. Brown, 157th N.Y., came over and mustered our Regiment at 1 P.M. today. There were altogether some 500 men mustered. This is a good number for a Regiment, as Regiments go nowadays, many being now reduced to 350 men. The men had just come off picket and did not look so well as usual; and their *best* is not very good. We have sent the muster rolls over to Col. B.'s quarters for his signature, and I intend to send them off to the Paymaster as soon as it is in any way possible.

Col. Peissner got a large hospital tent yesterday, and has had it put up in front of his own, for the purpose of holding officers' meetings in it. Tonight, for the first time, the Colonel has had a School of Captains. I could not be there on account of some business, but I guess it was pretty boshy; none of them know a hawk from a hand saw. The Col., now that he has broken the ice, will I hope persevere and try to make his Captains something like officers.

We are getting the Field and Staff parade into good order. We have a pioneer corps of 10 or 12 men, and they have made a nice plateau in front of our quarters around which they are to build a fence, which will in a measure secure us from intrusion. The Colonel and I rode out a short distance today, to the camp of the 33rd Massachusetts, to hear their band. They have some 15 pieces, and it is very agreeable to go over and listen to them.

Through some stupid mistake, there came back from Aquia Landing six discharged men, who had been stopped on account of some informality in their papers. When I came to investigate the matter, I found that the 1st Sergeant had lost the papers, which had been regularly signed at Genl. Sigel's Head Quarters, which had been given him to hand to the discharged men, and substituted others, which of course were worthless. I gave him such a lecture as he will not easily forget.

CHAPTER EIGHT

Waiting for Spring

March 1 to April 3, 1863

The Army of the Potomac was in thrall to what Theodore Dodge called King Mud, and only when the weather warmed and the roads dried—by sometime in April, it was hoped—could the spring campaign of 1863 open in Virginia. Meanwhile, there was drill and red tape and boredom and the sicknesses that always stalked an army in winter quarters. Most of the time, or so it seemed to Lieutenant Dodge, it was "half raining, half snowing."

Dodge himself was carrying an extra load in this period. On March 3 his father, the 119th's quartermaster, went home on sick leave, and Theodore took over the Q.M.'s duties in addition to his own regimental adjutant's duties. The elder Dodge's departure would mark the end of his connection with the 119th New York. When he returned to duty after a protracted illness, it was first in Washington; on his return to duty in the field in June, it was as quartermaster in another brigade.

In these weeks young Dodge's journal is marked with grumblings about the imperfections in his regiment and in his brigade that offended his sense of orderliness and military propriety. At last, the nomination for his promotion to captain came through, and word that his application for a ten-day leave came through as well. "So I have made all preparations to start tomorrow," he wrote happily in closing his entry for April 3.

March 1st 1863

Today a sick leave came back from Head Quarters for Capt. Hall for 20 days, which set the Q. M. on a new tack. For a week he has been much indisposed and evidently needs a change of air. Our camp is in as damp and unhealthy a spot as a man can find in a day's ride—marshy and inundated as soon as it rains, which it does most of the time. He got Dr. Aymé to write a surgeon's certificate, which was endorsed by Dr. Stein, acting surgeon, and made an application for a sick leave of 20 days. It was sent over to Brigade Head Quarters, "approved & warmly endorsed" by Col. Peissner. Now, over there they don't love the Q. M., because they have tried to pick several quarrels with him and have always come off second best. So in two or three hours back came the certificate disapproved &c &c. So we made out another more *en règle* and sent over; meantime, I went over and used a little soft sawdor on the Assistant Adjutant General and got him to send it to Division Head Quarters approved by Col. Krzyzanowski. At Division Head Quarters the way has already been paved by Col. P., who rode over today getting Genl. Schurz and Genl. Von Steinwehr (who commands during Genl. Sigel's absence) in a good humor and a promise that the application should be approved. So if the Q. M. should drop from the clouds into the St. Nicholas Wednesday or Thursday, don't be alarmed.

I rode up to Stafford Court House on several matters of business, and on the way home met Major Baldwin, riding down to Genl. Hooker's with Genl. Stahel to a dinner party. I had not seen him for several weeks. He told me that but one man in the Corps was yet confirmed as General, and that was Schimmelfennig; and none of the Brigadiers would be made Major Generals.

March 3rd 1863

The Q. M.'s application for sick leave went in, as I wrote you in my last letter on Sunday afternoon; and after the haggling at Brigade Head Quarters, experienced no difficulty in arriving to the Corps Head Quarters. Lieut. Col. Salisbury, Chief Commissary of the Corps, went in to the Medical Director's and spoke a good word for the Q. M., which had the effect of getting it approved; and as Col. Peissner had already seen General Von Steinwehr and got his promise of approval, it began its return march yesterday noon. The Colonel and I had been up to Stafford and assured ourselves of its success, and when we came back we told the Q. M. the result of our investigations; but so determined was he that he would not be disappointed if it did not come, that he per-severed in his unbelief.

Major Baldwin came over last evening to see the Q. M., and as the application had not yet got here, he went over to Col. Krzyzanowski's to hurry it on. Yesterday was Genl. Schurz's birthday, and Col. K. was giving a supper in honor thereof. The music and cheers reached us frequently until nearly 11 o'clock. Col. P. was over there, participating in the entertainment, which has been productive of a racking headache this morning. So the Major, eager to combine busi-ness with pleasure, bestrode his horse and rode over accom-panied by Harry on the "Irish Giant" (a big horse of the Q. M.'s), who was to bring us back news of the application. Harry stopped over there so long however that Joe was dis-patched after him to bring him back, it being the Q. M.'s opin-ion that he had forgotten all about the business in the pleas-ure. Harry came back with the news that "Three Cheers for Major Baldwin and Baldwin and Baldwin" was the order of the day and the application was given up in despair.

However it was not so with the Major; as soon as oppor-tunity offered, he got hold of the Assistant Adjutant General and made him send the application over; and about 10 P.M., after we had gone to bed, it came: "Leave of absence is hereby granted to N. S. Dodge, Q. M. 119th N.Y.V., for 20 days on Sur-geon's Certificate." This morning accordingly he has got off. He rode my mare down to the Landing as she is easier than his, and he felt so poorly—Joe went with him on the Lieut. Colonel's horse, carrying the carpet bag. He was to wait down there for the Lieut. Colonel, who will probably be on today.

The Colonel and I rode out yesterday to see the Major. He was in, and as he was just going over to see Genl. Slocum, we rode with him. Coming home, we met Lieut. Col. Salisbury, with whom the Major messes, and he insisted on our dis-mounting and taking dinner with him. As Corps Commissary he has many opportunities of getting good things, and he gave us as well assorted and well cooked a dinner as one gets at home. It was worth while going for. He invited us to breakfast some morning.

March 4, 1863

During the Q. M.'s absence, I am the acting Q. M. of the 119th, a place I by no means covet, as the requisitions come down like rain during a thunderstorm, now that a "green one" is in. Not to be called on too often, or to be overshadowed by troublesome taunts, I sign "T. A. D. Adjt. of the 119th for the Q. M.," which does not impose on me such duties as waiting on Brigade Q. M., seeing to the teams, &c. Last evening the Brigade forage master came in, and wanted to know how many animals we wanted condemned. He was told that all except 3 mules and 9 horses had already undergone sentence, and that he could not now call upon us for more than 2 teams at one time.

The order revoking General Orders No. 84, allowing the sale of commissary stores on credit to officers, was handed to me this morning by Harry (whom I had just sent over to Lieut. Smith for edibles), from that worthy commissary with a polite request to send the "wherewithal." The Q. M. had seen the order but forgotten about it, and I fear he has left no "mess fund" and my purse was not filled to overflowing by the Paymaster when last here; so I shall have to go to the Colonel to borrow some money, as we have to pay for everything we buy, except from Jimmie Christie, our own commissary.

Poor Dr. Aymé's application for sick leave came back today disapproved, with the remark, "Twenty days will not restore his health. He is constitutionally unsound. Signed for Med. Div. Dr. Peale." At an officers' meeting today, the Colonel spoke about Dr. Aymé, and Dr. Stein, saying he disapproved all signing of papers for or against promotions, it transpired that almost all the officers who had signed Dr. Aymé's petition had also signed Dr. Stein's. He spoke very highly of Dr. A.'s qualities, but indirectly of his unpractical-ness, and his promotion in consequence.

A telegram came from the Lieut. Colonel dated March 3rd, saying he would be here today and ordering horses to the Landing. Joe accordingly went yesterday. For the first time I took a musket and drilled the orderly Sergeants, which greatly pleased the Colonel. This A.M. in consequence we have had squad drill. This P.M. we shall have Battalion drill.

Joe came back from the Landing yesterday about 3 P.M. and as the Lieut. Colonel did not arrive, instead of riding his (the Lieut. Colonel's) horse, as I expressly bade him, the good for naught came back grinning and giggling on my mare, and when I had the saddle taken off and passed my hand down her back to see if it was tender, she winced under it. I was just of good mind to give Joe a cowhiding as ever I had to eat my dinner. I gave him one such blowing up as he never had be-fore, and he has not had a grin on his face since.

March 5, 1863

Yesterday we had Battalion drill of nearly 3 hours, and after drill Col. P. drew up the Battalion in front of Genl. Schurz's Head Quarters and presented arms in celebration of the 4th of March. Almost the last thing the Q. M. said to me was "Don't take cold" and as if there were a fatality in it, what should I do yesterday but take cold out on drill. A very sharp wind was blowing & sitting motionless on horseback was enough to give anyone a cold. Last night however I went to bed very early, taking a hot drink, and this A.M. my cold is bet-ter. However I had a bilious attack during the night and have taken some camphor and opium pills this A.M.

When we came in from drill yesterday we found the Lieut. Col. returned. It did me good to see him; of course he had spent a very happy fortnight in New York. He said he scarcely knew our camp again, we had so nicely fitted up Head Quarters. We have had our pioneer corps kept at work doing up odd jobs about the camp.

The Dr. has got a strong letter from the Colonel to Dr. Quackenboss, surgeon general of the State of N.Y., and I wrote him another this A.M. which the Lieut. Col. signed. He has also a Line officer's signature from each of the Companies. He sends all these papers today to the Q. M., who will dispose of them at discretion.

I was to have accompanied the Colonel down to Genl. Hooker's Head Quarters to see Genl. Butterfield, the A. Adjutant General, or rather Chief of Staff of the Army of the Potomac; but not feeling well enough to go, Lieut. Col. took my place. They left soon after breakfast. George, the Lieut. Colonel's waiter, went off today for Washington. I presume the others will work better now he has gone.

I have been thinking all the morning that today the Q. M. is at home, or rather with you, and wishing I was there too. Dr. Aymé has today sent in his application for leave of absence according to the new order.

March 6, 1863
Capt. Leubascher has applied for sick leave. Dr. Stein certifies that he has hemorrhage of the lungs. Capt. L. says he has never been troubled with his lungs before. Dr. Stein has been detailed to Division hospital. I am not well today but hope to be better tomorrow.

Dodge seems to have found his colonel, Elias Peissner, amiable enough, and he came to admire his skills as a chess player and fencer, but there were occasions (such as this one) when Peissner's indeci-

siveness and lack of military training left the young adjutant frustrated. With his father now home on sick leave, he was at pains to fill his journal entries with details of regimental goings-on for the benefit of the elder Dodge.

March 7, 1863

Today my fit of indisposition which was brought on by the cold I took has left me and I feel well again. The Lieut. Colonel had brought some medicine with him, and though it was the very thing I had been taking, two or three doses of that which he brought was entirely corrective—no doubt on account of the freshness & purity of the drugs. I have very little confidence in army medicines. They are put up in such enormous quantities and left in Government store rooms so long that they get stale and worthless; and several Army surgeons have told me that they have first to experiment with their medicines before they know the proper dose to give. Of course this is a bad thing for the patients. But I do not marvel at it, as the whole Medical Department of the Army is conducted in a most senseless and extravagant manner.

Two or three cases of presumptuous intermeddling by the Medical Department have taken place in our Regiment. Yesterday Dr. Stein, surgeon of the 58th New York detailed to the Regiment, was suddenly ordered off to Division hospital without any order having passed through the Adjutant's Department of the Brigade. or Division. The Colonel protested against the proceeding & retained Dr. S. until this morning, when an order came through the proper channel, on which of course the Colonel acted.

Now I want to tell you how the Colonel acted in reference to Dr. Aymé. Day before yesterday he approved of the Dr.'s application for leave of absence, and it was sent on to the Brigade. It was however sent back with an order requiring a new system of filing *all* official communications. When it went a second time, it was returned for not having been filed correctly, though in accordance with the order received (which had been written by a German), and a third time it had to be made out. Again the Colonel approved it, and it was forwarded. Shortly afterwards he called me into his tent and told me he really ought not to allow Dr. Aymé to go, as Dr. Stein was detached and Dr. A. was the only surgeon in the Regiment, and instructed me to write to Col. Theune, A. A. General 2nd Brigade, recalling the application. It consequently came back but by that time the Colonel had again changed his mind, the Medical Department might go to where sulphur came from, he didn't care a straw—send the Dr.'s application in again. So, in it went a fourth time, when in half an hour, no wonder, it came back disapproved by Krzyzanowski, saying the Regiment must not be left without a surgeon. So the good Dr. cannot get off and may thank whom? for his ill luck.

Yesterday Edward, the wagon-master, brought in nine express packages from Hope Landing and sent over to the Q. M. Sergeant to send for them. Soon after he (Edward) saw some men of the 119th lounging about and gave the boxes to them, telling them to bring them over to the Adjutant's office. They were brought over to the Regiment and wandered about from hand to hand until someone (whether the rightful owner or not) opened them, and I can as yet get hold of but eight of them. Thus is business done in style in the 2nd Brigade 3rd Division 11th Corps A. of P.

The weather is very changeable, now windy, now cold, and anon a lull with oppressive closeness of the atmosphere, and then rain, hail, snow and every variety of climate imaginable. Today rain & warmth prevail, but I do not go out of doors much.

Last evening's mail brought me the Q. M.'s letter from Washington, and ditto to the Colonel, both as full of information as his letters always are. I get on very nicely as Q. M.—

insist on frequent reports to myself tho' the active partners are the Sergeants. Have given the six ponchos or blankets which came from the Guard House to Major Hoffmann, A. A. General 3rd Division on his receipt. Henry works well, Joe also, much better since George left. Two boys can do perfectly well everything for the Field and Staff, except grooming. Cooper the butcher yields tongues, livers, kidneys &c, reports regularly, and has had a gentle hint that the "black trooper's" back was not healing as expected, which will prick him up to attending to it. Nelly has her regular exercise every day, ditto "Cornish Giant." Fanny prospers and is as fat as butter. Lieut. Col. L.'s wit revives. I guess he has not been allowed to vent it freely at home. Of course he has come back a new man, knowing that marriage has many cares, celibacy many pleasures.

I received a long letter from Mary Agnes two days ago. She is a fine correspondent. Dr. Aymé is very faint, yet fain to persevere. Now the Q. M. is gone, he falls upon me for aid and comfort. Good old Dr., he is as good and true as gold, but not worth as much in marketable value by a long chalk, and at about as much discount as gold is premium. But who can know him without liking him?

The demijohn is kept in close confinement. Even I do not touch him, but have substituted rhubarb for a week or so. Joe wanted a drink out of it the other day but I told him no one could have it. Only two drinks have gone out of it since the Q. M. left, both to cure my cold. Capt. Brandt has resigned under charges, and it has been approved & forwarded by Col. P.

March 9th 1863

About 20 minutes ago I woke up, and Harry, who was sweeping out the tent, said to me in a very cool manner, "It's quarter to 8." The deuce it is! thought I, and sprung up like a machine, with a misgiving that it could be only 1/4 to 7. But no, said Harry, & was positive. "Sergeant Major!" hallowed I,

"Sound the fatigue call!" for we have a fatigue party of 250 men to send out today. I soon invested myself in stockings and pants, when I proceeded to look at my watch, when lo' and behold, it was 12 minutes to 7. I shouted again to stop the call for fatigue, which was in fact checked just as two "poigns" and a "flam" (these are drum-stick words) had been sounded by the unlucky drum. I gave Harry a sound blowing up, and was so thoroughly awake that I did not care to sleep again, so this letter is the result.

For the past two nights I have slept on the Q. M.'s bed, which proves a much more comfortable one than mine. My ill turn has gone, but I continue my rhubarb 3 times a day. Last evening brought your letter saying that the Q. M. had arrived. Is your faith in furloughs confirmed now? Capt. Leubascher left on sick leave of 20 days yesterday morning; he was quite toned down by sickness, all the pluck of him gone. Lieut. Orleman is sick too, and 3 days have pulled him down to a nice skeleton; he is really very ill. Lieut. Schwerin is also sick. His turn comes next for leave of absence; he will probably go in 2 or 3 days, as Merritt's and Rasemann's time is up today.

It is a most lovely day, a warm and genial sun and cloudless sky, one of these incomparable spring days. It is still muddy but the ground is drying up fast. I got *Punch* and the *Illustrated News* from England yesterday—Punch was only pretty good.

7 P.M.—

I had quite a little accident just now. After opening my books, I took the one on sword play and showed it to the Colonel. We began to talk about sword play, when he said to the Lieut. Col. and me, "Come out and I will give you a lesson in sword exercise." Nothing loth, we went; we all of us forgot that our swords were sharp, the Colonel's particularly so. In one of the cuts, a bad guard brought his sword right over my wrist and made a cut about an inch and a half long quite to the bone. As this was more than I bargained for, I gave up the lesson. Dr. A. put sticking plaster and a bandage upon it, and it will heal up in a few days. It is very stiff however just now. I rode up to Stafford on the Willis mare and saw the Major, who is flourishing.

March 10, 1863

I write a few words before the mail goes. Yesterday was a most lovely day, today it's very opposite—a snowy, wet, windy day, just as uncomfortable as can be. We have a large fatigue party out. I pity the poor fellows. They are corduroying the road from Stafford to Falmouth. Capt. Willis is in charge of the party. There are probably 3,000 men at work on the road. They say it is being very well built.

The Colonel has had his big hut fitted up splendidly. A large fire place, in which we can burn whole logs of wood, blazes away on one side of the tent, and the other is lined with benches for officers' meetings. The whole is floored and is very comfortable. We celebrated its inauguration last evening in a whiskey punch. Our Head Quarters are now the pride of the neighborhood: a nice grand plat railed in front of the line of tents, a row of evergreen shrubs decorating the sides, tall flag staff and banner, the regimental colors displayed every fine day fluttering in the breeze, sentinel pacing his beat in front of the quarters, horses or rather "proud steeds" (more likely sorry hacks with very sore backs) champing their bits and pawing the ground in eagerness to gallop away, and all that sort of thing you know.

Our having just got nicely fitted up is surely indicative however of our speedy departure. We had an officers' instruction last evening, and the ignorance of the Regiment was fully displayed. With the exception of one Lieutenant, the whole of them did not know enough to fill the brain of a Corporal. I heartily wish that, instead of mustering so many good officers out of the service in the consolidation of old Regiments, they would muster out these ignoramuses and put the old officers in their places.

Today we have drawn ten days' rations, which we shall give right out to the Companies. They say we are to get 14 lbs. hay per diem for our horses. I hope it may be true.

This celebration of Krzyzanowski's brigadier generalship turned out to be premature, as noted in Dodge's March 14 entry. Although he would serve through the course of the war, Krzyzanowski only became a brigadier general by brevet in March of 1865.

March 11th 1863

Col. Krzyzanowski is at last General. Last evening our whole corps of officers went over to Head Quarters to congratulate him. He and Staff had just finished tea, and we were invited in and liberally treated to claret. We each congratulated him separately as we entered his tent and, after having seated ourselves and having been supplied with cups of wine, the new fledged General arose to return thanks. He made an "oration" in point of modulation of voice and action, but as wretched a "speech" as one can imagine a Polish Jew to make on sentiment or language. Still, to ordinary German ears it was an "oration," and American ears were at its close suddenly startled by "Three cheers for our General, hip, hip, hurrah!!" from Capt. Van Borries. The cheers were rather weak and undecided, giving no very visible impression of our Polish tendencies to the new General. He had said in his speech that to be sure the 119th was a new Regiment and yet untried, but he still had no doubt it would do its duty; that it had the name of being a singular Regiment, but that he had no extraordinary grounds of complaint against it; and much more in an uncomplimentary strain.

After a few minutes, Col. Peissner rose to say a few words. He spoke well, slowly in a conversational tone: "We were a singular Regiment and we intended to be so; we did not perhaps mix much with the other Regiments; well, it was not our way; we didn't cheer much but that need not be construed as any want of enthusiasm; we had a mind of our own and we intended to keep it. As long as our General did his duty, we should do ours; that this was the only true basis of military discipline, &c &c." We then rose to go, after drinking once more the General's health.

Last evening Lieut. Merritt invited several officers to his tent. He has recently come from furlough and had brought some good things with him. I was of the party. The Adjutants of the Brigade were all there, and we had a nice punch and many good things. Story telling was the order of the day, and we had a very fine time.

The yesterday's mail brought *Harper's Magazine*, for which I am much obliged. Col. P. would like to have the Q. M. bring his foils, mask and plastrons from Schenectady, if it will not be too much trouble. Fencing will be a pleasant pastime if we get them.

We have sent our whole Regiment out on picket today: 3 Captains, 8 Lieutenants, and 330 men—all we have fit for duty.

Nathaniel Dodge's "pamphlet" was a paper on the organization of army transport that was being considered by Hooker and his chief of staff, Dan Butterfield, in planning the spring campaign. The journal entry for March 14 explains the project further. Captain Otto Van Borries, the subject of young Dodge's derision (March 14), would temporarily command the 119th after Chancellorsville by virtue of being the senior captain.

March 12, 1863

The mail, which came an hour ago, brought a letter from dear Mrs. G., a paper (*Illustrated News*) from London, and Mother's of the 7th inst., enclosing George's. I send Mrs. G.'s (which is to the Q. M.) and return George's, both of which are exceedingly interesting.

Our whole Regiment is on picket for 3 days from yesterday, and Dr. Aymé was detailed as picket surgeon for the Corps—by no means an agreeable thing for the good old gentleman. However, he took his detail very philosophically and slowly, and being (as a matter of course) furnished with a horse and rations by me, went off yesterday after dinner. This morning he sent word to me (the impracticable old Dr. all over) to send him out a hot breakfast. He is 3 miles from here, and how he expected a hot breakfast from camp is a marvel to me. I sent him a large package of sandwiches, but had nothing else. If he only had a servant now, how much more comfortable would he be. The "Cornish Giant" was the horse he rode. He promised to send him back last evening but did not, and probably will keep him the 3 days.

By the way, we have changed our dinner hour from 1 to 5 o'clock, and then take dinner and tea all at once. The Colonel likes this much better and so do I. As there was very little to be done in camp, the Colonel, Lieut. Colonel and I rode down to Falmouth this A.M. to see General Butterfield, Chief of Staff of the Army of the Potomac. I rode the Q. M.'s bay mare, as Fanny has not quite recovered from her sore back. We took about two hours going down, and the same returning, cutting across country where we could find the best roads, only pursuing the general direction. On our way down we met a Lieut. Farley (a Union College boy) who stopped the Colonel as he was riding by. As I was introduced he said he had seen a sister of mine at Rochester. Does Mary remember him? A small, fair-haired fellow, rather insipid?

Major Genl. B. received us very graciously, spoke about the Q. M.'s pamphlet among other things, and entertained us most pleasantly for an hour or so, when we took our leave. He seems to have a plenty of business on hand. He is a young man, scarcely thirty, rather handsome, wears a black mustache, stoutish face and figure, very cool and collected in his manners, and very gentlemanly. We also went in to see A. A. General Kimball at Genl. Patrick's Head Quarters. Kimball is the same fine hearty fellow as ever, and gave us as fine a glass of sherry as one might desire. He is coming over to dine with us on Sunday if he can get off duty. He spoke much of Mother and Polly whom he greatly admires. He is a nice fellow.

The wind is blowing a hurricane tonight and I have to tighten up the cords of my tent every little while; we are pretty well protected here. On the hill they rather catch the breeze, I fancy. It is March weather altogether. There is now no number of Field and Staff about and I really don't know but I could get leave despite Order No. 10, if the Colonel would send in an application for me. But I fear the Colonel needs my services too much. However I shall try it, if we do not move before the Q. M. gets back. Mrs. G. writes she hopes I will not get fat about the neck. Unfortunately I am one of the thin necked beings which could not possibly get even decently fat there.

March 14, 1863

I sit at the table with a fat letter on official business to Dr. Aymé (sent through Head Quarters A. of P.) staring me in the face. As I write this, up drives an ambulance and out comes the Dr. himself from picket, dirty, tired and cold, tho' in good spirits. He opens the letter, and much to my disgust, for I had been hoping some great thing for him since the letter came in from Head Quarters last evening, it was only an invoice for hospital tents drawn by the Dr. before we left Stafford the last time. Capt. Lloyd comes in tonight from picket, and the rest

211

will soon follow. Col. P. is detailed on fatigue duty, building a corduroy road from here to Potomac Creek for 4 days with 450 men from the 26th Wisc. and the 58th N.Y.; and has gone off in anything but good temper. The hours of work each day are from 8 A.M. to 4 P.M. with 1 1/2 hours for dinner. We shall therefore dine at noon. The Lieut. Col. is president of a court of inquiry, and I am therefore left to "run the machine," as the only active member of the Field and Staff present.

Yesterday the Sergeants of Company H spent their money on not a few bottles of so-called champagne (probably a mixture of spirits of wine, sugar, water, and cream of tartar) at $2 per bottle. This precious mess they bought of the sutler of the 75th and jolly drunk they both got; after which they set to fighting and gave each other a mutual merciless beating. Col. P. put them under arrest, which did little good. They ought to have been reduced to the ranks, put in irons and then on guard duty a week hard running. This would have effectually checked their "flow of spirits." As it is, they are as merry as larks, having enjoyed their spree without any lasting disagreeable consequences.

Yesterday I rode over to Stafford and saw the Major; he said he had written to the Q. M., and should write again soon; he gave me a very good glass of ale, a thing I had not tasted before for a long time. Lieut. Schwerin left on leave of absence yesterday and Capt. Van Borries ditto today. The latter will go to the St. Nicholas, and says he shall see Mr. Dodge. If Mary and Mother wish to see a puppy let them see Capt. and prospective Major Van Borries (he already has his letters directed so). The other evening the distinguished Captain came swagging to the Colonel's tent. "Haw, what's the lesson today, I declare I've not looked into the book." "Captain," says the Colonel, "I'll give you $100 if you will answer the first question correctly," & sure enough he could not. But nothing daunted: "Why, yes he could have answered, only he didn't understand the question exactly &c &c." He is the laughing stock of the officers. Capt. Willis is decidedly improving, much to the gratification of us all.

One of the Corporals is under arrest under charge of sleeping on his post. The charge he denies and says the patrol addressed him in German, which he did not choose to answer. He will be court martialed, but it will be a nice little point which will come up, viz. Can German be used as an official means of communication? No recruit, says the Regulations, "shall be received unless he shall have a good knowledge of English." How can they come over that?

The first fruits of "Army Transportation" are as follows:

> Chief Q. M.'s Office, 11th Army Corps
> Stafford March 10th

Circular

In compliance with orders received from Head Quarters A. of P. the following will be the full allowance of means of transportation:

For a Regiment with 700 men & upwards present: 6 wagons.

Of 500 to 700: 5 wagons. Under 500: 4 wagons.

All Q. M.s will at once reduce the means of transportation in their commands to this standard and turn over any excess to the depot Q. M. at Hope Landing.

> J. G. C. Lee
> Actg. Chief Q. M. 11th Corps

Capt. Worms has got back and matters which have gone on smoothly during his absence, have begun again to froth and bubble. He begins by declaring that we have not 500 men present and that the Adjutant's report shews it. The last report was 507 men and 20 officers, so I can throw that in his face. He ordered Carpenter to take two wagons to Hope Landing and said he would see we got but 4 teams when mules were drawn again. Only one wagon went, and I should like to see him keep back one team from us. I will lose nothing by a row with him.

One caterer is now allowed to bring wines and ales to a Regiment. Our Brigade has not yet got them—probably Worms will be the man.

8 o'clock P.M.—

Jake, our pet teamster, has got into trouble today. He began (as is always the case) by getting too much liquor aboard, and then hit on his particular grievance—his extra pay. "We gets him," says Jake and starts off on his "yaller" (yellow) horse to Capt. Worms. Here his remonstrances ended in his being ordered out of the office; whereupon he returns to our department and says to the teamsters that he was going to get ahead of him (Capt. W.) and forthwith rode off to Stafford to Capt. Lee, Acting Chief Q. M. 11th Corps—all this of course without my knowledge. There he found out that Capt. Worms had this morning drawn $1,200, so back he came by way of our camp, and after sharing his news with his fellow teamsters, he again made for Capt. W., when he made such a hubbub that the Captain arrested him and put him in the Brigade jail. He (Capt. W.) afterwards came to tell the Colonel that of these $1,200, $940 odd belong to the pioneer corps and the rest he must use for the 58th, who are in arrears for a year's pay. So our boys will remain unpaid. Today Jake was released and came over with a very smiling face feeling quite the hero, but I cut him short with a good blowing up. Capt. W. swore he should never be a driver again, but I guess we shall keep him.

Major Baldwin and Capt. Kent were here a short time ago and spent near an hour. Our Corps Staff are getting up a chess tournament and want the Colonel to join them. The Dr. is again going to send in his application for a leave, and Major B. has promised to do his best to help it through.

Note. The news has come today that Genl. Krzyzanowski, who was felicitated and fêted on his appointment as General, has passed thro' reconsideration & been rejected, much to the delight of the Q. M., who thoroughly despises him.

March 16, 1863

I did not write last evening to send off by the morning courier, for the Col. and I spent the evening at Stafford. I told you about the chess tournament proposed between the Staffs of the 12th and our Corps, and they are anxious to find out the best players. Col. P. is strong at chess, and Lieut. Col. Meysenburg, A. A. G. of the Corps, is also a great chess player; so Major Baldwin invited both of them up to his quarters to play a game or two. Col. P. went up after 3 P.M., and I went with him. He vowed he would not play, for he wished to get back to camp before dark, but no sooner had he arrived than he was inveigled into one game, which shortly became two and then three, so that it was 10 o'clock before we got off on our way home. Meanwhile I took supper with non-players, and lounged about occasionally watching the game. Col. P. lost I believe two out of the three games, altho' as good a player as Col. M. The former plays a more brilliant, while the latter plays a solid German game.

A great thunderstorm sprang up, accompanied by violent wind and hail and torrents of rain, while all this was going on, in which our poor horses and Jack the orderly were forgotten and were of course all thoroughly drenched. When at last I got the Colonel away from the chess, it was as dark as pitch, the only glimmer being from the snow on the ground, and we had a shocking road to get back to camp and two creeks to cross—all, too, in a violent thunder and hail storm. We got through however without breaking our necks, altho' our poor beasts stumbled about like drunkards, and came down on their heads every little while. The road is all cut thro' pine woods and is consequently full of little stumps. Arrived at camp we were fain to go to bed, instead of taking up the pen.

I went to Stafford yesterday and saw an artillery inspection. I should like to be an artillery officer—it is a splendid service. I had rather be Captain of a battery than Colonel of a Regiment. There were three batteries out and some splendid maneuvering. I heard at the same time that Stahel and Schurz had both been confirmed as Major Generals, the latter probably to get the Corps, and Stahel the command of all the cavalry about Washington. Joe dressed up in his "good clothes" and looked just like a chimpanzee. He is a good, strong looking nigger when he has on his working gear, but he looks horrid in his Sunday togs. We called him "Deacon Johnson of the South Baptist Church." He wanted to go down to the Landing, but could not on account of the late dinner. Capt. Kimball did not come yesterday; some business I presume; besides it is a long distance. George thinks he can get some sketches inserted in one of the London illustrated journals and I think I can get some made at Corps Head Quarters. Major Baldwin knows some good sketchers. I got by mail last evening the tooth brush and stamps all safe. Many things may be sent that way which take so long to come by Express, and are not sure to reach at all. Don't let the Q. M. come on till he is *quite* well. It will not do.

P.M.—

Today Col. Peissner has been in command of the Brigade. About 10 A.M. an order came: "Col. Krzyzanowski having had to go to Washington, Col. P. will take command of the Brigade," which he accordingly did, when about 4 P.M. another order came: "Col. K. having returned will take command again of the Brigade." Col. K. travels pretty quick. He must have special fast boots to have gone and returned so soon. I rather think he issued his order, and then found he could not go after all.

Today another of those miserable petitions came round for signature. It originated in this manner. Lieut. Col. Matzdorff, of the 75th Pa., when he heard of K.'s confirmation as Brig. Genl., congratulated him in these words, "If you, Sir, had not been confirmed I would have resigned my Commission." Now that the Senate of the United States have refused to confirm him, this valorous officer must do something. Accordingly *he* gets up a petition, ostensibly, but really the petition savors of Col. K.'s own clerk's pen. The officers of the 75th sign it, and then those of the 58th, and then it comes to us, the "independent" Regiment. The officers hold a meeting, whereupon Colonel P. said to them, "p. 220 Revised Regulations forbids such a proceeding" (which in effect it does); "petitions have several times brought us into trouble & therefore I am opposed to it." Accordingly this is endorsed on the petition and it is sent back with a note as follows: "Col. P. and officers respectfully decline signing this paper."

We are not liked in the Brigade and no wonder. They abuse us and we have sometimes a chance to retaliate. Anyhow the petition was a manifest absurdity: "America owes a debt of gratitude to Poland," and more such twaddle. Col. P. has been relieved as Corduroy King, at which he does not grumble. Lieut. Col. Lockman is on as Brigade Officer of the Day for 3 days.

Don't let Father come back till he is entirely well. Everything goes on swimmingly in the Q. M.'s Department. Don't patch him up, but let him recover thoroughly.

March 17, 1863

We have just finished officers' school. I attend it because the Colonel says, "I like to have the officers see that you know something," but it is very dull nevertheless. We had Battalion drill this A.M. for several hours. It was very cold when we went out, but pleasant when we finished at 11 A.M.

March 18th [1863]

In the 3rd Division our picket duty is done in the following manner. The two Brigades alternate every three days in furnishing a picket, about 500 or 600 men strong. This takes about half the infantry of the Brigade, so that our Regiment goes out about 3 days out of 12. This is not very hard on the men, but the fatigue duty does sometimes press sharply on the poor fellows, and they hate to go out and work. In most cases the older a Regiment gets, the more unwilling it is to do fatigue duty, and the less work can be got out of the men.

Our Regiment came off picket last Saturday, the 14th inst., and so does not go on again till next week. The respite is devoted by the Colonel to drill, and every morning the Battalion maneuvers over the hilly fields of Dame Lawrence Cliff, whose domain has been robbed both of fences and produce. She, you will remember, was the crusty old lady who of her teeming abundance refused us a turkey for our Xmas dinner. I fancy that all her turkeys will not now amount to much, for her "safeguard" is removed. Is not this a retribution?

It is wonderful how the whole country round here is literally stripped of its timber. Woods which, when we came here, were so thick that we could not get through them any way are now entirely cleared—the pine being used for building and making roads, and the cedar and hard wood, of which there is a great quantity, for fire wood. This struck me specially the other day on the road to and from Falmouth. You can now scarcely see a wood anywhere, and at times it seems a marvel where the camps could get their supplies from.

My mare has completely recovered from her sore back. She is fat and frisky as a two year old. I dare not ride her at drill till after I have trained her a bit, for she is far too playful. Jenny (Father's horse) does a good deal of work now. I ride her at drill daily, and she goes into Stafford besides.

March 20, 1863

I was sure from the last letter that the Q. M. would not be able to come on at present and we do not wish him to do so till he is quite well. The Colonel is satisfied and in event of a march all will go on smoothly under my superintendence. The Q. M. Dept. is conducted by the two Sergeants under my supervision, and no complaints whatever have been made. We drew 8 mules, nice fat ones, yesterday, and now all our wagons are in good order again. Today we have chosen a sutler who has two wagon loads of goods at Aquia Landing. His name is Rubenbender, and he seems a fair and honest man (the only one of the applicants who did look so) and I fancy will do well. He was also the only one of the applicants who had his goods here.

Captain Brandt is in Washington, to appear before Col. Ricketts' Board of Enquiry. He is dropped from the rolls and will probably be dismissed. It has been snowing all day, the equinoctials, I suppose, and I hope the breaking of the disagreeable winter. The ground is covered with snow. The Colonel is Corps Officer of the Day.

March 21, 1863

Nothing of note has been transpired today and I have scarcely been out of the tent, as it has been half raining, half snowing all day long. The roads, which were getting quite good, are again spoiled by the storm, which I hope is the breaking up of winter. It will be at least a week before the roads will again be in a passable condition. Cooper, the butcher, today went out shooting and brought in some nice fat robins, which we had deviled for supper. The Colonel has given him a shooting commission and he is to supply the mess with game, if he can. Some shot is to be got for him and he hopes to get a few snipe for us. These Enfield rifles make very good shot guns, as I hope the Rebels may soon find out as well

219

as the robins.

Our Ordnance Department is being brought into trim. The men are to carry 60 rounds, and trains 100, so that we shall be well supplied with ammunition. An officer in each Division is to have charge of the Divisional Ordnance Department. Capt. Koenig is the officer chosen for our Division. It is pretty certain that Genl. Schurz will get the Corps. I wonder whether he won't want a likely young man on his Staff? I know of one.

March 22, 1863

Mr. Sprague has been installed as Chaplain, and as the day was not suited to divine services, he gave the officers a lecture in the Colonel's tent on Biblical Ethnology. It was just like Sprague (he is a controversial Universalist preacher), though very interesting. He makes 3 different Adams—or races created at different times. Thus from Genesis 1st Chapter 1st Verse to 2nd Chapter 3rd Verse is the first or Ethiopian race of whom it is said geologists have found fossil remains in the chalk formation two millions of years before our date of creation. From Genesis 2nd Chapter 4th Verse to Chapter 4th inclusive is the second or Red or Malay race. From Genesis 5th is the third or Caucasian race. So the Adam of Genesis 1st is not the Adam of the 3rd, 4th or 5th. Mr. Sprague's theory is ingenious, to say the least.

It has been a most glorious day overhead, and as wretched underfoot. Lieut. Schwerin returned today and Capt. Willis goes in his stead. Schwerin brought the package for me. Tomorrow the whole Regiment goes on picket and I shall have little to do for 3 days.

March 23, 1863

We sent almost the whole Regiment as detail for picket this morning & consequently there is not much to do. I always enjoy these days when the Regiment is on duty, and I can fold my hands and do what I like. Col. P. is still Officer of the Day for the Corps. Capt. Yates 13th N.Y. came over to see us today and is going to stop the night with me. He is a member of a court martial which is adjourned till tomorrow, and as his Regiment is down at the Landing, he came up to seek a shelter. Down at Hope Landing it seems they fare excellently— fresh fish from the Bay and all the products of the Washington market. Cooper went down to Aquia Landing yesterday to see a friend of his, Capt. Mott, skipper of a ship in Government employ. The old fellow was up at the camp awhile and I saw him and got invited down to his ship; and he sent me yesterday a bottle of excellent bitters and word if I would come down on board he would give me as much as I could carry away. You may be sure I will go if I get a chance.

March 24, 1863

The weather is very mild. This evening it has begun to rain. Col. Peissner will be relieved as Corps Officer of the Day tomorrow. He has done his duty faithfully and will be quite fatigued by his 5 days of work. I have twice ridden out to the pickets today and nowhere found the line so good as where our Regiment stands.

There is a good deal of humbug in this Corps in decrying the 119th, as a little incident will show. Today Col. Peissner found a man of the 58th off his post. "To what Regiment do you belong?" he asked. "To the 119th," replied the man. "That's not so," said the Colonel, "for I know every one of my men by sight." The man then owned up, and told to what Regiment he belonged. The Colonel had him arrested and he will be court martialed. It is in this sort of underhand way we get an unenviable reputation. However this sort of thing is getting played out and altho' we have not yet been in action, we are a long way better drilled than the "old 58th," and the 75th, of our Brigade.

Although Lieutenant Dodge had been acting captain of a company of the 101st New York on the Peninsula, and for nine months regimental adjutant of both that regiment and the 119th, he only now received his captaincy, to date from March 25. He apparently was not notified of the promotion before he went on leave. He here detects signs of Hooker mounting a campaign.

March 26, 1863

Everything has gone on swimmingly in the Q. M.'s Department ever since it has been under my care till today, when everything has gone wrong. Last evening Capt. Worms got an idea into his head and had a report written setting forth that our teams were so poor that they could not draw an empty wagon; and furthermore that he had ordered the Q. M. to report to him, which he had not done. Now, so much was true as that through a fault of his own. Greenwood (one of our drivers) had that day broken down and had in consequence been ordered back to his Company by me. Worms' report was handed in to Col. Krzyzanowski, who sent it to Col. Peissner to report thereon. Col. P. gave the report to me, & thereupon I made a statement as to how things stood, viz. that our teams have always been ready for and done their duty when called upon, except in this particular case, which had already been punished, and that Capt. Worms' order had been verbal, and so badly delivered as to be incomprehensible, and that I always obeyed *written* orders.

This roused the valiant Worms and today he came over and tackled Col. P. This first thing he found fault with was Greenwood's team (which is really in poor condition) and Col. P., instead of seeking for an explanation or trying to justify his own Regiment, and taking part with his own officers and men, at once flew into a great passion and reduced Q. M. Sergt. Carpenter to the ranks, put the old Q. M.'s Sergt. (Shenan, a miserable fellow) in his place, and raised the old nick generally. He was so unreasonable that I refused to have anything more to do with the Department, and was accordingly relieved, altho' reluctantly on the Colonel's part. I never saw a man behave so childishly. Every word of Worms' he took as Bible truth, and raved and tore round generally at our supposed misdemeanors. At one time he ordered every one of the teamsters back to the ranks, but recalled his order soon after at the suggestion of Worms himself. I gave orders to the Q. M.'s Sergeants to report directly to the Colonel, and hope to goodness he may have the bother of the Department for a week or two.

Black Joe went into Washington today to meet the Q. M. We have been expecting a telegram from him as he promised.

Alas! I now come to the greatest of my troubles. The order has come suspending any more leaves of absences, and just too as I was on the point of being able to go. Had it come a week ago, I should have cared but little, but for three or four days I have been making up my mind that I was certainly going, and accordingly feel greatly disappointed. For one thing I really need a leave, viz. my teeth, as they need a dentist's care every much. However as that is not a thing to cause "permanent disability" or "risk to life," I can't found on it a claim to a "sick leave."

A verbal order to reduce our baggage has come in; 10 lbs. is all which will be allowed an officer, but I guess as the Adjutant's papers take up a large space, I can continue to fill in a few little accessories to comfort. "Fighting Joe" is doing things quietly. The order suspending furloughs and the order reducing baggage are both verbal so, as we suppose, to avoid publicity. I fancy we are about to march.

March 27, 1863
We have had an inspection today by the new Division Inspecting Officer, Capt. Lendig. It has been beautiful weather

and the men had good opportunities of making themselves clean and neat. They looked well with the exception of one Company, Capt. Willis', which really looked wretchedly dirty, though he has the best men in the Regiment. He got a thorough blowing up from the Inspecting Officer. Col. P. is sometimes droll in his ideas and today, as the Inspecting Officer was not a field officer, he gave the command of the Battalion over to me and left as soon as he had brought Capt. Lendig out to the parade ground. We got on well enough together. He could pick no flaw in my Department and altogether I think the Regiment had a pretty good record.

This evening Lieuts. Schwerin, Odell & Hamilton came in and played a rubber of whist. After that we began playing poker and got to gambling for chips, putting a nominal value on each marker. I soon beat them all out of the field, and won (in markers) 15 or 20 dollars. We passed a very pleasant evening.

March 28th 1863
A rain storm sprang up last evening which lasted till late this afternoon, so that the roads are once more in a wretched condition, and the low ground on which we are camped is almost inundated. There is a prospect of its clearing up tomorrow, and at this time of the year the ground dries much easier than at any other season.

Col. Peissner has been taking to sculpture the last two days. Last evening about 1/2 past 11 he came into my tent with a huge piece of sandstone, on which he had cut a woman's head with a jack knife. It was quite well done. Today he has been working away at the same piece of stone gradually reducing the size of the woman's face, until this evening it is only half the diameter it was last night. He is quite clever at it.

He has been working at a lengthy report on some improvement in our system of picket duty, to accompany his report of 5 days' duty as Corps Officer of the Day. Col. P. has a very good head for organization, but not sufficient business qualities to carry out his ideas.

Mr. Sprague, our new fledged Chaplain, has been amusing me today with his ideas on spiritualism. He was telling me of a Mr. Fellows, out of whom he drove a wicked spirit, and into whom he conjured the spirit of his (S.'s) Mother, and who has ever since been a wonderful clairvoyant. Sprague is a queer, fantastic man, but he has a good deal of superficial knowledge in him. He has been giving Lieut. Schwerin and me our phrenological characters, and really he hit the point very often in his analysis. He is what he himself calls a Bible Spiritualist. He pretends to reconcile everything with the Bible.

Three men were sent to us by the Provost Marshal today, arrested as deserters in New York. One was a citizen who in a drunken spree said he belonged to the 119th New York, and has been 5 weeks in prison. One is a man who was regularly discharged months ago, and lost his papers after he got home to Newark, N.J., and one was a poor crazy fellow who deserted in Centreville. The citizen thought he wouldn't get drunk again in a hurry.

How is the Q. M.? Joe came back from the Landing today.

The Lieutenant Henry Schwerin who was moved to "dismal visions" by the appearance of casualty forms for the coming campaign was prescient. He would be killed in action at Chancellorsville.

March 30, 1863

This evening's mail brought a long and very interesting letter from George—a horse letter, and just such a one as I have been wishing he would write me. There was one to the Q. M. in the same envelope. It was very kind of George to send us saddles; it is just the best present we could have at this time.

Lieut. Col. Lockman is again Brigade Officer of the Day, and goes his rounds three times daily. I generally accompany him in the afternoon. Each morning now we have Battalion drill for 3 or 4 hours. This A.M. we were out from 9 to 1. The signs of moving culminate. This A.M. Lieut. Schwerin told me with a long face that blanks were being prepared with columns headed "killed," "wounded by shell," "by sabre," "by rifle ball," "by bayonet," &c &c, which no doubt produced sundry dismal visions to his mind's eye.

I hope I shall not have another such summer as I had last; & I do hope, if fight we must, we may do it quickly, which alone is the way to spare life. Have the thing fought out square. I shall send all superfluous clothing off, as we are ordered to reduce our baggage, so I shall not retain my portmanteau. It will be but 20 lbs. in all.

March 31st 1863

During all last night it rained and snowed, and this morning the sun has melted all into such "slush" as will render the roads again impassable. This morning an order came detailing all our available men on picket, to relieve the 26th Wisc., as the weather has been so bad that 3 days hard-running was considered too fatiguing.

I rode to Stafford this P.M., and Lieut. Col. Hilding of the Corps Staff, who had been very intimate with Major Baldwin, told me that he had heard from him (B.) that he had been appointed by the President A. A. Genl. of Stahel's Corps. In this case he will have to resign his place in the Regiment and I shall be the happy man to succeed him; so at least it will be if the Colonel is true to his word. I am confident he will nominate me, and I ought to have influence enough to secure the Commission.

I have not heard for several days, and am anxiously awaiting news from the Q. M.

Hooker's breakup of the Grand Division structure of the Potomac army left General Sigel in command of a "mere" corps, and he resigned indignantly. Carl Schurz, Dodge's divisional commander, was in line to succeed to command of the Eleventh Corps, but Hooker considered Schurz unqualified and instead put Oliver Otis Howard in the position. While Captain Dodge and what he called the "American element" of the corps expressed pleasure at the appointment, the corps' large German element did not.

April 3rd 1863

As we were drilling this morning, an orderly came in with an order for a review by our new commander (Genl. Howard) at 2 o'clock. So we hurried home to get our dinner and be ready to turn out again. At 2 we marched out to the parade, where the whole of the 3rd Division was turned out. Genl. Howard came 1/4 before 3 and we passed in review before him. He is a good looking man and I am glad for once that the Corps is turned over to an American commander. The American element among the officers has long enough been depressed, and now, as there are comparatively few of us, we shall stand a good chance. I am sorry for Genl. Schurz, but he will get a Corps elsewhere, I presume. I am in hope that my leave of absence will come back approved tonight. So I have made all preparations to start tomorrow.

CHAPTER NINE

Defeated at Chancellorsville

April 14 to May 7, 1863

The Eleventh Corps would find itself at the epicenter of the Chancellorsville battle (and controversy), and Theodore Dodge's journal furnishes the best and most complete eyewitness account of the corps' ten-day experience marching and fighting. Joe Hooker's plan of campaign was bold and innovative. With three army corps, some 40,000 men, he would march upriver in complete secrecy, force a crossing of the Rappahannock, and sweep back down the south bank of the river and into Lee's rear at Fredericksburg. At the same time, two corps would cross the river below Fredericksburg in order to fix Lee in position. All the while, a massive cavalry raid to the south was under orders to destroy Lee's railroad lifeline.

Dodge returned from ten days' leave with his homefolks in New York (exactly on time, in pointed contrast to many of his comrades) just as the campaign was scheduled to open. Then, as he notes, the rains came. As he waited impatiently on the weather, General Hooker put the army back into its routines of drilling and training. Captain Dodge slipped back into his own routine, plotted his advancement to the rank of major, and took heart in the improved parade-ground performance of the 119th New York.

Camp near Stafford Court House April 14, 1863

I left Washington this morning at 8 A.M. and the boat made a splendid run of 63 miles to Aquia Landing inside of 3 hours. After some search at the Landing, I found Mike with the horses. My mare looked well and was very spry after her ten days' rest. I came to camp, 7 or 8 miles from the Landing, on a dead trot inside 3/4 an hour, which on our roads is very good traveling. When I got to camp I found everything in confusion from sudden receipt of orders to march tomorrow morning, an order for inspection at 3 P.M., and various orders to turn in tents, extra baggage, extra arms and accouterments, and to send the sick to Division hospital. It really seems as if we were about to march tomorrow, and now (9 o'clock) we do not know how things are to turn.

I had to strike my tent and turn it in towards 3 P.M., and shall have to quarter on the Colonel tonight. The Q. M. had a large trunk here which I was obliged to send to Hope Landing, as it could not be carried with any safety. My own trunk I am going to risk. The men have got 8 days' rations to carry, an unprecedented thing, as 3 days is the maximum. Nothing else is allowed to be taken; all is turned in. One blanket to sleep under and one extra pair of shoes and stockings to march in, 60 rounds of cartridges. What will the poor boys look like at the end of our march? I am very tired tonight and must therefore cut the journal short.

Old camp, April 15/1863

During the night a terrible storm of wind and rain sprang up, which put moving quite out of the question. The rain is falling in torrents, and I am mighty glad we are not caught in it marching. Dr. Hewett and I slept on the floor of the Colonel's tent, and I slept well, tho' he, getting under a leak in the tent, got as wet as a fish. The old mess has been broken up and I have settled with the members in the Q. M.'s name. After long persuasion I have taken the post of caterer for a new mess, and expect to have lots of trouble with it, but as I am the junior officer, it was forced upon me. However I don't mean to lose money by it, as is usual; for I intend to foot up monthly and divide expenses amongst the members.

Today, as the old mess was broken up, we were really in danger of getting nothing to eat. The mess is composed of four: the Colonel, Lieut. Colonel, Dr. Hewett and myself. Dr. H. is the new surgeon, lately assigned to us from the 107th N.Y., and a nice man apparently, a thorough gentleman, tho' perhaps a man of the world—just the kind of man we want. He seems clever and energetic, which dear Dr. Aymé was not. The latter good old soul has not yet returned, and perhaps may not, tho' he may get a surgeon's berth in another Regi-

232

ment. He really is not fit for an Army surgeon in active service. The right place for him is in a hospital in a city, and there he would be invaluable.

Everybody was glad to see me back again yesterday—Col. P. especially—as he had been in constant fear of moving before I got back, he says. You know that an order has been issued lately from the War Department that all Regiments falling under 510 men shall at once be consolidated into 5 Companies, the Colonel and Major mustered out, and the Lieut. Col. command the Regiment; and that in Regiments of 800 men no more appointments shall be made than shall be necessary to the command of the men. Now, this will play mischief with my nice plan, as they will not commission a new Major if the old one resigns. I fear, if I am to get a Majority, it must be in another Regiment. But let us wait and hope. I shall certainly after all the plans be greatly disappointed if I don't get a Majority. Confound the order anyhow (privately, of course) tho' it may be good for the service. I got 4 months' pay in Washington.

Note. By today's papers it is said that the order referred to was so sweeping and so disastrous in its workings that Genl. Hooker sent it back to the Department with a refusal to promulgate it in the Army of the Potomac. So we hope it is not to go into effect. Undoubtedly it would sweep away much rubbish in the way of inefficient officers, but it would take nearly all the veterans also, as the oldest and bravest Regiments are specially those which are most thoroughly decimated.

April 16, 1863

The storm of wind and rain which began Wednesday morning lasted till midday yesterday, and quite deluged the country around. It is however rapidly drying, as the subsoil is sand & nothing but the surface is affected.

Today Dr. Hewett and I rode a long distance together on some business, and this P.M. I had to ride to Stafford again, to send a telegram, so that tonight I am very tired. I had not taken much exercise North, and find the long ride wearied me. I had to turn in the hospital tent, which the Q. M. and I had used so long together, last Tuesday, and Dr. H. and I have been sleeping in the Colonel's tent the past two nights. Today however, Capt. Willis turned in his wall tent, which he has been using through the winter, and we took possession and fixed it up for our use. We are very comfortable in it and I am now writing in said new quarters.

April 17, 1863

The Regiment went out target shooting this morning, I superintending the whole. Many of the men made very good shots; indeed some crack shots were made. While the men were firing, I took a notion to try my revolver, and I made two shots which astonished the beholders. At 100 yards I put two out of five balls into the 6-inch ring, which greatly raised my reputation. I don't think I shall dim my laurels by any further exhibition, as the shots were probably chance ones. I am a decent shot, but 100 yards is almost beyond pistol range; besides, I was mounted.

This P.M. there was a Brigade drill of the 1st Brigade under the supervision of Genl. Schimmelfennig and Genl. Schurz; and tomorrow there is to be a Division drill by Genl. Schurz, which is likely to be a very tedious affair, as such things generally are.

Dr. Hewett has a thoroughbred horse in camp and a good runner, if well ridden. Today he and I had a short run, on pretty even terms—he being a very heavy and clumsy horseman. A Captain, commissary in the 1st Brigade, was watching us and when over, offered to make up a sweepstakes match, $5 entrance fee, of as many horses as chose to be entered, as he has a colt he is very confident of. The Dr. intends to run his horse, and has a nice little jockey in camp for him.

We have not yet moved, nor do we see much prospect of it. The 8 days' rations are kept constantly on hand and all seems to be ready, however.

April 18, 1862

Our Division drill turned out much better than I had anticipated. Genl. Schurz, instead of making the drill routine of book maneuvers, imagined the enemy in a certain place and took all the dispositions for action, and we skirmished and charged and shelled the woods quite gallantly—considering that not a single gun was fired. We marched out at 8 A.M. and back again at 1 P.M., and everyone was pleased. General Howard and several visitors looked on. The field was about 1 1/2 mile from camp, and being very rolling there was ample opportunity for displaying readiness in the disposition of troops. Genl. Schurz stands higher in my estimation than ever.

After drill I rode to Brooke's Station to meet Capt. Caswell of ours, direct from the Q. M. in Washington. He had some business for me to do here for the Q. M., & tomorrow I intend to ride down to Falmouth to do it. Our racing match is progressing and the Dr. and I had our horses out training today. We shall have some fun anyhow, unless a march nips it in the bud. This evening there has been a chess match between the Colonel and Capt. Van Borries. The Dr. and I bet a claret cup for the party on the two games out of three—my man, the Captain, losing; and I am writing while the same is being brewed.

Sunday, April 19, 1863

This A.M. early, I started for General Hooker's Head Quarters near Falmouth, to see Genl. Butterfield and get his signature to a paper for the Q. M. I got there and saw him about 10 o'clock, and he signed it "with great pleasure," speaking at the same time very highly in favor of the Q. M. I then rode to

Aquia Landing thinking to find Capt. Caswell there, who promised to carry the papers back to Washington, but found he had left yesterday. Tomorrow however we are to send Joe into Washington and he can take them. My ride before dinner was nearly 30 miles, and over roads by no means good.

During the P.M. the Field and Staff rode out again a few miles thro' the woods and the Colonel and Dr. got lost, while the Lieut. Colonel and myself keeping together found our way out. The Colonel and Dr. did not get home till dark. Genl. Schurz paid the 119th the compliment of saying that Col. P. was the best Colonel on the ground—tho' that might be & not be much.

While they waited, the officers of the 119th devoted their free time to fencing and chess, with Colonel Peissner serving as tutor in both activities. In his April 23 entry, Dodge labels the colonel the "Admirable Crichton," after the celebrated sixteenth-century Scotsman James Crichton, master scholar and swordsman. Dodge finds the English saddle sent him from London by his brother George to be superior to the McClellan saddle, the army's official issue, a product of then-Captain McClellan's prewar tour of Europe's military establishments.

April 20, 1863

It has been a rainy day and nothing has occurred but sending Joe to town to fetch some things for us. Colonel P. has begun to drill the Lieut. Colonel and me in small-sword fencing. We have a pair of foils, but no masks, jackets or gloves; however we manage nicely. It astonishes us that we do not move. How different this from last year! Then we were hurried on and complained of because we did not march by the 1st of March. This year nearly two months later and no word said; and were we to stop till June little would be said.

21st April 1863

I have been tinkering today *"pour passer le temps,"* and with such implements as camp affords and a plentiful infusion of hot water I have transformed a bacon barrel into a hip bath. I dare say the idea of bathing in a bacon tub makes your hair stand on end, you who dwell amidst the appliances of civilized life; but you do not understand its advantages: for instance, it is cheap, and besides answers some of the purposes of a sea bath. I expect to inaugurate my patent bacon-barrel-hip-bath this evening; and I have no doubt whatever but that I shall fancy myself at Newport. When you live in a tent, bathing is a public exhibition and reminds you of Japan, where all the people bathe in public, before their houses. To a certain degree a tent is transparent as the light casts the shadows on the canvas, and the outsiders can witness all the performance, if they feel so inclined.

April 22, 1863

This noon Joe came back from Washington, bringing George's beautiful saddle and bridle with him. I have been out riding upon it this P.M. If feels queer after so long using a McClellan, but it is undoubtedly the best. Major Harper, the Paymaster, has come and perhaps we shall be paid tomorrow. He has a tent over at Brigade Head Quarters, for which we are so glad, as it is a great nuisance to accommodate 3 men extra in one of our small tents.

April 23, 1863

All day it has been raining fearfully, notwithstanding which the men showed no reluctance to marching over to Brigade Head Quarters and standing hours in the wet to be paid. As usual there are some pitiable cases of men who have been left off the rolls entirely, and of others who have not received as much as they ought, through some mistake in the papers. All day long we have been bothered by the cry of money, money, which if it don't happen to belong to you is a very disagreeable word.

There is a boy against whom I collected a cheque in a curious manner. A box had been sent to a member of Company A; and he being absent in hospital, the fellow in question managed to get hold of and appropriate it. I was told of the theft, and had the culprit up and, as he was sorry for the offense (or rather being caught in it), I let him off by making him promise to pay the value of the box. The owner of the box placed the value at $20, no doubt five times its value. Anyhow, I made out an order for the amount, and today he finds himself two months' pay short. He is very young and I fancy the lesson will not be forgotten.

Our Field and Staff have taken to chess playing & fencing, both of which help to fill up our leisure hours; and these are many tho' not quite 16 hours a day, as the retired banker estimates his to be. The Colonel is the "Admirable Crichton" in both these accomplishments, and beats us all unmercifully. We have had a nice set of chessmen from Washington, which stands all day long on the Colonel's table. The foils are the Colonel's and were sent from Schenectady; we have unhappily no masks and therefore cannot "pitch in" as well as we otherwise could, for fear of accidents. I gave Capt. Schwerin a black eye the other day with the foil button, for which he did not greatly thank me, I fancy. Everybody is in admiration of my new saddle, and I have already had several offers to buy it. It is quite the thing.

April 24, 1863

It has rained most of the day and not till evening have I been able to get out at all. Towards 5 o'clock I took a ride of a mile or two. After dinner today the Colonel, Lieut. Colonel, Dr. and I played a game of chess, the two former against the

Dr. and me. We played so that there was no communication between the partners, and of course often one would destroy the play of the other. Each partner played in turn; the game lasted nearly two ours, when we were beaten.

We have this evening been fencing, till it got too dark to see, the Colonel holding the ground against all comers, and some of the German officers are very good swordsmen. No news except a rumor that Hooker has resigned, on account of the weather, 'tis said, all folly of course.

Captain Dodge predicted the start of the Chancellorsville campaign with perfect accuracy—the Army of the Potomac did indeed march two days hence, on Monday, April 27. Hooker issued orders for the usual Sunday inspection to scotch rumors of an early march and protect the security of his plans. Dodge notes the small caliber of the camp rumors then circulating. Generals John Charles Frémont and Franz Sigel may have been much admired by the German troops of the Eleventh Corps, but neither was destined to have any further connection with the corps.

April 25, 1863

Everything seems tending towards a march: we have been thinking all day that we should march tomorrow, until this evening, when the order came for a Sunday inspection, which of course put all conjectures at rest. However I should not be at all astonished if by Monday we were on the road. What plan is to be adopted no one can tell or guess. Our position for attack is so very poor, that only a master mind can originate a feasible scheme, and a master in the art of war carry it out.

A rumor (more absurd than usual, if possible) has been circulated today: that Frémont has superseded Hooker, with Sigel as Chief of Staff!

A strong wind has been blowing all day, which is drying up the roads very fast. I should fancy we ought to have seen the last of March weather by this time, and we are hoping for a little warmth—it must come eventually but it will be very late anyhow.

April 26, 1863

Still no immediate signs of moving, though orders may come later in the day. Tomorrow or the day after we shall probably leave this place. We have drawn 3 new wall tents. They are being pitched now as the others have to be turned in. If we do not march tomorrow, I will write.

These entries for April 27–29 detail the march upstream of the Eleventh Corps, in company with the Fifth and Twelfth Corps, to cross the Rappahannock and then the Rapidan. The cavalry fight at Kelly's Ford in March that Dodge mentions, if somewhat less brilliant than the newspapers labeled it, at least showed the Union cavalry willing to fight. Dodge's belief on the 29th that the Army of the Potomac was bound for Gordonsville or Culpeper to the west was for a time shared by General Lee.

Camp 2 miles south of Hartwood Church
Monday April 27, 1863

We have just arrived here—the end of our first day's march this spring, and the opening of the campaign. Orders came yesterday noon that the Corps would march today. Towards evening, 5 1/2 o'clock was named as the time when we were to be ready to start, and we went to bed full of the thought of the morrow.

Reveillé waked us this A.M. at 4, and within the hour everything was in marching trim. We started at 6 1/2, the column being composed of the 11th and 12th Corps. We very slowly took our way towards the southwest, after destroying everything we could not take with us, and cutting down our flag staff.

Those who knew told us we were going to Hartwood Church. Our plan seems to be to make several crossings (of the river) at the same time. One true attack and several feints. We may have to do the work of a great many; at all events I guess we shall cross the river tomorrow, and all agree that there will be a big fight within two or three days; possibly to-morrow.

It has been a lovely day and very warm; we have marched about 12 miles. A pontoon train is near the river ready to be thrown across. Our horses are turned out to graze their fill in this beautiful young clover, and enjoy it fully. Promise of a fine night and a fine day tomorrow, tho' our mules are braying— sure sign of a rain within a day or two.

April 28th 1863—3 A.M.

I am writing by the light of a large fire while the servants are cooking our coffee for breakfast. We march at 4 1/2 A.M. After I wrote last evening, we had supper and then pitched our tents—shelter tents 6 feet square and 3 feet high—a little den to creep into out of the dew, & two or three officers in each. We talked a long time, before going to sleep, of the dear folks at home.

We are within two miles of the river. No signals are al-lowed to be blown, and everything is as still as if there was not 100 men in the neighborhood. The fire is burnt so low I can't see to write more. *Adieu.*

2 P.M.—

Instead of crossing the river near Hartwood Church as I imagined we should, we have marched 16 miles west and are now within half a mile of Kelly's Ford—the scene of the bril-liant cavalry exploit a month ago.

This we shall cross early tomorrow morning. The enemy is strongly entrenched on the other side, and our Division is to be the first to cross and storm the rifle pits. It will be pretty brisk work, but I am confident we shall be successful.

It has been raining a little all day, but has ceased now. I hope tomorrow may be fine, for fighting in the rain is by no means agreeable. The last fighting I did was in a thunderstorm at Chantilly, and I hope the result will not be the same now. However if it comes I must take it. I was mistaken yesterday in saying there were but two Corps in this attacking force. There are some from the 5th, 6th, 11th and 12th, under whose command I don't know, but they must amount to from 50,000 to 60,000 men. Half of the Army is certainly here. Now if the enemy does not outflank us again as they have done twice before, we shall have the best of them in one respect—for they received a jolly good drubbing just here a month ago. Poor Polizzi! (my Italian friend) died of the wounds he received here! He was a brave, noble fellow and a soldier to the core.

Col. Peissner feels elated at the idea of a fight, but the Lieut. Colonel regards it as I do, as a disagreeable duty. I shall be glad to have had the Regiment in action once, for it will transform them from new troops into veterans. They have marched splendidly today, better than any Regiment in the Corps, say all the Staff officers. We shall probably start early in the morning.

Love to all dear ones. I think of you oh! how often.

6 P.M.—

A short time ago we got orders to be ready to move, and shortly after, to move at 5 1/2 P.M. We are in line now ready to march. We had made all ready for the night, promising ourselves a good rest, and are by no means jolly over the prospect of the movement. However, jolly or not, we have to go.

All the troops are in the same case as we. The reason of this sudden start we do not know. Many reasons may be and are given, and they are each in turn discussed by the assembled officers; but the *real* reason is not probably known. It is said the pontoon bridge will be laid at 2 A.M. tomorrow.

Wed'y April 29th [1863] 8 A.M.

We stood to arms at 6 P.M. last evening and marched towards the Rappahannock, which we crossed at 10 P.M., on the pontoon bridges. We had received notice of a warm reception on the other side, and were considerably surprised at about 2 A.M., after having been maneuvered round a swampy ground in the dark for 2 or 3 hours, when we emerged out upon the Culpeper Turnpike and began to march west without any resistance. We made about four miles along the road, when we halted and lay down to rest—the men thoroughly jaded out.

At 6 A.M. the shelling of the woods by one of our batteries awoke me, and I have just washed and taken breakfast. I feel as if two hours is scarcely enough for a night's rest following such a tramp as yesterday's; however I am better off than the poor boys who had to go on picket after their long march. We sent 100 men on that duty and I picked the poor fellows.

The weather is still overcast, and I fancy it will rain today. Last night it was very foggy, though there was a bright moon. It was nice weather to make the passage of the river interesting. Another report says only the 5th, 11th and 12th Corps are here—not the 6th. I should not wonder if we went to Culpeper shortly. I don't know what the chances for a fight are today. I have not heard any opinion from Head Quarters yet.

Several prisoners have passed here this morning, among them a Lieutenant, quite a young man, particularly well dressed and good looking. This dress does not corroborate the stories of destitution in the South. He may however have newly received his Commission.

The choice of roads lies between Culpeper and Gordonsville; the latter place I now fancy to be the destination.

11 P.M.—

We marched at noon today, after the 12th Corps, and took line of march through a beautiful open country (the finest part of Virginia I have seen) towards Fredericksburg, Culpeper & Gordonsville being "played out." At 7 P.M. we halted at the Rapidan River—over which there was no bridge—for the night.

We have however just been waked and are to march at once (i.e. in half an hour), the bridge I suppose having been already built. You would laugh to see me sitting on a roll of blankets against an old rotten tree, with a choice end of tallow candle in my hand, which is ever and anon burning me by running down my fingers, writing these words. I wish I could take a photograph of the surroundings. But Mike, my man, wants the blankets to pack. So, *adieu.*

As the flanking column under General Henry Slocum, Twelfth Corps, crossed the Rapidan and advanced eastward toward Fredericksburg, Dodge found morale among the marchers to be very high. Thus far the surprise of the movement seemed to be holding.

Across the Rapidan—April 30th/63 2 A.M.

Since the last was written we have crossed the Rapidan, and are now encamped till the whole of the Army are across, which may be until noon. So Dr. Hewett and I have pitched our shelter tent and, while he is writhing under the operation of having his wet boots pulled off, I lie down on my stomach—the only position tenable for writing in a shelter tent—to write a few words.

Col. Peissner from his tent is calling out lustily for broiled partridge and Urdow Cliquot Mousseux, or a milk punch. The Lieut. Colonel from his, is moralizing & chanting ditties, by turns. Dr. H. is quoting poetry and going to sleep, and I guess I will follow his example as to the latter.

Crossing the river there was a foot bridge for the men. Mounted officers crossed the ford, which the horses had almost to swim. My boots were luckily watertight, and so my feet were kept dry. Huge fires were lighted on either shore to enable the men to see their way; the remains of the old bridge—nothing but the piers were left standing; the shadows of the men on the water and the aforesaid fires all combined to make a most weird picture.

We surprised the Rebels at the Rapidan yesterday morning. Our cavalry came up the river and found a party of pioneers building a bridge, 75 of whom they captured. They evidently knew nothing of our movements. I believe this move of our forces is entirely unexpected by the enemy. Thus far we have been very successful. I hope it may be so all thru'.

8 A.M.—

We have had a most refreshing sleep and feel ourselves once more. We are again to march in ten minutes, and may reach Fredericksburg today—being now about 14 miles from there. We are camped on a large rolling plain, a splendid place for an action. This section of Virginia is full of such plains. Now and then we pass a beautiful farm, which lies so peacefully, showing no sign of the devastation of war. They are ploughing in many places along the road. As we pass, the inmates of the houses come out and sit on their door steps watching us with interest, if not with pleasure.

The weather has been dull ever since we started—raining every day. Notwithstanding, we have made very good progress, and no ill results can have happened from it I think. The 3 Corps with us are under Genl. Slocum, who also commands the 12th. He will make a reputation if he conducts this attack, or, rather flank movement, successfully. The spirits of the men are excellent. We have marched fast, but our Regiment has lost but 4 men by straggling. Really the 119th has marched better than any other Regiment I ever saw.

4 P.M.—

We did not leave our camp on the Rapidan till 12. Since then Dr. H. and I have been acting as foragers, and have visited all the houses on the road. At one we stopped for nearly an hour and they baked some corn cakes for us. The lady of the house was strong Secesh, but nevertheless treated us very kindly. Her name was Mrs. Semmes. We had some Confederate coffee there, made out of rye.

We are waiting here now till the train comes up. There is some cavalry skirmishing about in our rear, and we fear it may be captured; we are on the extreme end of the column. The Rebels have been trying to plant a battery to shell our column some few miles from here—with what success I have not yet heard. I hope we shall camp tonight for I am getting tired of marching every and all night. It now seems that Fredericksburg is our destination. We are to flank the batteries there. I should not wonder to find them evacuated.

At this point in the journal is a pasted-in copy of Hooker's April 30 address to the troops. "Our enemy must either ingloriously fly," Hooker announced, *"or come out from behind his defenses and give us battle on our own ground." In the event, that happened exactly. Dodge's entries of Friday morning, May 1, to Saturday afternoon, May 2, reflect the continued prevailing optimism, despite sharp fighting on May 1 that halted the Federal advance.*

Camp 12 miles west of Fredericksburg
May 1st/63 Friday 9 1/2 A.M.

We were put on rear guard last evening, and did not reach camp till 10 o'clock P.M. The 400 cavalry did not show themselves; tho' Capt. Stoldt A. A. G. of Brigade and I rode back a mile or two in search of them. When we came past Head

Quarters Col. Krzyzanowski came out and showed us a circular from Genl. Hooker thanking the 5th, 11th and 12th Corps for their successful operations. Heintzelman they say is at Gordonsville, and they have almost caught the Rebels at Fredericksburg; at any rate they must retreat or come out and fight us on ground of our own choice.

10 A.M.—

Bravo for Hooker! So far this movement has been beautifully planned and executed. This is May Day, a most lovely morning it is too, one of those misty mornings which always betoken a hot day. We shall probably march towards noon—not before, as we have to stop to kill some beef, the rations being all gone. The chances for a battle at Fredericksburg are I fancy almost over. The struggle will be nearer Richmond.

Twice today we have been almost burned up by the grass taking fire. We have just, all hands, been out beating it out with blankets and brush, I with someone's overcoat. My mare too came near being burnt. They are firing heavily towards Fredericksburg—some very heavy volleys of artillery have been fired; probably shelling the outworks or something of that sort. I send you the printed orders spoken about yesterday. It is very hot. I am lying off under my shelter tent. They say we shall not march till tomorrow.

3 P.M.—

The heavy cannonading has continued (at Fredericksburg, we suppose) since noon. Our Corps, so says a recent order, is to be the extreme right of the Army. For a time past, Col. Peissner has been getting a reputation. Genl. Howard thinks a great deal of him, as also Genl. Schurz. Just now he was ordered to take a section of artillery, supported by the 119th, and guard a cross road.

I believe a part of the Army is now engaged near Fredericksburg. Our own Corps and the 12th are at present guarding a position where an attack is expected. The Rebels apparently don't know which way to get out except by Culpeper, and we are lying in their way. A strong column has just taken up a position on a hill about half a mile from here. They look finely. I have my glass with me and can examine them at leisure. The battle is to be between Fredericksburg and here. The news of yesterday that Fredericksburg was evacuated is not true. They cannot do so.

I have not told you how I am equipped for the march. I ride my grey mare on my nice new saddle and use one of the Q. M.'s horses (the black trooper) as a pack horse, on which my eatables and blankets are packed. I carry nothing at all on my horse, my own weight being enough for her. Mike leads my pack horse in the rear of the Regiment, and altogether I am well off, faring better than we usually do.

7 P.M.—

The enemy is shelling our pickets 1/4 of a mile ahead of us. We are drawn up in line, the 119th first in the line—probably the action will take place tomorrow. Some shells have exploded near us but no one hurt as yet.

Saturday May 2nd [1863], 5 A.M.

After writing the above we moved over to support the 68th New York, who under Genl. Schimmelfennig were trying to take a battery; but were afterwards ordered back without firing a shot. At 9 P.M. we lay down on our arms to pass the night. I have had a good long sleep and feel refreshed, all except a wash, of which there seems to be no chance. However we can get on without that one day.

The battery on our left has been protected by a line of rifle pits cast up during the night. It is posted on a fine commanding eminence, in front of a field of considerable extent, and might do execution. Some think however that the enemy has escaped us during the night. If so we shall probably march into Fredericksburg at once. But of course no one can conjecture what has or will take place. A most lovely day again.

8 A.M.—

Since I wrote the above I have had a good wash and ditto breakfast, and a short ride to survey the surrounding scenery. I expected we should move as soon as we got up, but perhaps we may not move today at all. Genl. Hooker passed about 8 A.M., riding down the lines. Whether we are to have an action cannot be known except by the leaders. Cannonading is going on at a distance. All troops are in line and position.

Noon—

Still in the same place. The 11th Corps is the extreme right of the Army, which extends from Banks's Ford to the present position. This moment news has come that the enemy is making a demonstration on our right flank. A cavalry officer has just passed with his company, which has been driven back from its position on the picket line; he says they are 1/4 a mile from here. We are just alarmed by a very heavy volley of musketry on our right, but nothing has yet come of it. Severe cannonading is going on all the time.

Stonewall Jackson's surprise flanking attack on the Eleventh Corps is described here at the first interval the shaken Captain Dodge had a few minutes' peace to write. Krzyzanowski's brigade was hampered in its attempts to form by fugitives from the first units hit by Jackson's hammer blow. In his later book on Chancellorsville, Dodge revealed that the 119th New York was additionally hampered when Colonel Peissner, caught up in the excitement of his first battle, gave a confusing order that (in Dodge's words) "brought the regiment in line with its back to the enemy." Thus from the start the regiment "lost confidence in its officers." On May 2 Dodge had exchanged horses with his commissary sergeant, and afterward was thus in search of his favorite mare, Fanny. On May 3 the battle raged on without the routed Eleventh Corps, and Dodge envisioned help from the army's left wing under John Sedgwick.

6 A.M. Sunday May 3/1863

About 7 P.M. last night we were again alarmed by a quick sharp volley of musketry in the same place we had heard the last, viz. on our right wing, and this time not without cause. The firing increased, and in 1/4 hour from the time of its beginning, the Rebels had broken our lines.

When the firing began we were eating our supper, but we soon stopped that, and took place in line of battle. The Rebels were so much stronger than we that they drove in our pickets at once, and Schimmelfennig's Brigade retreated in great disorder. These men rushed through our Brigade, which was then exposed to a most galling fire. The 119th stood well against great odds, until they saw old Regiments break and run right through them, when it was impossible to keep them in line. They broke and retreated by Companies, slowly though not in good order. Rally them we could not. Poor Colonel Peissner had received his death wound and fell waving his sword. The Lieut Col.'s horse had been shot under him, ditto mine, which reared and threw me, falling heavily on me. I got a little group around the colors, but when the boys who had never been under fire before saw others running, they could not be kept together.

The Rebels drove us some 2 miles, and then we rallied, & assisted by another Corps, checked them. Our Regiment now has 200 men out of 450 answer to the roll. Several officers are wounded. The firing was kept up till late at night, and has been renewed this morning. The 11th Corps, which was badly cut up yesterday, has been taken 2 or 2 1/2 miles to the left and rear, and the 12th and 5th Corps moved ahead. The latter are now fighting and fighting well, if one may judge from the sound of the cannon and musketry.

Poor Col. Peissner! He was a brave man. Shortly before he was hit he turned to me and told me to dismount. He and the Lieut. Col. were then both dismounted. This was the last I saw of him. He was waving his sword and shouting to his men, when he was hit in the breast and fell flat on his face. I have since heard that he was carried to a field hospital. I hope that he may not be mortally wounded but fear there is no hope.

Schwerin is dead. Lieut. Peissner is wounded in the thigh, Lieut. Lewis in the arm; other officers I do not know of. I have lost about all I had. First my horse shot under me, then my pack horse gone with all my rations, blankets, dressing things, &c, and last but not least my English saddle. When my horse fell, I took the saddle & bridle off and gave them to a boy near me, telling him I would give him a good reward if he would bring it somewhere where I could put it on another horse. He carried it over a mile, but when the Regiment broke had to abandon it. Some Rebel officer is probably delighting in it now. I would rather have lost almost anything else.

I thought I had lost my Fanny yesterday. I saw a horse just like her very badly wounded and running away. Jimmie Christie was riding her just then, and I was riding his. The firing now going on is terrific. I hope it may result in our favor.

12 M.—

We are lying in the same position on the left of the Army, which makes a semicircle or bow, each lip of which rests on the river. Ours is at United States Ford. There has been very heavy firing of musketry and cannon about a mile & half from here, at Hooker's Head Quarters, which must be I guess one third of the way from our (the left) wing to the right.

It is said that Genl. Sedgwick has Fredericksburg, and is advancing from there with his whole force to join us. The Rebels have been repelled at every point this morning and his coming will I hope put an end to the action. The 5th and 12th Corps have been fighting today.

We had our share last night. Oh! that our Corps had stood its ground! I am ashamed that even any number of the enemy should have been able to drive us from our position. To be sure we were the right flank of the Army, and when outflanked we were the first to suffer. But is any explanation enough to justify our being so badly beaten? One singular thing is that all the Schenectady men are wounded. The Colonel, whom we hear is now in hospital, his brother, Capt. Schwerin and Lieut. Lewis. And Capt. Becker has also been wounded.

On May 4–5 the battle continued, with the disgraced Eleventh Corps acting as the army's reserve. Lee reunited his divided forces, and at the same time prevented Hooker from uniting the two wings of the Army of the Potomac. By night on May 5 Hooker had determined to recross the river and give up the campaign. Captain Dodge here remains optimistic to the end. When the Chancellorsville casualties were officially counted, the 119th New York had 12 killed, 66 wounded, and 42 missing, for a total of 120. As Dodge feared, the dead included Colonel Peissner.

Monday [May 4, 1863] A.M.

We had a tough little skirmish last evening before we left our position on the left. The Rebel sharpshooters peppered away very merrily. Right outside of our picket line was a house inhabited by some ladies, which Genl. Howard ordered burned for fear it might be used by skirmishers from the enemy. It was full of furniture and valuable things which the ladies, who were brought within our lines, greatly lamented, especially their piano. The sight of the burning house was magnificent.

About 9 P.M. we were told to rest for the night, and shortly after the Lieut. Col. and I had lain down, we got another order to move. The 12th Corps relieved us and we took up a position about a mile to the right, which we are now holding. We have been skirmishing all the morning with the enemy, though they have not made anything of an attack on us.

I am so angry about my horse. The Lieut. Col. has lost his, and the Colonel's has not been seen since the fight of Saturday; so that my grey mare is the only one on hand, and I have to lend her to the Lieut. Col., and walk myself. It is hard work, I tell you, when you have got used to riding. The Lieut. Colonel almost refused to take my horse, but of course I insisted.

We reckoned our loss last night and found it to be 132. This takes a slice of 1/3 at least of our Regiment. We have got the name of being the only Regiment who really made any good stand on Saturday evening. We have been fighting now four days if you count today. I wonder when it will be over. They say that if we beat Jackson and Lee here, the enemy will not make any further stand in Virginia. I hope it is so. Hitherto all has been a success. May it continue so, and we shall have made a long step towards wiping out this wicked Rebellion. The balls are occasionally flying by us, but no one hurt this morning in our Regiment.

Monday May 4, 3 P.M.—

Lieut. Hamilton, our acting Q. M., came over from the other side of the river today and brought us some bread and ham, off which we made a very creditable meal. He told us for certain that Sedgwick had got Fredericksburg; good news. All the morning we have been skirmishing with the enemy's pickets, but towards noon they retired and since, everything has been quiet as Sunday afternoon. We have put up a shelter of blankets, under which we are lying off. They say the Rebels are trying to cross the river above us, perhaps to try a raid on Washington. Our cavalry and artillery have gone up to oppose them.

5 P.M.—

On examining my overcoat today I found a buck shot through it. I am glad it came no nearer. There has been firing up the river this P.M., tho' not very heavy. The pioneers have just been making a road for the artillery, at right angles to our breastworks, for batteries to come up in case of need. We have been thinking that we should move towards Fredericksburg this evening, but from this indication I fancy we shall not.

We are all very anxious to hear from the Colonel. Many say they saw his dead body being carried towards the ford upon a stretcher yesterday, but one does not really know what to believe. This irregular living makes me very bilious, and my mucous membrane, my old bane, is again getting into trouble. Coffee and sugar with hard tack does not agree with me. I fear I may get ill again, if we have a long campaign, like I did last year. I really should like being garrisoned in Fredericksburg. I am not much of a rover.

I received a letter from the Q. M. thro' private hand this P.M., dated 29 April. At that time he did not know of our moving. This battle (of Barryville as they call it) is the 7th in which I have been an *active* participator. I wish it was to be the ending of the war.

5 1/2 P.M.—

The Rebels have begun another attack on our line 1/2 mile to our right. Of course we have fallen in, and now rest on our arms.

Tuesday 5th May/63—8 A.M.

We moved, shortly after the attack, towards the right, and took up a new position, which we now hold. I should fancy we were now near the centre. I have just breakfasted and washed, and the Rebels have begun another attack on our right. We are shelling them merrily, and the musketry is sharp. They seem to be getting nearer. This is the 5th day's fighting. When will it cease?

They say it is Sickles they attacked last evening, and he drove them back right nobly. This attack seems to be in the same place. Our great nuisance in sleeping on the ground here is the wood ticks. The Lieut. Col. has just found 4 stuck to him. I have not yet had any. It is a foggy morning, presaging a hot day. I fear we shall suffer from the heat here and we have no shelter.

8 1/2 A.M.—

Sergeant of Co. E has built a shelter for us, so that the complaint above made is without cause.

We have just displayed our colors on our breastworks. They are full of holes and covered with blood. The lance of one of the colors was broken Saturday night. One of the most affecting sights I ever saw was in the color guard the evening of our fight. The color sergeant fell pierced by 3 balls. Corporal Carter of the color guard seized the flag, when he also fell. Orderly Sergt. Carter (his father) who was too ill to carry a musket in the action, was just behind him. As his son fell he rushed forward, seized the colors with the exclamation "poor Joe, poor Joe, come on boys!" and carried them thenceforward and from the field. The color sergeant and three corporals fell. The sergeant was a splendid young fellow. The boys on the color guard were all young men—everyone of them fine, handsome and brave. Together as they lay there face to foe, it was a noble sight to look upon. Just now we have been filling the color guard up by volunteers, and have once more 7 or 8— our full complement.

11 A.M.—

Another skirmish—our pickets driven in, and the whizzing of a few bullets. Now only a desultory fire on our right. We do not know what to make of it—whether it be real or a feint.

12 M.—

The skirmish did not last more than half an hour—a few of our men only were wounded. An orderly sergeant of the Regiment was just brought in, a ball through his body. He only lived a few minutes; his body is lying close by me. Poor boy! He leaves a wife and 4 children! When men fall fast around, one does not think of individuals; but a solitary example like this one, makes me feel sad. He was a fine fellow!

From his eyewitness knowledge, Theodore Dodge here corrects the newspaper accounts regarding the sequence of events during Jackson's attack on the Eleventh Corps. What Dodge did not know, however, was that on May 2 Hooker had sent due warning of the Confederate threat to corps commander Howard, who paid no heed. In any event, Dodge admitted, the Eleventh Corps "lost the day—and sorry enough I am to admit it."

Old Camp at Stafford Court House
May 7th 1863

I have not journalized for the last 48 hours, for it would have taken a man of more than iron to have written a word under the wretched stress of marching and weather borne by us since we were in line near Wilderness [Church] day before yesterday.

We got notice at 5 P.M. that day [May 5] that we should probably be attacked, but just before the time, a fearful thunderstorm arose, which not only drenched us thoroughly, but dissipated all thought of an attack. This lasted nearly two hours. During the interval we stood admiring the unfolding leaves; the trees looked bright and fresh, just as they often do after a shower; and it struck me how little beautiful nature looked like the awful struggle then on hand between the contending armies. A slow, dull, but cold and piercing rain then sprang up which has lasted till this morning.

At 8 P.M. we got an order to fall into line and be ready to move at a moment's notice. This we did and so stood till 1 A.M. I scarcely ever suffered so much from cold as then. At 1 A.M. we moved a few hundred yards to the rear, being relieved by the 26th [Wisconsin] behind the crest of a hill, and were allowed to build small fires. How great a boon this was I cannot express to you. The Lieut. Col. and I lay down in the rain, so overcome were we by weariness, and slept for a few minutes.

At 2 o'clock we again began to move. We knew then it was to recross the river. We arrived at United States Ford at 4 A.M. and crossed. The enemy shelled our retreating columns, and when our Corps had crossed, attacked with infantry, which however was speedily repulsed. All day yesterday we marched—marched—marched, with but one halt, at 1 P.M. to get our breakfast. It rained and poured and blew by turns, and the mud was worse than when we made the famous "muddy march" under Burnside. The Lieut. Colonel and I rode by turns—ours being essentially a one horse Regiment. Sad and weary and worn we tramped on, expecting to arrive at Brooke's Station, but at last we "turned up" in our old quarters, having been on foot 10 days—and once more been thoroughly drubbed.

I have seen a New York paper this A.M., and wish to state two or three facts. Three times was notice sent to General Hooker that the enemy was turning our right flank, several hours before the attack commenced on Saturday night, but no answer, no reinforcements came. Genl. Schurz's Division did not "throw down their arms and retire without firing a shot," nor were they the first to retreat. The 1st Division was the first attacked, and the ones who first ran. *They* broke our line. Our Division [3rd] was drawn up in line prepared to make a stout resistance, when the 1st Division came flying back, passed through our lines and formed, or attempted to form behind a line of breastwork in our rear, and then *began firing into us*. Thus, not only were we exposed to a fire from the enemy on our front and flank, but from our own men in our rear—which lost us as many in the time it lasted as the enemy's fire.

Thus circumstanced, who could expect the men to stand? Our Regiment retired in comparatively good order. But the Corps—I grant our Corps lost the day—and sorry enough I am to admit it. But for the Corps we might have been successful in our movements. Well—I am sure I did my duty, and it was not my fault my Germans didn't stand.

It will take several days to make our camp respectable again, as we destroyed everything before we left. This is the third time we have returned to Stafford Court House after defeat, or what is equivalent, want of success.

Ned, the Lieut. Col.'s boy, is the only negro who is here. I hear Henry has gone to Washington. If he comes to you don't pay him; for I won't pay him a cent unless he comes back. Poor Colonel, we can't hear anything of him. We fear he must indeed be dead; he fell gallantly. My English saddle, the black trooper—saddle bags and everything are gone. I shall have to buy a new saddle &c &c in Washington.

CHAPTER TEN

Respite between Battles

May 9 to June 10, 1863

The Army of the Potomac returned to its old camps around Fal-
mouth and Stafford Courthouse and took stock. Hooker's lieutenants
revealed their discontent with his generalship and contrived for his
replacement, as they had contrived against Burnside before him. The
army was further disturbed by the departure of thousands of two-
year men and nine-month short termers. Hooker postponed any
plans for a renewed offensive, and General Lee stepped in to seize the
initiative. As he had following his victory the year before at Second
Bull Run, Lee laid plans for crossing the Potomac and marching
north.

Captain Dodge, turning twenty-one and now a veteran of half a
dozen battles, contemplated life in the much-depleted 119th New
York. Colonel Peissner's death at Chancellorsville was finally con-
firmed, and Lieutenant Colonel John T. Lockman took command of
the regiment, to Dodge's considerable satisfaction. Working to-
gether, the two were able to spruce up the 119th until it was the pride
of the brigade. In due course, by the time the army marched in June,
Lockman would be confirmed as the 119th's colonel (a position he
held for the rest of the war). Dodge, however, would not make major
while in field service, despite his best efforts and a supposed promise
by Governor Seymour of New York. Thus it was as captain and ad-
jutant that Theodore Dodge prepared himself for what proved to be
his last campaign.

May 9th 1863

Since Thursday we have been making out reports, getting
clothes for the men, &c. My journal will contain nihil till we
again march, when I will again journalize.

To Father, May 9th. Poor Colonel! I fear he is gone! All our
officers are resigning—3 Captains and several Lieutenants.
What do you think of the Dutch skedaddle? I am sorry I was
in it but never mind. I hope you will get your promotion. How
wonderfully I was preserved in the late engagements; most of
our officers were riddled by balls. I had but one on me.

The Majority business goes on slow, and not sure I fear. What about a new Regiment now? I would take a place in one or I can stay where I am. I am content. I saw Capt. Worms; he says it was reported in Washington that both Lieut. Col. and I were killed. I don't wonder—it was enough to kill anyone.

Dodge was obviously bothered by the conduct of his regiment, and indeed the entire Eleventh Corps, at Chancellorsville. He thought the newspapers had apportioned the blame unfairly, and so he wrote this careful account of the May 2 fighting for his older brother George, in London. It was George who had sent the English saddle that Theodore so much regretted losing during the battle.

Head Qrs. 119th N.Y.V. nr. Stafford C.H., Va.
May 10th 1863

Dear George,

I have kept a regular journal all through our late movement and "Seven Days Battle No. 2," but I have no doubt you will like to hear a few words direct from me. And first, I would give you *true statement*, which the newspapers do not, of the action of May 2nd, in which our Corps was so utterly beaten.

Genl. Howard, who does not now stand by many pegs as high in my estimation as before the beginning of this month, has been in command of this Corps a short time only, and not only, as he himself says, has he not yet got confidence in the men, but the men, who are almost entirely Germans, have no confidence in him. During our forced march to flank Fredericksburg he did very well, and was complimented as was also the Corps, by Genl. Hooker in a circular, and was placed in the post of honor, on the right of the Army, when a position was taken up at Wilderness [Church]. The position was very good but as we stood entirely on the defensive, entrenchments ought to have been dug, and more especially ought our right wing to have been curved so as to present a front to the enemy if he should attack us on that point.

Our Division, the Third, was the centre of the Corps, the Second being on our left, the First the extreme right. During the while morning and afternoon we were talking among ourselves of the probability of the enemy attacking us on our right, and at noon, some cavalry even were seen and fired on in that direction by our men. Word, they say, was sent to Genl. Hooker that the enemy was turning our flank but no heed was taken of the message. Well, at 5 o'clock that afternoon a most terrible attack came, and the First Division, on which the shock fell first, broke and ran like sheep. I do not believe that an average of two rounds was fired by the whole Division. When the attack came of course our front had to be altered and in such a hurry that the best positions were not taken up.

However, our Division stood the brunt of musketry, artillery, and charging in the front and left flank for at least 3/4 hour. Three of our Regiments, the 26th Wisconsin, the 157th and 119th N.Y. standing heroically. However we were compelled to fall back, and as the only line of retreat was along the main road where the artillery and cavalry were mixed with infantry, and vying who should get to the rear with most speed, after making two or three rallies, our Regiment was broken up into many parts, some of whom marched to the rear and others joined to troops who were trying to hold the enemy in check.

We were surprised through the fault of the Generals, and therefore it was not our fault that we were driven back; but I never saw men run as did these Dutchmen. Our boys stood— all American Regiments did—but the panic among the Dutch was fearful. It shows where the mettle is. This is the first fight I have been in where individually we retreated. The old Regiment and the old Division *always* stood. Well, I suppose, to be

263

a thorough soldier, you must also know how to run away scientifically, the same as a perfect rider must know how to fall
scientifically. A "skedaddle," to use a very vulgar word, is not
calculated to make one's spirits rise or to give one much confidence in one's men. However, I know that I did my duty—
that is enough.

My losses were considerable. Of all I lost, however, I regret
nothing so much as my saddle & bridle. I had had it but a couple of weeks & had got to like it so much that I cannot bear a
McClellan now, and that is the only one I have. I hope my losses
will not be so heavy next time. I should be ruined very soon.

About the Majority, nothing has as yet turned up. I fear in
this Regiment there will never be a Major made. However,
then it will cost me nothing & I am contented with my present
condition. The Quarter Master seems to have great hopes of
my getting one, and may know more about it than I do. Anyhow, if there is a Major made in the 119th, I shall be the one.

I get the *Illustrated News* and *Punch* regularly now. Many
thanks for your sending them to me. I hope all of you at No. 4
get along nicely. I often envy you your comforts when trudging along, wet through and tired out and with no prospect of
a dry change of clothes or a dry room, but perhaps to go
where fires are even prohibited. I tell you that soldiering
comes hard on a man sometimes.

My best regards to Mr. G. and all London friends. Love to
little Lady and believe me

Ever your most obliged & aff. Brother
T. A. Dodge

*The Federal casualties at Chancellorsville came to 17,300, greater than
Dodge estimates here. Almost 6,000 of that total were the missing,*

most of them taken prisoner. His observation that the Rebels would soon reestablish communication with Richmond referred to the cutting (very briefly) of the Fredericksburg-Richmond rail connection, the minuscule fruit of the Yankee cavalry raid during the campaign.

Head Quarters 119th New York, May 11/63

Yesterday we had a review by Genl. Schurz, which was a very stupid affair. There is no doubt the Corps is greatly demoralized, so much so that Genl. Howard has been obliged to issue an order to cheer the men up, saying that the same disaster might have befallen any other Corps. It might, but was not likely to, for *Americans* will make a stand even if outflanked and surprised.

The weather is very warm and coming on warm fast. No signs of an immediate move are apparent, tho' I suppose Hooker will want to do something soon to retrieve his reputation. I must confess my inability to see any great success in the late movement. We seem to be in exactly the same position we were before and nothing gained that I can see, & much lost in the brave dead—alas! how much!

The enemy now again hold Fredericksburg, and, I have no doubt, will soon reestablish communication with Richmond. So what have we gained by the loss of ten or twelve thousand brave men? Our men have drawn clothing and knapsacks within the last day or two, and are again fully equipped. An enormous deal was lost on the 2nd of May. I have lost almost everything. All my toilet articles have been snatched up by some Rebel, and I am at a loss out here how to replace them. As to greater losses, I spoke before.

I wish I could get into Washington for a day or two. Our mess, of the six who composed it, only the Lieut. Col. and I are left as the sole representatives. My boy Henry ran away on the 2nd. So Ned, the Lieut. Col.'s boy, cooks for us; he is not much of a cook however and our table is only passable.

May 12th 1863

We have had a Corps drill this P.M., which went off pretty well, though drills on such a large scale are almost always a bore. General Howard seemed well pleased. The weather was hot, but there was a refreshing breeze. I think the move did the men good. Inspection is announced for 7 A.M. tomorrow. Today we could only turn out 150 men. How the Regiment has run down and been in only one action, too!

May 14, 1863

We have had bad news of Col. Peissner. Dr. Suckley, the Corps Medical Director, who has been on the other side of the river with our wounded, has written to Corps Head Quarters that the Colonel is dead. However it seems impossible to be certain, and so Lieut. Col. Lockman will not write to Mrs. P. till some more news comes. Of Capt. Schwerin we hear nothing. He was a brave and good officer, and fell in his first engagement. I always think it particularly sad for a man to be shot down in his first action.

Washington May 17, 1863

I wrote the above before I had any idea of coming to Washington. Later letters will explain how I was interrupted at Stoneman's Switch by a telegram about the Colonel's body. Capt. Schwerin's body was also found to have arrived, when we returned from escorting the poor Colonel's remains to the boat at Aquia Landing, and I was sent on by the Lieut. Colonel to bring them here. Shortly after I got my pass, a Dr. Van Voorst of Schenectady came in, sent by Mr. Schwerin, to try to hunt up the remains of the Captain, and he also came on with me. I telegraphed the Q. M. that I was coming, and he made all the necessary arrangements so that Dr. Van Voorst and I had no trouble at all.

This is Sunday. I return on Tuesday. Genl. Schurz said to me just before I left: "Why don't you ask leave for 10 days?" "I don't wish to be absent now, General," said I. "That's the right spirit, Adjutant," said he, shaking my hand heartily. He has been particularly kind and pleasant to me ever since the battle. *Adieu.*

Despite upheavals in the Army of the Potomac's high command after Chancellorsville, morale in the ranks did not fall sharply as it had after the Fredericksburg defeat. The 119th New York is a case in point. Under the strong leadership of Lieutenant Colonel Lockman, and with Adjutant Dodge's assistance, the regiment's conduct and appearance began to sparkle. This gain survived even the bombastic (but temporary) command of Captain Van Borries (May 29).

Head Quarters Brooke's Station, Va.
May 20, 1863

A complete change has come over the 119th since we changed camp. We have now a beautiful location about a mile from Brooke's Station. The new camp is laid out in fine streets, and the boys, encouraged by their officers, have made their tents as neat as a row of pins. Lieut. Col. Lockman has taken the right course, viz. a consistent one. Every order he gives he sees carried out. He is up and about at reveillé, and he has his eye everywhere. At guard mounting he is present, inspects himself each man; dirty ones are put down on the black list and doomed to fatigue duty. At Company drill he is always present among the Companies, showing them how to execute certain maneuvers and correcting wrong ones. He is also consistent in his punishments, severe but strictly just. While the Colonel was supposed to be alive he would not change a single thing in the organization of the Regiment, but after the news of his death became certain, he began to treat the 119th as his Regiment, and the results are plain and gratifying.

May 21, 1863

We had a general inspection yesterday and the 119th was complimented as the best-looking Regiment in the Division. This is the result of three days' work; wait but 3 weeks! I am thorough in my admiration of Lieut. Colonel Lockman as a man and a soldier.

Since Saturday, during my absence in Washington, I did not journalize. I will try to make up for it. On Saturday A.M., when I left with poor Capt. Schwerin's remains, the Brigade moved, the 119th being excused till after the funeral ceremonies. The processional, which was well got up, moved to Brooke's Station and the body was conveyed to the Landing in the 8:30 train under my charge. Dr. Van Voorst, a friend and physician to the family, was also with me. We reached Washington at 4 P.M. and met the Q. M., who had made all the arrangements for us. The body was placed in an air tight metallic coffin, and sent on to his friends. I stayed with the Q. M. till Tuesday A.M. and drew my pay. Dr. Hewett was also with us in Washington, and Tuesday morning the Dr. and I started for camp, which we reached in the P.M.

The new camp is in a beautiful spot and from Head Quarters we have a view for ten miles around, taking in a circle of half the horizon. The Company streets are in a pine wood, which has been thinned out enough to be just healthy, the tall and large trees left standing affording sufficient shade. Head Quarters are on a sandy grass plot at the edge of the wood, and though we have no shade, we are so high that we have constantly a cool breeze; a very desirable spot it is on the whole, and we are all very well satisfied.

It would seem as if we were to stop here some time, an order having been just issued allowing regimental commanders to go on leave of absence. When we are next to be led to slaughter, I don't know.

May 22, 1863

Lieut. Col. Lockman and I go almost every day to the Division hospital, which is only about a mile from here, to see our wounded boys. Whenever we can, we take condensed milk, biscuits, oranges, lemons &c, whatever little delicacies we can lay our hands on for them. On such occasions Joe accompanies us on the mule, laden with a large pair of bags, and then goes through the tents distributing the goodies. Of course Joe takes the greatest delight in doing this, and the poor boys hail his black phiz with joyous exclamations whenever he appears. The Lieut. Col. is very careful to see the poor fellows every day, if possible, and has always some kind words to say to them.

He thinks of going on leave of absence for a few days. The Regiment will be under Capt. Van Borries, our senior Capt. If he does, we shall have a gay time. But as there are no present signs of moving, I presume everything will go on comfortably.

I feel once more set up, as the Q. M. has kindly loaned me his saddle. I so dislike a McClellan saddle now. Yesterday Dr. Hewett and I went all about the camps to find a horse for him. We found several good animals ranging from $125 to $225. One bright chestnut specially pleased him, but the price was better than the horse. However as he wants it so much, I think he will buy it. He has plenty of money.

The weather is perfectly charming; not too hot and a cool breeze prevailing.

May 23rd 1863

Lieut. Col. Lockman has just received leave of absence, and has left us for New York. Capt. Van Borries is in command. Dr. Hewett is on a court of inquiry. Some stupid young Dr. Ganel, whom Hewett snubbed the other day on the other side of the river for a mal-operation in Rebeldom, has brought the most laughable charges against the Dr., so that he has demanded a court of inquiry before a court martial, in which he is resolved to give Dr. Ganel and his abettors fits. The charges are drunkenness, malpractice, and the like. The specifications are perfectly frivolous. One was that he was so drunk that he fell down and wallowed in a pool of blood. I told the Dr. that I, as his tent-mate, would testify that his habits of personal neatness were such that were he "beastly drunk," he could not be brought to do such a thing. Capt. Willis and I are his counsel. The weather is fearful: it is so hot and sultry that we can scarce keep alive. Writing is a bore.

May 24, 1863

Dr. Hewett has been to Falmouth to see his old friend in the 66th N.Y., and has returned quite tired out. We had a short service today by Mr. Sprague at dress parade. Mr. S. expects to go on furlough to see about his Commission. It is very hot, so hot that we are expecting a thunderstorm. A Mr. Landan, an old friend of the Colonel's, was here today. He spoke very feelingly of him. Everybody regrets his sad fate so much! Everywhere we go, all speak well of him. His loss is greatly lamented.

May 26, 1863

This A.M. Dr. H. and I rode down to the Landing to get a horse which the Q. M. had bought in Washington for him. She proves to be a perfect beauty. Her name is the same as mine, so we call them Fanny Gray and Fanny Brown. The Q. M. also sent out two boys. One of them I like very much and I shall take him. The other will doubtless find a place in the Regiment. Now that the 119th is in the hands of Capt. Van Borries, I cannot tell you how things go on. He and I keep on good terms, tho' he is a great humbug. I shall be obliged to have another horse as mine cannot do all the work.

May 29th 1863

I have neglected to journalize somewhat this week. Reason why, I have so much to do. I have taken to drilling the non-commissioned officers. Capt. Van Borries insists, during the Lieut. Col.'s absence, on battalion drill every day. I will tell you after what manner it is conducted.

On our way to the drill ground, says the valorous Captain, "Haw, Adjutant, in the cavalry we do," so and so and give such and such commands. "How do you do in the infantry?" I then proceed to explain what he wants to know (and ought to know), upon which he answers, "Haw, yes, of course it is so, I *supposed* so." Once on the drill ground, before every new movement, it is, "I say, Adjutant, in the cavalry it is so and so," &c and I of course have to give more than half the commands myself, our competent Captain disdaining to inform himself so as to give them properly. He is the greatest bungler you ever saw, and he told me today that he had never looked into the Tactics more than two or three times in his life; more shame to him.

Today I had a few words with our "good tempered Capt. Willis." He is peculiar in arrogating extraordinary powers to himself. This morning I was waiting for him to send them in his pay rolls (the Paymaster is here) so that I might send in all together. His were the last. At length he came in and said he was going to take in his himself. I replied that the rolls must all go in together, and I had been waiting some time for his, &c &c, and I finished the matter by ordering him out of the tent. However his anger don't last long, for he soon came back fetching the pay rolls to make up.

Dr. Hewett and I have had a visitor with us for two or three days, a Mr. Whelpley, quite a nice fellow. He will return to Washington tomorrow. I sent my new darkey into town today, to bring in some eatables. He is to find a good cook for us, as since my old Henry went away we have been at odds

271

and ends for a good table. The weather for a few days has been very pleasant, moderately cool and a nice breeze. Today it is hotter.

Near Head Quarters we have had a gymnastic apparatus put up. Some of the German line officers are very good gymnasts, but I still hold my own in my old *forte*. We have a meeting daily. Our muscles get sore at first, and I am lame all over.

June brought increasing signs of a movement by the army, which derailed Dodge's hopes for a leave and (as it turned out) his hopes for promotion. Regimental morale—and certainly Dodge's morale—was boosted by the resignation of the boorish Captain Van Borries.

June 2nd 1863

The great event of the day is the Lieut. Colonel's return. When he got upon the mail boat, he was stopped because he had not a pass from the Provost Marshal, in addition to his leave of absence (the regulation concerning passes is changed about every week), and so he could not come on. We had sent to the Landing for him, but he was not there. However Joe had the discretion to wait a while, and about three o'clock an extra boat came in with Genl. Neill, on which the Lieut. Colonel was lucky enough to get a passage. Contrary to everybody's expectations but mine, he came without his eagles. During his absence, Governor Seymour had appointed a new Lieutenant from the 157th N.Y. Vols. to our Regiment, and this has set the Lieut. Colonel to work, and he will propose names for all the vacancies. He will also work for his own promotion, which I hope will ensure mine also. I rode again to Hooker's Head Quarters today to see Genl. Ingalls, Chief Q. M., on business for Father. It was a hot and dusty ride.

June 3rd 1863

Lieut. Col. Lockman came home yesterday as I wrote, and today everything has gone on admirably; we were all overjoyed to see him. Our quondam *pro tem* commander, Captain Otto Van Borries, the German baron with his proud bearing, coupled with low-lived behavior, has come to grief. I went to his tent today for some little matter, and found him gambling with some of the privates of his Company. Of course I was compelled to report it to Lieut. Col. Lockman. He at once preferred charges against him and put him under arrest. The high and mighty baron thereupon resigned, "immediately and unconditionally." His resignation was forwarded with the remark that the service would be benefited by its acceptance, which it undoubtedly will be. Every officer in the Regiment rejoiced.

The Lieut. Colonel went up to see Genl. Schurz about his promotion. Genl. S. gave him a very handsome letter, which was also endorsed by Genl. Howard. Col. Krzyzanowski also put in his mite. This will be forwarded to Governor Seymour and will doubtless be effectual.

June 4th 1863

Last night about 12 M., I was waked by an order from Head Quarters to turn out at daybreak and stay till half an hour after under arms. I did not think it worth while to wake the Lieut. Colonel, as reveillé was to be sounded at the proper hour. At 3 1/2 A.M. it did wake us and I had the Battalion formed in short order. Everyone was inquisitive and anxious, but I who got used to this sort of thing on the Peninsula, when we had to turn out every night, thought little of it. The "funny man" who exists in camp as well as in town (Lord knows we need him) says that one of our pickets saw 3 Rebel scouts bathing in the river, which fact, in passing along to Head Quarters, grew to be an Army Corps crossing, which sorely

273

alarmed the Fighting Old Boy, so that he ordered the Army of the Potomac under arms.

We have received from Mrs. Peissner today, by the hand of the Chaplain (old Corporal Sprague who has returned today with a Commission in his pocket and a good coat on his back), three large photographs of the Colonel. They are very lifelike. They were dedicated in Mrs. Peissner's hand—one to Genl. Schurz, one to the Lieut. Col., and one to the Regiment. This little act pleased us much. I have just got news of Father's promotion. How glad I am you can't tell. We are all here very joyful that his application has succeeded so well. He is now Captain and Asst. Q. M., which in the Q. M. Department is very good.

June 5th 1863

This morning I rode the Doctor's mare down to the Landing, having some $1,200 from three of the Companies to send to their families by Adams' Express. I took occasion to vary the scanty bill of camp fare by taking some ice cream in a saloon there, where they make it very good.

There has been a terrible hour's cannonading down at or beyond Fredericksburg. I don't ever recollect of hearing sharper firing at a distance. It has ceased now (7 P.M.). We are under orders to be ready to move at a short notice. I do not think it will be tomorrow though. The weather is cool today and feels like rain, which seems "holding up" by just a thread. If we should move tomorrow I will enclose a word in this envelope and send it if possible. If we move, I shall be cheated out of my five days with you. I have just received notice of Father's promotion. How thankful I am.

June 6th/63

We have not yet moved, and from the present appearance of things we are not likely to this time. There has been a thunder shower which has cooled the air amazingly.

June 7, 1863

An order has just come that we may have to march early today, tho' I do not think we shall. However there is no telling. I hope we shall not till I get a chance to see you. I desire this very much. We march with three days' rations.

We have passed a very quiet Sunday despite the order to be ready to march at about 5 A.M. I always rise at that hour now. An order came from Brigade Head Quarters which ought to have been sent last evening, to the effect that we might have orders to march at any moment. However we have not yet moved. Tomorrow is Monday and we may begin the week with a march. We generally start on Monday. We had Sunday A.M. inspection, the Lieut. Colonel making a very minute personal examination of each man. At 10 o'clock Mr. Sprague held divine services consisting of reading, prayer, and a 7 or 8 minute sermon. The service was short but interesting; there were but few present as the attendance is optional.

After service, Lieut. Col. and I went down to the hospital; most of our boys have been sent to Washington, or have received furloughs. All the bad cases were sent to Washington at first, so we have but two cases of loss of limb left. The boys are always so glad to see us, that it is a treat to go down. Coming home we rode past our old camp, and stopped a moment at the old winter quarters. The huts are all standing and are likely to for years to come. We also stopped at our Brigade cemetery. There is the headstone of poor Berger; he died 4 months ago. Capt. Schwerin and I were the only officers present at his death bed; he because Berger was Sergeant in his Company, and I because he was my clerk. How much did we think that in three months one of us two would be no more.

Some think we shall march tomorrow; I opine not. If we do, I shall have to get on without a pack horse; which is a very desirable thing. I often think of Copake, and wish I could fly thither for some days. Love to all.

June 8, 1863

Weather coolish, so much so as to make a cold bath at 4 1/2 A.M. (which I always take at that time, in another pork barrel, the old one being lost) quite a thing to dread.

I am on the lookout for a horse. My own needs rest, and I intend to send her to the Q. M. at Washington. He will not use her as hard as I am obliged to. The Lieut. Colonel bought a new horse today, the "Willis Mare," as we called her, which used to belong to Father. When he bought her she was a real beauty, but riding over 200 lbs. and very hard injured her greatly. After the Lieut. Colonel bought her, he transferred his mule, which is a U.S. one, to me. So now I have got a pack animal for the march, I am at ease. I now own a Fanny and a Jenny, the latter being of the donkey persuasion.

Dr. Hewett also bought a cheap horse the other day. The Doctor's court of inquiry turned out decidedly in his favor, even the witnesses summoned against him testifying in his favor. We are all much rejoiced at the result.

In this entry, Theodore Dodge could not be more proud. On the brigade inspection books, the 119th New York is now ranked first. And on drill before "Mrs. Crockery" (the wife of brigade commander Krzyzanowski) his men showed their mettle. The "appointment" his regimental commander speaks of here is what Dodge calls his impending majority.

June 9, 1863

This A.M. at 6, we had Battalion drill. It was the first we have had under Lieut. Col. Lockman, and the best I have seen since I have been in the Regiment. Lockman is a good drill master. This P.M. we had a Brigade drill, with a woman on a grey horse (Mrs. Crockery) as a spectator. We traveled over considerable territory but all the harm we did the Confederates was to trample down Old Secesh's sweet potato patch. The 119th New York is coming up. We used to stand 5th on the Division inspection books; lately we stand first, distancing all other Regiments. All this is owing to the commander. Everyone who sees the camp and the Regiment is pleased.

We have not marched; many thought we should this morning. On account of this all leaves have been stopped. I hope to get a pass to go into Washington but may not. Dr. Hewett will probably get his sick leave. He will leave his mare either here or in Washington. I am on the lookout for a horse. I shall never find one which satisfies me as well as Fanny, but her color is so bad for the field.

Has Baldwin yet resigned? There is a rumor that Prince Salm-Salm is coming to command the 119th. I would not serve under him. Lockman has spoken about "my appointment" several times. When there is a vacancy, all will be right.

June 10, 1863

The most striking event of the day is the kick of a horse administered to your humble servant. The Lieutenant Colonel and I were going down to Division hospital when, passing a spring on the way at which some Christian mortal had left a cup, I dismounted to get a drink for both of us, when getting too near his horse's heels, I received a blow on the inside of my knee which made me squeal. Ever since I have been hobbling round like a Chelsea pensioner. This is the second kick I have received in Uncle Sam's service. I shall be a veteran before long.

Joe asked me today for half a dollar. In joke I told him he would gamble it away. Dr. H. also said he had been gambling last night, at which he protested he had not, and in proof pulled out his purse and showed us some money. "Yah, Yah, I didn't bin gambling. I'se got some money left, Yah, Yah." He evidently thinks gambling is only *losing* money.

We have had some trouble with one of the Lieutenants, for refusing to go on picket duty. He is an impertinent fellow and has got himself into hot water, so he will either have to resign or be dismissed. He has two or three times tried to quarrel with me for blowing him up on drill, and I rejoice at the prospect of getting rid of him.

Our life is nowadays very regular, up and dressed by 5 A.M., have breakfasted and inspected Company's streets and camp generally by 6 A.M., when we march out to drill—generally Battalion drill. At 7 we are back in camp and guard mounting at 8. Sergeants and Corporals drill at 9; and then the morning's work is over. Drill at 4 P.M. Dress parade at 6, which ends the day.

Lieut. Colonel Lockman and I play a good deal of chess together. We generally retire between 9 and 10 P.M. The weather is very pleasant, very hot, and we have had but little rain this season.

CHAPTER ELEVEN

On the Road to Gettysburg

June 11 through July 5, 1863

On June 3, 1863, Robert E. Lee started his army west from Frederdericksburg, then northward along the Blue Ridge and in the Shenandoah Valley. By the 16th, Lee's leading corps, under Dick Ewell, was crossing the Potomac into Maryland; a week later Ewell was moving into Pennsylvania. Longstreet's and A. P. Hill's corps followed. Joe Hooker took the roads north in pursuit starting on June 11, with the Eleventh Corps moving out on the 12th.

Theodore Dodge's journal offers a full and careful account of the 119th New York's twenty-day odyssey leading to its fateful appointment with Ewell's veterans on July 1 outside the market town of Gettysburg. Again, as at Chancellorsville, the Eleventh Corps was routed, and this time Dodge did not escape unscathed. A Rebel bullet shattered his ankle, and his fighting days were over.

It is not until his June 19 entry that Dodge mentions the enemy invading Pennsylvania, and then it is by report from the newspapers. But, of course, he knew as soon as they turned northward that the movement was not an offensive but rather a response to the Confederates. Beyond that, however, the army's course was a matter of rumor. When Hooker announced that he was waiting for the enemy to develop his plans, Dodge was acerbic: "I fear, Monsieur, the Enemy will finish his plans before we see the development."

Although the marching was hard and the weather scorching, Dodge continued to be appreciative of the moment: "in this lovely country it is impossible to turn any way without beholding something pleasing to one's sense of beauty." When finally the moment of battle came, Adjutant Dodge was at his post, at the side of his colonel at the center of the action, trying to hold a wavering line, and both men fell wounded within moments of each other.

June 11th 1863

We seem to be on the point of marching. Orders have come to have all citizens and superfluous baggage moved to the rear, to have wagons reduced to the lowest standard (which leaves the 119th four), and to be ready generally. The

3rd Corps has moved southerly today, it is said, and we may move tomorrow, certainly very soon. The Brigade surgeon says we shall go to Catlett's Station; others are of opinion that we are to go down the river; but nobody *knows* of course.

Joe went to town today, to return tomorrow. If we move we shall be in a pretty fix, for Master Joe will be left behind. *He* will not be very sorry but *we* shall. It will be wretched without him, for he is the factotum of the Field and Staff. My leg has got almost well. The inflammation and swelling have subsided, and I can ride once again.

June 12, 1863. 1 1/2 P.M. Friday

Moved at noon—much confusion. This is written on horseback, at a short halt 1 1/2 miles from camp. Our destination today Hartwood Church, the same as our first day's march last move. May this not prove like that!

3 1/2 P.M.—

We are resting in the ravine where we camped in the march from Berea Church, after the muddy march, to Stafford Court House; we are to go some 6 or 7 miles farther. A band of 1st Brigade is playing merrily, and everyone feels in good heart. Our boys have marched well today, despite the heat and dust, which are very aggravating. I am sorry to have to take my grey mare on another march. She has been getting very thin this month past, and this will do her no good; but we left so suddenly we had little time for anything, much less for changing horses.

6 1/2 P.M.—

Arrived at Hartwood Church & camped. The horses are now feeding near us and the cook fires burning brightly. We have marched 9 miles today and have made it well. There has been no straggling of any account. We have marched through a country containing quantities of handsome marbles. Huge pieces of it lie about everywhere. I did not know before that Virginia was rich in marble.

Dodge's reference to the "marching and fighting Division" is Phil Kearny's division, on the Peninsula and at Second Bull Run. The Eleventh Corps' march took it to Catlett's Station on the Orange & Alexandria Railroad, thence to Centreville near the Second Bull Run battlefield, then north by west to Leesburg and the Edwards Ferry crossing of the Potomac.

June 13, 1863

Rose at 2 1/2, breakfast at 3, and were ready to start long before the starting time, 4 A.M. We are waiting now for the 1st Division to file past us. We shall probably take a long march today. If to Catlett's Station it will be over 20 miles—a longer march than I have made since I left the old "marching and fighting Division." Whether the 11th Corps alone are marching this way, I don't know. I think we saw another Corps taking the same direction. We shall march along the Warrenton Pike today. Along the route we pass many beautiful homesteads embowered in groves. Some of the most picturesque groups of trees line the road. Oaks many hundred years old (apparently) form prominent features of every view, and in this lovely country it is impossible to turn any way without beholding something pleasing to one's sense of beauty.

11 A.M.—

We have made no less than 14 miles this A.M. We are now having 1 1/2 hours' rest for dinner. The boys have marched splendidly. The road has been through a beautiful rolling country, and mostly through woods so that the sun which has been somewhat shaded by clouds, is partly deprived of its power. We have had no water since we left, so that our horses have just now been watered for the first time since yesterday afternoon. However they have now made up for it. I have got a pack mule, one the Lieut. Col. used to have, and manage very well. I forgot to say that Joe came back from Washington and joined us last evening, bringing us many good things. We were right glad to see him.

5 1/2 P.M.—

We have finished our march of over 20 miles, and are now in sight of Catlett's Station. We are all tired and shall be glad to camp here for the night or longer. I hope we shall not march again tomorrow. It would be pretty hard. If we stop here I shall send into Washington for a horse the Q. M. has got there for me. My mare is poorly and the march is hard upon her.

It has been coolish all day and we have not had an over bad time. I have kept a wet sponge in my hat and it has kept me very comfortable. Colonel Lockman and I sleep together in a shelter tent.

Sunday 14th June [1863], 9 A.M.

We hoped to stop some time at this place, but just now a sudden "Assembly" (call to fall in) was sounded from Brigade Head Quarters, which brought us to our feet and a sudden consciousness that we are again to be on the tramp. Our A. A. General says our destination is Manassas. I should hate to fight again there, for though things look well, yet the prestige of the enemy on that field would do for them a great deal.

The day is cool and the 10 miles to Manassas will be easily done, if such is our destination. I had half made up my mind that I should be able to send into Washington for the horse the Q. M. has got for me there. My horse needs rest for a month or two in pasture.

3 P.M.—

Have halted for dinner, which we have just dispatched. It consisted (as usual) of hard tack and coffee, and as a great luxury some hung beef and butter. I am now going to lie down. *Addio, buona notte!*

A little accident has just happened. An ambulance was standing within 10 yards of us, with Drs. Hewett and Daly in it. The horses took fright and dashed away, one each side of a tree which smashed up the ambulance, but hurt neither of the doctors; but a poor fellow who was sitting near the tree was thrown 12 feet and badly hurt. One would think that after so long a march, horses would be too tired to run away.

Monday 15th [June 1863], 4 A.M.

At Centreville! Centreville, don't it seem as if we had been running down to Falmouth for nothing? When we made the march last winter, it took us 6 days. Now we have done it in two days. It was a hard march yesterday & we did not reach camp till 9 o'clock; and the poor boys were very tired. How glad I always am that I do not have to take it on foot now! We are to start again this A.M. The last two days we have made respectively 22 and 20 miles. This is like old Kearny's marching. Colonel Lockman and I slept in the open air last night, on an old railway embankment. No trains disturbed our repose, but this morning when we got up we were soaked through with dew.

8 A.M.—

Our Corps has taken up position about a mile from Centreville, towards Bull Run. We shall probably stay here 2 or 3 days. I sent Joe into town to get my horse.

5 P.M.—

We are still in line in front of Centreville fortifications. The men have put up their shelter tents on their muskets, inverted, with the bayonets stuck in the ground. The Corps officers are lying under a tree, *very* hot and uncomfortable, among them your humble servant. Col. Lockman and I have just ridden over to our old camp on the other side of Centreville; there is very little remaining of it, the place where the tents stood being only recognizable. There are troops passing us all the time, marching either towards Chantilly or Fairfax. I fancy part of the Army has gone to the Shenandoah Valley, and part to Harper's Ferry.

June 16, 1863

Dr. Hewett got a pass to go to Washington to report to the Medical Officer there. He is really ill. Shortly after he left, Dr. Aymé came into camp from sick leave; we were all glad enough to see him. We may move today, but it is more probable we shall stay, as we have just had a detail for picket, which looks like another 24 hours sojourn.

Col. Lockman and I rode out to the old 9th N.Y. Militia, his old Regiment, and I was introduced to some of his friends. The officers are as a whole a fine looking set of men. I expect Joe with a horse today, which the Q. M. has bought for me. He will ride out from town I think.

7 1/2 P.M.—

Joe came out with a nice little brown mare, arriving about 1 o'clock. I shall send him in with my grey tomorrow. The weather is very fine; hot but pleasant, if not on march. We are in the woods at present bivouacking, as if on picket.

The Chain Bridge crossed the Potomac upstream from Washington just inside the District of Columbia line, and, as Dodge soon discovered, was not the army's destination. As it turned out, the resourceful factotum Joe would make his way back to the regiment and continue to deliver his essential services. The firing heard from the west was indeed cavalryman Pleasonton clashing with the Rebel horsemen. Dodge's handling of a straggler (June 18) suggests that he had learned to temper the martinet in his military nature.

June 17 [1863], 7 1/2 A.M.

We were waked up at half past 3 this morning, with but half an hour to get ready in. We used it however to such good advantage that we marched off at 4 o'clock. News was spread abroad that we were going to Chain Bridge, 8 miles from Washington, and the Colonel, on faith of this, sent Joe into town for several things, more particularly to take my grey mare in to the Quarter Master. I was very loath to part with her.

We have now marched some 3 miles on the Aldie Turnpike from Centreville. We are not going to Chain Bridge, but to Aldie; and it will be some time before we see Joe again, I fancy.

10 1/2 A.M.—

We are about ten miles on the road to Aldie. The Adjutant of the Brigade just told me that we are going to Leesburg, which is 30 miles from Centreville. If we have to do this, we shall not get there until midnight on a steady march. *Adieu* Joe! He will be at Chain Bridge this evening, and we shall be at Leesburg. Alas! for staff officers and rumors. They are on a par: the first don't know anything, the last always wrong. Chain Bridge indeed; no such good luck.

12 1/2 P.M.—

Driest and hottest day on record! Drought through the land; springs all dried up; no water here where we halt for 2 hours for dinner. We have made 14 miles this morning, and not one half our boys were in the ranks when we reached here (we are in the woods) just now. They are gradually coming up however. It has been a terrible march this morning—what for I do not know, as they say we are going to camp some three miles from here for tonight. Oh! the heat! We are almost suffocated. Col. Lockman and I have taken off our coats and are lying down under a tree, our horses standing near us eating some oats, which we always carry with us on our pack animals. Oh! the heat once more!

Goose Creek, 6 P.M.—

We have camped for the night, having made 19 miles today; the men are almost done out. We are 6 miles from Leesburg, and 6 from Edwards Ferry on the Potomac. They say we shall cross tomorrow. Cannonading is heard towards Harper's Ferry, probably Pleasonton engaging the enemy. The march has been very severe. It has been fearfully hot and men and animals are almost worn out. I have had nothing to eat since noon, and feel very hungry withal. Luckily we are near water, which has been scarce all day and the boys are enjoying a good wash. I will imitate their example, in the wash basin instead of the creek.

[June 18, 1863] 5 1/2 A.M.

We received orders at midnight to march at 4 A.M., but we did not march at that hour, and some time after a circular came round that "This Corps will not move until further orders." Probably we shall wait until the sun is very high and hot, and then start off.

There is a great lack of water about here. The men have suffered much the last two days' march from want of it. It is a very hard duty (which falls to my lot) to stop the men falling out of ranks at wells we meet on the way. The water is poor anyhow and in the canteens gets undrinkable. Many are the hard words that I get inwardly from the poor boys no doubt, and I do not wonder, nor blame them. Another hard duty is to keep those men in the ranks by threats when you can't do it by cheering them up. When you see a man almost exhausted, it is very hard to force him on; cheer him up you can't, and I frequently have to ride them almost down, before I can get them forward.

The other day one of my boys brought his piece to a "ready" against me, when I rode towards him, after he had disobeyed my order to rejoin his Company, which he had left.

He was so sorry for it afterwards though, and such a good boy generally, that I did not punish him. It was almost an involuntary act which he was sorry for as soon as he had done it. These 20-mile marches on these awfully hot days are very hard. No one knows how hard, until they have made them themselves, with 60 lbs. on their back.

6 P.M.—

We changed our position to a hill about 1/2 mile from Goose Creek at noon. We now overlook all the country looking north and extending between here and Blue Ridge. We have had a thunder shower this afternoon and 'tis raining still. Dr. Aymé and I are under my shelter tent, on the roof of which this rain is pattering heavily and about a tenth part coming in through the thin canvas. Altogether I feel very uncomfortable.

I have just got a chicken which one of the drummers caught (or foraged) for me at a house near by. Anyhow I paid for it. It is cooking for supper. I have been giving my mare "Dimple" some medicine (the bark of the red oak, boiled). She has lost her appetite out here, not having got acclimatized yet. This is her first campaigning. I send you some little wild flowers plucked on the hill here. What they are I do not know. The rain is so powerful, I am fain to stop writing.

June 19 [1863] 8 A.M.

Despite the heavy rain I slept very nicely. This morning the rain ceased but it is still very cloudy, and the air is fresh and cool. There is some firing off in the direction of the Shenandoah Valley, but whether it is minute guns or not, we cannot determine. I fancy the batteries are clearing out their pieces after the heavy rain. We saw a newspaper the other day and as the Rebels are stated to be in Maryland and Pennsylvania, we do not see why all this delay takes place. A supply train has left the station this morning to get forage at Fairfax, full 25 miles from here. Why we are not on the move is a mystery to me. Probably someone knows, though whether there is good reason for it, I doubt.

Saturday June 20 [1863], 10 A.M.

Still at Goose Creek, waiting (as Hooker's telegram to Howard says) "for the enemy to develop his plans." How suggestive the name of this place is? I fear, *Monsieur*, the Enemy will finish his plans before we see the development. When is a war, carried on such principles, to be expected to finish?

The weather is overcast. Last night it rained very hard, again and again, & I got very wet. Today is scarcely propitious for drying, for I fancy the rain will come on before long. It would seem that we are lying in line of battle, covering Washington. The different Corps are posted, I believe, from Manassas Junction to Leesburg and the river at Edwards Ferry. All this while the Rebels are quietly devastating Pennsylvania. An order has been sent round to reduce baggage, and the wagon inspector made some objection to my small trunk; but by proper management I got him to let it pass. Col. Lockman and I had to reduce our mess kit though, and we have been down to the wagons contriving to squeeze it into proper limits.

We have some beautiful flowers around here. Somebody brought the Colonel a splendid bouquet today. The raspberries and blackberries too are getting ripe. I had some today. Strawberries and cherries are scarce, on account of the multitude, but we had some beauties two or three weeks ago. I got a shelter tent out of the trains today and have set up an establishment all by myself. You have no idea what a change it is from two persons (with saddles and baggage) in 5 foot 6 inches square and 3 ft. high at the apex, to one only. I feel almost lost when I get into my tent all alone.

You poor beings in houses little know of the magnificent luxury of a shelter tent. It really is curious how little will content a man and make him comfortable and happy, when he can't get more. Now, if you at home could look down upon us here (as we often wish you could) when taking our meals, or sleeping during a thunderstorm in a shelter tent, you would dub us the most miserable of mortals. But really I am happy and contented, and though a home dinner and bed would be desirable, I manage on what I have very well indeed.

One of Col. Lockman's servants (old Ned by name) is quite a character. He was formerly a slave near Fredericksburg, and ran away. He knows all the country round about there. The other day I asked him if he was married. "Not exactly," says Ned. "Have you got a wife?" "Got some, I reckon," says he. "How many?" "Wal, don't know—*some few*." His ideas of the married state are rather too liberal, I fear! He says he's somewhere between 30 and 50 years old. He don't know exactly. He is a capital horse doctor, although I didn't know it before yesterday, when he cured my mare completely. "That mare wants some bark," says old Ned; so he went into the woods, cut some bark off the north side of a red oak, and dried it by the fire enough to pound it up and gave it to the mare in a feed of oats. She was quite well half an hour afterwards. The green feed she had picked up had disagreed with her. Old Ned wants to get to Washington. He is afraid he will be taken prisoner, and then he knows he will be hung. Every gun that goes off in the distance makes the old fellow prick up his ears. There is no real fear however of his getting caught.

Theodore's father, Captain Nathaniel Dodge, served during the new campaign as a brigade quartermaster in another division of the Eleventh Corps. The 119th's posting here was on Goose Creek, a few miles south of where it emptied into the Potomac at Edwards Ferry. In this relatively untouched section of northern Virginia the Federals foraged extensively. This was also part of "Mosby's

Confederacy," where John S. Mosby's partisans roamed, and Dodge notes the efforts to catch what he terms "Mosby bushwhackers."

June 21st [1863], 10 A.M.

We were making ready for service this Sunday morning, when an order came for the 119th to break camp and report at Head Quarters. Howard had sent Schurz an order to detail a Regiment with efficient officers to guard some forks of roads and fords over the creek. We are now about three miles from our camp on the hill (Camp Hill, over Goose Creek), and Genl. Schurz is showing Colonel Lockman how he is to post the Regiment.

It is very cool today, the sky quite overcast, a good day for marching. There is a deal of cannonading in the direction of the Valley, though it does not seem so far. I should not wonder if the enemy had developed his plans sufficient to allow Hooker to move. The Signal Corps has been busy on the hills around. That is a fine branch of the service. We have one of our Lieutenants in it. I sent a letter to Washington last evening by some ambulances.

3 P.M.—

There has been heavy firing at Aldie all day. Col. Lockman and I have established our pickets, as I think, in a good style, and now the Rebels may come. It is very hard work this placing pickets. Jimmie Christie, our commissary Sergeant, has just come out with a load of rations, and tells us that Capt. Dodge is attached to the 1st Division, 1st Brigade, 11th Corps. He has seen him today. This is good news.

Monday June 22 [1863], 7 A.M.

I saw Father yesterday. He rode into camp. He is with Col. Von Gilsa's Brigade, Dutch, but good enough. He was of course very glad to see me, and I him.

Last evening about dusk two men came running down the road from Guard No. 3, saying that large forces of skirmishers were to be seen advancing upon us. I thought it was queer, but as the man said Captain Volkhausen, Capt. Guard 3, had sent them, I galloped up there thinking there might be something after all. Captain V. pointed out an open space on the north side of the creek where he had seen some skirmishers, as he thought. I rode out to Guard 1, commanded by Capt. Willis, and found out that a patrol sent out by the 1st Division had passed him and instead of marching in a body, they had marched in Indian file, which had alarmed Capt. Volkhausen. We had quite a laugh over the fright in camp, and I had quite a gallop.

During the night it rained considerably, but cleared up at midnight. At 4 A.M. Colonel L. and I mounted our steeds and went out to see things generally. We first went to Guard 1 at Gulick's Ford, and from there followed up the creek through the woods to Ball's Ford, and here we found the post of observation. Returning the direct road we stopped at Mr. Wm. Moffitt's and bought a pound of butter, and at his brother's, over the way, we bought a loaf of wheat bread. Our meal was completed at Mr. Thrift's by a canteen of milk. Thus we united pleasure to duty in our round.

At camp we took breakfast, consisting of lamb (cold roast), veal cutlets, fricasseed chicken, and coffee. The fact is that the animal creation about here are very pugnacious, and insist on attacking our picket line so often that our boys are fain to bayonet them out of pure self defense. Of course there is no foraging done. Oh, no! only when lambs, chicken, sheep, and calves will rush to an untimely fate. *Quid faciendum?*

I have got the whole drum corps tied up this morning. A lady living nearby came and complained about their depredations, and I have got them all tied to trees. I am going to keep them there all day.

Father has just come out to see us. He is looking well. We are continually arresting men around here. We have sent many into Head Quarters and are going in search of them every hour. They are mostly men suspected of being guerrillas.

Head Quarters 119th N.Y.V. in the field.
Leesburg Va., June 23rd [1863], 2 P.M.

It is just about the time George is drinking Father's health and mine in London. I was at the Q. M. Department of the 1st Brigade and we talked of the dinner supposed then about to be eaten. At precisely 1/4 2 P.M. I looked at my watch and thought I could hear the toast proposed, even at the distance of 3,500 miles. Toasts are effective, for behold on the very day George wishes us all manner of prosperity, your humble servant is nominated to Governor Seymour by Colonel Lockman for promotion to the Majority of the 119th. Capt. Lockman to be Lieut. Colonel. Captain L. however is in very delicate health and he will in all probability resign before long, and then *"qui sait"* but I may be Lieut. Col. Dodge. But I had better not be building castles in the air, for they are very fragile, and besides, I remember a certain fable about a nice young woman and her pail of milk.

But to my journal. About 2 o'clock yesterday we were relieved by a Brigade who proceeded to post pickets in the most abstruse and incomprehensible manner, the result of which seemed to me to be a triangle of sentries looking inwards. Anyhow they used five times as many men as we did and were not guarded as effectually. We left at 3 P.M., and by Genl. Howard's order were (as an "efficient Regiment") set to catch guerrillas (not gorillas). It seems that there are about fifty of the above mentioned enclosed within our lines somewhere, precise location to within 30 miles not easily ascertainable. The 119th is located apart from the Brigade, at a certain point where it is hoped the said gentlemen may be nabbed. So we are in a state of constant watchfulness, sending out patrols at every point. Yesterday we caught 3 of Mosby's bushwhackers. Up at Corps Head Quarters they have a man who has cut the throats of five of our stragglers. He confesses as much, and says he don't care if they do hang him. His wife and children came crying for mercy to Genl. Howard, but he (the fellow) told them to go home. "They may hang me, damn them," says he, "for I have killed 5, and Jeff Davis will hang 4 for me and that'll make 9; so let them hang me and be damned." He seems a regular desperado.

We got a big mail yesterday. I had nearly a dozen letters, among them the Wilderness round-robin, and also a letter from Mrs. G. endorsed by George. How excessively kind of him to order a new saddle for me. I hope I may never lose another. My new mare I like much. She is a nice animal and pretty and a fast goer besides. The weather is fine, clear, breezy, and we have had such a spell of bad weather, I think we shall have it fine now for some time.

Edwards Ferry June 24 [1863], 1 1/2 P.M.

Just as Col. Lockman and I were preparing to ride over to see the Captain (N. S. D.), up came an orderly with orders to march. We had just got nicely fixed up, and were in a splendid place where we could roam at will and monopolize all the farm houses around, and we growled considerably. But it was no help, so we drew in pickets, packed up, and in half an hour were on the way to join the columns. Since then we have come about 6 miles and are at Edwards Ferry over the Potomac, 30 miles from Washington.

I bought a horse yesterday, $30—a speculation. He has a splendid rack, trot, canter, and gallop, and jumps like a hunter, but his back is very sore. Our veterinary, Cooper (at present with the Captain), says he can cure it and I promised him $10 if he can do it in a month. The horse is then worth

$125 easy, if well, and I guess he will pay. I use him for carrying a pack now. Dr. Aymé will give me $50 for him today.

The captain referred to in this entry is Theodore's father. The First, Third, and Eleventh Corps crossed the Potomac at Edwards Ferry on June 25. Sugar Loaf Mountain in Maryland was used as an observation post by both sides at various times during the Antietam and Gettysburg campaigns. The "Libby Hotel" (June 26) was Libby Prison, for officers, in Richmond.

June 25 [1863], 9 A.M.

We broke our camp at 4 A.M. this morning. The Captain slept with me in my shelter tent, and was very sick during the night. This morning orders came to send all unable to march, to Washington by the canal which runs along the river. The Captain felt so poorly that he determined to go, too, and as Col. Von Gilsa had requested him not to take the Department in hand till the 1st prox., he went. An ambulance took him to the canal boat. Joe rode his mare into town; Cooper (who is with him), now a paroled prisoner, staying behind to take care of his goods and chattels, and the grey mare (who by the way is getting fast better) is in the Q. M.'s Department where she gets all she can eat.

Our camp was in a beautiful place for the horses last night: an immense clover field miles in extent afforded the animals of the whole Corps ample and good forage. Oats are somewhat running short. As the sun rose this morning and just as the first sign of the big golden ball appeared above the hills of "My Maryland," we put foot on the pontoon bridge which had been thrown across. The river is about 500 yards wide, and 75 pontoon boats were necessary. Even these were insufficient, for, as Goose Creek (whose confluence with the Potomac is at Edwards Ferry) had to be crossed as well, the pontooniers had to erect a trestle bridge some way into the stream on the Maryland side. There is a curious swaying motion of a pontoon bridge in crossing it, which would be apt to make some men giddy and sick. Something unsteady about it. The men have to march as unequally as possible in crossing, for a steady tramp would break down the bridge.

The country we are now passing through affords a rare contrast to Virginia. The land is fruitful and cultivated and the immense fields of corn (wheat) are a sight well worth seeing. The scenery of the banks of the Potomac of which we catch every now and then a glimpse is magnificent. We are near Sugar Loaf Mountain. It is impossible to march 5 minutes consecutively without catching sight of it. It is a perfect nuisance in fact, and they say, last year, when the Army was moving round about here a great deal, that the soldiers used to swear at the mountain. You cannot camp within a circuit of 25 miles from here without seeing Sugar Loaf Mountain.

We just passed a delightful sight, actually two young ladies (whose home we could see, a beautiful house in the distance), on horseback; pretty girls too they were, and I could not but sigh as I passed them and saluted them. Alas! for a good long talk with one of my lady friends. It would be the very most refreshing thing I know of. I wish I was a good enough sketcher to let you have some of the scenes we see. Such beauty as we pass is not seen everywhere. We are now halting in a lovely grove, having marched about 7 miles this morning. The country around here is very rocky, and the rail fences are replaced by stone walls, like New Hampshire. The soil is rich however and fertile.

Jefferson, June 26th/63, 7 A.M.

About as uncomfortable as a fish out of water, or rather a land animal in water. We halted yesterday about noon for two hours, during which time the sky covered with clouds, and about 5 P.M. it began to rain; not to shower as if promising a speedy cessation of the drenching, but first to drizzle, then to sprinkle, then to rain in that dogged kind of way which always augers a lasting storm. I do not mind a rain coming on after my shelter is put up, but to have to put up a shelter tent in a storm, with everything as wet as can be, is very disagreeable. Added to this, Jack, who has been riding my Jim all day, had fallen into the canal with horse and all blankets on him, so that even the luxury of a dry blanket was not at my disposal. However I made the best of a bad job, & I did sleep heavily. Last year at this time I was worse off still. Coming as near as I did to having a room in the "Libby Hotel" or some worse place, I fancy. The Battle of Seven Pines [Oak Grove] was on the 25th of June.

I have not told you that instead of going to Harper's Ferry, as we thought we should, we marched to Jefferson, a beautiful little village in the most superb country. The scenery around here is particularly beautiful, rolling and well cultivated. The farms are much more numerous than in Virginia, and everything wears a healthy appearance which is a great contrast to the broken-down looks of a county in Virginia. Everyone is at work, and 'tis pleasant to know that one half of the men you see at least are Unionists. In Virginia everyone is Secesh.

We supposed we were to march this morning, but we have not yet received any orders. I for one am content to stay here until we get dry. There are rumors of Longstreet's being in the vicinity with 30,000 men; also of our going to Frederick; but we know about nothing. There is enough in our little sphere to occupy us. It is rather tantalizing to see the village of Jefferson within a stone's throw of one, and not be able to go there, against which there are stringent orders. One envies the Generals though, in nice comfortable houses with (*qui sait?*) nice girls to wait on them. Oh!

Middletown, 6 P.M.—

We left Jefferson about noon, marching with music through the town. I put a letter into the post for Mother there. We reached Middletown about 4 P.M., and made some show through the streets of the town.

Middletown is a place of about 2,000 inhabitants, situated in a most exquisite section of country. The beauty of the scenery I cannot give you any idea of. Plenty of water abounds, and little creeks running across the road every few hundred yards. Cattle and grain are seen on every side, and the country people look very happy. All along the road groups of girls and boys watch the columns pass and occasionally one sees a refreshingly pretty face. In Middletown we were welcomed by the women with flags and handkerchiefs waving. It is the first Union town we have passed.

Camp near Middletown, June 27, 1863

The sun has come out today, and it promises a chance to dry our wet blankets. We expected to move this A.M. early, but are still in camp, I believe waiting for the 1st Corps to pass us. I have been in town this morning, to post my journal to you. One part of it (as you will see) went to the Captain in Washington, and as he had left, Prof. Marix sent it again to the 119th, which it reached by mail this A.M. just in time to send it off again with the rest.

It seems so pleasant to be in a town again! I bought two collars, and when I got to camp Col. Lockman inveigled me out of one. I wish you could see the view spread out before me this moment. A valley, through which runs a beautiful stream, is bounded by a rounded hill of wheat waving in the summer breeze, about half a mile from where we are camped. Beyond this we see the spires of the pretty town. To the left is part of the Catoctin range of hills, enveloped in mist. To the right a beautiful picture of hill and vale, woodland and fields, farms and mills, which to a military eye is improved by a long wagon train and camps as far as the eye can reach.

Joe Hooker, increasingly at odds with the administration and undermined by his own generals, resigned his command this day and was replaced by George Gordon Meade, of the Fifth Corps. McClellan would have been Captain Dodge's choice. Dodge erred about Frederick; Maryland's capital is Annapolis. The army was moving fast now, with the Eleventh Corps reaching Emmitsburg, near the Pennsylvania border, on June 29 after a twenty-five-mile march—"tough work," said Dodge, "for any length of time."

June 28, 1863

We lay in camp till 3 P.M., when we got news of Hooker's removal and Meade's appointment. Oh! that Little Mac were the man! At the same time notice to move. We are now on the road to Frederick, where we shall halt for the night at least, perhaps for longer. Colonel Lockman has friends there and we should not mind halting there a day or two. It would be so pleasant to visit inside a house once more. The 1st, 2nd, 3rd, 11th and 12th Corps are now here or in this vicinity. I watched my old Division file by in Middletown this morning. They are a tough set of men, and though the Regiments are small, the old Division still numbers quite a lot of men, there are so many Regiments in it.

28th June 9 P.M.—

Have just arrived at Frederick and camped; we march again tomorrow at daybreak. Frederick is the capital of Maryland, and has a population of some 5,000. From Middletown we had to cross the Catoctin range of hills; we have marched about 10 miles.

29 June 1863

The country here is less hilly than nearer the Potomac. Vegetation is flourishing and seldom do you see a waste piece of land, as you see acres upon acres in Virginia. There is comparatively little woodland about. The farms look prosperous, the barns being twice the size of the house, and more handsomely built, if anything. You very often see little villages; and pleasant places they are too. The people are courteous and intelligent, all (with few exceptions) good Union men. Although we do not get any very good rations ourselves, nor clean clothing, we are lucky enough to have plenty of forage for our horses. This is a great blessing as, if the horse has to carry you, he needs food more than you. Last winter when we had little forage, I often felt as if I could go without food for myself to get food for my horse. "Dimple" stands the march much better than any horse on the road, and after 20 miles is as frisky as a lamb. 20 miles at the slow pace of infantry, i.e. 2 miles per hour, is very trying for a horse.

June 29th, noon—

It is too rainy to journalize on the road. We have marched 14 miles and are now at ———— town [Creagerstown]. We have ten miles further to Emmitsburg. Roads good. All our men marching like bricks, despite disadvantages; little straggling. Emmitsburg is on the Pennsylvania border. Col. Lockman and I are now sitting near the fire, on which are stewing two spring chickens. The horses are ready saddled for a move. The men are stirring round like so many bees, some packing their knapsacks, some cleaning their pieces, some quarreling, some singing, some laughing. In the distance towards the west rises the range of the South Mountain, the top covered with mist, this side of which are fields upon fields of corn and wheat. The weather is wretched, always drizzling or raining. For the last 4 days we have not caught a glimpse of the sun. However, as all things

301

must come to an end, so we hope may this bad weather. Campaigning in the rain is not pleasant.

Emmitsburg, Maryland, June 29, 1863, 6 P.M.—

We have made 25 miles today, and over bad roads too. It has cleared up the last 3 or 4 hours and tomorrow may be a fine day. I fancy we march again tomorrow. If this is Meade's work, he begins sharp; five and twenty miles a day is tough work for any length of time. We are close on the borders of Pennsylvania. If we march we shall probably enter the state tomorrow.

June 30th 1863, 9 A.M.

We received orders to march at daybreak this morning, and accordingly at that time we were packed up and ready to start; but a move was not made. We had struck our tents and so we sat down by the fire to await whatever was to take place, but as it was raining pretty heavily and we had waited for something to turn up for an hour or two, towards 6 A.M. we pitched our tents again. We have been lying off some time now, and we are to move over a couple of miles towards South Mountain, and camp again. It is probable we shall stay in Emmitsburg during the day.

July 1, the first day of Gettysburg, was another black day for the Eleventh Corps, and for Theodore Dodge his last day of battle. West of Gettysburg, Confederates of A. P. Hill's corps clashed with John Reynolds's First Corps, killing Reynolds. The Eleventh Corps, called up in support, was hammered by Ewell's corps advancing from the north and was driven back through Gettysburg to Cemetery Ridge south of the town. By the account Dodge gave to a comrade, Captain Robert Brewster, Dodge's new horse bolted at the first cannon fire, and he went into battle on foot. "Our men retreated firing, the 119th

in good order, some other regiments in confusion," Brewster's account reads. "At this moment Theod. felt a terrible shock and fell instantly." At almost the same moment, Colonel Lockman was wounded. The Confederates soon overran the field and took both men prisoners.

July 1st [1863], 9 A.M.

Early this morning a circular came from General Meade, calling upon every man and officer to do his duty in the approaching battle. This is the first we have heard of the Rebels being in our vicinity. At 7 A.M. we were on the road to Gettysburg, where the enemy are supposed to be. We know however nothing of movements. There is more taciturnity on the subject than usual in this Corps. Well, if we are to have a battle, I hope it may be such a one as will annihilate Lee's Army. But what dare we hope?

10 A.M.—

We have now crossed the border and are in Pennsylvania. The 11th Corps has arrived in the free states, on a hostile movement. I believe we are on the left of the line this time. The country round here is very rocky, and not so well cultivated on that account as the section we have passed through since we crossed the Potomac. There are more roads too. The marching is wretched and the atmosphere so oppressively close that the men scarcely make any way at all. If we march ten miles today we shall do well.

Noon, 2 miles from Gettysburg—

There is firing in the front. They say the 1st, 3rd and 5th Corps are engaged. May they be successful! There is more infantry than artillery firing. It is not as yet very heavy.

2 P.M. Beyond Gettysburg—

We are engaged. We lie in column supporting a battery (Dilger's) with skirmishers in front. Shells are flying and bursting at a considerable rate. The Rebels are about half a mile off. The country is open and we can see everything. We see their batteries and the men at work very plainly. Our batteries are working hard. Reynolds has fallen, and in him we have lost much, but he died bravely and took 1,200 prisoners before he fell. Our Corps is to hold this position of Gettysburg. God grant we may have victory!

July 2nd [1863], 7 P.M.

I am lying on a bed at the house of a Mr. Benner's, 1 1/2 miles from Gettysburg. The action of yesterday was short and sharp, Ewell's (late Jackson's) Corps again driving the Germans with fearful strength from the town. I was hit by a minié ball through the ankle just as we started, fell, and was taken prisoner. I fear my foot will be stiff for life, for although the bone is not fractured, it is considerably injured. The Confederates treated me kindly.

July 3rd [1863], 4 P.M.

The battle has raged incessantly since I came to Mr. Benner's. We are within shelling distance, but have a red flag (hospital) hung out, and till now, thank God, no shells have struck us. I am unable to use my right leg at all; have lost all muscular control over it, and it is rather painful, but I thank a kind Providence it is no worse. I suppose I shall be paroled and sent to the Union lines whenever this battle is over. I suspect the slaughter must be fearful. Such cannonading I have not heard since Malvern Hill; last evening it was more like rattling of musketry at short range, so quick was the firing.

I must tell you a queer little incident. There is a Confederate General in this house. His negro servant came into the room just now and looked round without saying anything, until his eye caught some new pennies on the table. He asked me if it was silver. I told him, No, they were cents, and gave him one. He then said, "Would you like some chicken for dinner?" I said I would pay him for anything he would bring me. Shortly after he brought me some stewed chicken and some coffee, which was a great luxury, as I could get none anywhere else. He says he will fetch me some supper.

My foot is considerably swollen, but I keep away inflammation by frequently bathing with water. The wound looks well, I think. It is just beside the ankle joint, in the right leg, going in on the outside and coming out in the inside. I hope it may not lame me for life; but the Confederate surgeon who looked at it the day before yesterday, said that he feared it would, as it had injured the bone. I can move my toes but not my foot. I have to keep my leg in one position all the time, which is very irksome.

After I was hit, day before yesterday, I lay for some time between the two fires, our men having retreated, and the Confederates making a pause. It was not a pleasant position. After their line had passed me and I was a prisoner, my sword and belt was taken away. I then cut off my boot and bound up my ankle with my pocket handkerchief. After a while an orderly Sergeant of the 119th, who was also taken prisoner, came up to me, and with the help of a Confederate soldier, got me to a grove in the rear. Here he helped me bind up my wound afresh, and then I waited till after dark, when they came and carried me on a stretcher to Mr. Benner's. I was very lucky all the way through, one of our drummers, also being a prisoner and with me, keeping my foot wet from his canteen while I was on the field. When I got here, I lay down on the floor on a blanket, and with the aid of a dose of morphine, passed a tolerably comfortable night. Yesterday was the longest day I ever remember. The 1/4 hours seemed whole days. The firing began early, ceased towards noon, and at 5 P.M. was recommenced in a tremendous style.

There is a French boy of the 107th Pa. Vols., Francois by name, who waits on me, and as I can talk French with him, likes to make me comfortable. So you see that I am pretty well off.

July 4th [1863], 7 A.M.

Still at Mr. Benner's. The Confederates have, it would seem, evacuated the vicinity of this place, whether or not the town, I cannot say. Part of their cavalry pickets have just left, but a few straggling shots still indicate their presence on the Chambersburg Pike west of the town, on which they are probably marching. I fancy our troops will be here today. This would be glorious and I should not have to be paroled after all. I wish I knew the facts.

Dr. Habschmann of the 26th Wisc., the surgeon in charge of the 11th Corps field hospital in Gettysburg, came out here and paid us a visit yesterday evening. He bound up my foot and told me to keep it constantly wet, which I do. I dress it myself every morning and evening, during my leisure minutes, which are many, I pick lint & make bandages from an old sheet Mr. Benner gave me.

Afternoon—

About noon we managed, by sending a message to Genl. Howard, to get permission to send ambulances to this place, which is nearer the Rebel pickets than ours; and I expect to be taken some time today to the Corps hospital, established in rear of the town. It is raining hard this afternoon.

I have just seen a couple of slightly wounded boys from our Regiment. They tell me that Colonel Lockman was wounded. Also that many of our officers and men were killed and wounded. I have sent them into town, to see if they can't bring a doctor out here. I much want to get to some civilized hospital. I fear inflammation is setting in my foot.

The July 4 entry concludes Theodore Dodge's journal. After powerful assaults on July 2 failed to dislodge the Federals from Cemetery Ridge, on July 3 General Lee staked all on Pickett's Charge—and failed. On July 4 the Confederate army started on the road back to Virginia, leav-

ing any captured wounded such as Dodge behind. These letters trace Dodge's prognosis in the Eleventh Corps field hospital over the next days. By Captain Brewster's account, "On Sunday [July 5] the surgeons held a consultation and on Monday, amputated, which seems to have been necessary, as the ankle bones were utterly destroyed." Dodge's right leg was amputated about four inches above the ankle, and his career on the Civil War battle lines was over.

**At Mr. Benner's on Harrisburg Road
nr. Gettysburg, Pa. July 4, 1863**

Dear Mother,

I was wounded in the foot (ankle) shot thru' by a minié ball on the 1st, since when I as above, *very* comfortable and in good health and spirits. My wound is getting on well. I may get into Corps hospital today. Am now between picket lines of Rebels and Unionists. In no danger, tho' not much to live on. Shall probably be in Washington in a week or so. Truly in love—Theod.

Dear Father,

I am as above, very comfortable quarters. Thinking you may perhaps have returned from Washington, I send this. Come and see me. I was shot through the ankle joint on the 1st inst. Ever aff., Theod.

Commander 119th New York
Sir:

I have respectfully to inform you that I was wounded on the 1st inst. in the ankle. I am now as above. This for your information. If you can send this slip to Mrs. Dodge, Copake Iron Works, Columbia County, N.Y., you will greatly oblige me.

Yours respectfully,
T. A. Dodge
Adjt. 119th N.Y.

P.S. I am very well, & comfortable, though unable to use my leg.

July 5, 1863

Dear Mother,

Several doctors say I may preserve my foot, others that I must have it amputated. Anyway I shall stay here for ten days or a fortnight. Can you come out here and see your selfish boy? In love, Theod.

[July 1863]

Dear Mother,

I hope to go home in about a fortnight. I consider myself lucky not to have lost more in that terrible fire. It will be two months probably before I can hold my leg down and six before I can think of an artificial foot.

I was very averse to having it off and refused to have amputation performed till convinced that it was absolutely necessary, the bones of the ankle being fractured to shivers, when I made up my mind and had it done at once. The stump is now healing.

APPENDIX

Left Wounded on the Field

One of Theodore Dodge's first efforts as a military historian was this article, published in the September 1869 issue of Putnam's Magazine, *describing his battlefield experiences at Gettysburg and based on his wartime diary and journal writing. Dodge intended it to be a generalized view of Civil War combat. To achieve that effect, he was deliberately nonspecific. He does not name his regiment, the 119th New York, nor his corps, the Eleventh, and offers few specifics of the engagement on July 1 that cost him his leg. His unnamed regimental commander was Colonel John T. Lockman; the critically wounded Union general who shared his ordeal was Brigadier General Francis C. Barlow, commanding First Division, Eleventh Corps. Some six months after this article was published, Dodge retired from army service, and in due course devoted himself to the writing of military history.*

"Left Emmitsburg at 7 A.M.," says my pocket-diary of 1863, under the heading of Wednesday, July 1.

We had been marching northward about two weeks from our quarters at Acquia Landing, had crossed the Potomac at Edwards Ferry, and well knew that we were in pursuit of Lee, who had made one of his splendid feints, got away under cover of it a good two-days' march ahead of us, and was in Pennsylvania. Full many a rumor reached our ears, of Harrisburg sacked, of cornfields burned, of devastation and vandalism, but how much to believe and how much to reject, we could not tell. We had received no New York papers (on which regimental officers always relied for such information) since we started; and except at Army, or, perhaps, Corps Headquarters, precious little is generally known of the why and the wherefore, the cause and the effect of the marchings and counter-marching of a large army. Generalities we could, of course, guess at, or hear about; that we were up in Pennsylvania in pursuit of the "Army of Northern Virginia," we were

311

well aware of; that we should not go much farther without a "big fight" we could easily imagine; but just where Lee was, or what battle-ground he would select, or how many days hence the collision would occur, we had no conception of.

Nor did we seriously bother ourselves about it. Our Colonel, brave fellow, had fallen in the awful mêlée at Chancellorsville; our Lieutenant-Colonel was in command, and I was his Adjutant. There were no other mounted officers in his regiment, and we had enough to do to keep the command in good order, and ready for the hard work we knew was sure to come, without trying to find out the when and the where.

Colonel —— and I were on very intimate terms. We had each been in service since early in the war, and each had joined this regiment (a new one) after a probation in the field; he under McDowell, I under gallant Kearny, which had made us veterans as compared with the other officers, none of whom had seen service until within the last few months. This had always made us good friends; and we had, from the first, shared our meals, slept under the same shelter-tent, and been officially and personally as closely allied as ever two officers could be. The Colonel let a good half of the duty fall upon me, and reposed great confidence in my discretion. My position in the regiment was a pleasant as well as a responsible one.

We marched along leisurely enough, making about two miles in the hour, and then enjoying our ten-minute halt, as is usual when there are no orders before the marching. Nothing was farther from our thoughts—at least to us uninitiated fellows—than the prospect of an immediate engagement. To be sure, we had broken up at three that morning, and by eleven or twelve o'clock had got within six or eight miles of Gettysburg—name unfamiliar, then, familiar since to all the world—but it was not till about two or three in the afternoon, that we heard the booming of guns ahead, and began to prick up our ears at the probability of an approaching action.

The booming went sullenly on, bearing no definite tidings, for half an hour or more, when our Brigade A. A. G. (little aware, poor fellow, that before sundown his life-blood would be ebbing out) rode down the column with, "Keep your men well in hand, Colonel, and close them up—there's fighting to do ahead!" and passed on with the message to the regiments in the rear.

Now is the time to watch the countenances of the men. Here one whose face may be a shade paler, but his eye is none the less lustrous, nor his lips less firmly knit, as he weighs his inclination with his duty. Beside him lags a dead-beat, who five minutes hence will complain of sore feet, and make every excuse, and look for every chance to drop out and straggle; not far off, the bragging fellow, whom you would dub a lion from his words and a hare from his deeds; who will talk loud, and vent his gasconade on every side, but who will be as far to the rear in the coming broil as he can get, by sneaking or deliberately running away. The boy, fair-faced and small, scarce eighteen years old that trudges behind him, whistling to keep his courage up and drown the remembrance of mother's kiss and sister's smile left far behind at home, a pigmy compared with his file leader, and probably often a sufferer from the bully's coarseness and ill-nature, is yet an unconscious hero. *He* will be in line when the braggart is skulking in the rear; he will do the work which the dead-beat avoids; he will march on with sore and blistered feet; he will stick to the ranks till he is shot down and crippled. At such a time it is easy to tell who is to be relied upon, and who to be spotted as a shirk or a coward. As a rule, for a volunteer company, give me the well-bred lad of less than twenty. Easy to manage, relying upon his officers for guidance and example instead of his own discretion, less conscious of danger, too young to be bound by any habits, the boy will generally out-march, out-work, and out-fight the older man; and you may be sure that in a tight place he will stick to you gallantly, and if you will only *lead*, he will *follow* through thick and thin. I do not refer to the old, trained soldier; I only speak of volunteers.

We had been keeping up the accelerated pace, probably two miles and a half an hour, for some little while, when several staff-officers, one by one, came down the line to urge us on, and every now and then stopping to answer an inquiry about the news. Once told, it soon got abroad. "The First Corps has had an engagement some five miles on, at Gettysburg, and Reynolds has captured a whole rebel brigade!"

"Bully for Reynolds!" is the universal comment.

Then, a few minutes later, comes another rumor: "General Reynolds killed!"

"Close up, men! Captain, keep your men well together!" is the instinctive comment on this.

By this time every one has forgotten any symptoms of fatigue which may have been creeping over him, in the exciting anticipation of an approaching fray. Every one's blood flows quicker, every pulse beats louder, every nerve is more sensitive, and every one feels that he is living faster than he was half an hour since.

Nor this from faint-heartedness. The bravest men will feel a certain dread on going into action, at least every man who has a high-strung nature and a gentle blood. I have seen men whose *sluggishness* never left them, even in the deadliest struggle; who had no dread because no appreciation of danger. I have seen men who were continually saying they would rather fight than not, who were on their muscle continually, "spoiling for a fight," as they say over in Erin; but my humble experience, gathered on some scores of hard-fought fields with the old Third Corps, has taught me that such men are generally unreliable, and that they do not make good officers. Some of them may do for a charge on a battery, where ten minutes will do the work; but for your steady, cool leader, who will neither lose his head in the flurry of an action, nor let slip a good opportunity from sheer inertia, commend me to the man who has the nerves to feel his danger, and the nerve to do his duty.

Ever and anon there was a lull in the firing ahead, and then it would break out again with fresh vigor. We hurried on without the hourly halts; but for fear of bringing the men into action too tired to be effective, no double-quick was ordered. Finally, early in the afternoon, we hove in sight of Gettysburg. Passing on through the town, with much ado preventing the men from dropping out to get the tempting drinks of water, ladled out by women and maidens at nearly every house, we reached the outskirts of the place, marched into the fields, and were drawn up into double column in the place pointed out by the proper staff-officer.

We then had a few minutes to ourselves. The men were allowed to rest in line, and each one sat or lay down in the most comfortable position just where he was, some reclining at full length and closing their eyes, some merely squatting down to discuss hard tack and the situation, while the first sergeants called the roll.

The Colonel and I sat under an apple tree (our regiment was in an orchard), and speculated upon the coming encounter, and its probable results. He was a married man; I not, as yet. He had been wedded to his fiancée some eight months before, on the very day he started to join his regiment, and had left her immediately after the ceremony and informal breakfast, a wife by only half. They had been married so that, in the event of his being wounded, she might have the right to go to him, and nurse him through his sickness. Our talk was naturally more or less of our dear ones at home and each committed to the other messages and directions, often given before, in case of mishap.

We were both members of the Episcopal church. The Colonel was an upright, conscientious Christian, who did his whole duty not only with military precision, but with scrupulous fidelity to himself; and I verily believe that no soldier was ever more upheld in a strict path of duty by his sincere religious feeling, than our good Colonel. In some things, I used to think, he carried his religious scruples too far, but in the main I always saw the benefit of his piety.

As he and I sat apart from the rest of the officers and men, and somewhat secluded from their observation, the Colonel said to me in the midst of our conversation: "Adjutant, we are going to have some hot work shortly—let us ask His protection." I readily assented, and we knelt down under the tree, and uttered, each in his own heart, a prayer to the God of Hosts. It was a sincerely unaffected act, prompted only by the solemnity of the occasion, and, I feel sure, had its good effect on both of us.

Not long after, the firing, which for some time had been hushed, broke out again about a half a mile on our left, where the First Corps was still holding its own, despite the loss of its gallant leader. The ground was open, and we could see the opposing lines of infantry pouring, now a scattering, now a more concentrated fire of musketry into each other's ranks. Occasionally, a regiment would show signs of wavering, then again would rally with a cheer and return to its former steadiness, the while the mounted officers rode along the lines, and the staff and orderlies galloped to and fro between the front, and the Commanding-General in the rear.

"Fall in!" rang along our own line, from regiment to regiment, as the tune of skirmish firing was suddenly taken up in our own front. But there needed no command for that, as three or four of the cracking rifles ahead sufficed to tell us that beyond the woods the enemy's skirmishers, preceding their advance, had suddenly encountered our own. Quickly formed, we were marched in line of double columns at deploying distance, forward through the fields, tearing down the fences in our way, or climbing them in confused ranks, and re-forming on the other side. Our whole division thus advanced some three or four hundred yards, when we were ordered to halt and deploy, the brigades in reserve remaining in column. On deployment, we stood, as far as we could see over the level ground to the left, and extending to some woods on the right. How our flanks were protected we could not see, though we could readily imagine. All we expected was that there was work enough cut out for us in front, and we concentrated our whole attention towards that point.

And now for a ludicrous event—for such will happen at all times. My favorite horse—"Fanny Grey"—I had been obliged to send into Washington for a rest, as she had completely run down by hard work and little or no feed in the Chancellorsville campaign; and, in her stead, my friends had sent me a little brown mare, which I nicknamed "Dimple." Now Dimple was a very nice little beast of Morgan breed, and very serviceable; but she had never, as yet, smelt gunpowder. From the time we had come within sound of the cannonading, Miss Dimple had been getting more and more excitable, and by the time we arrived within the immediate range of the enemy's artillery, when an occasional shell would whiz above our heads, or explode near by, I had had extreme difficulty in managing her, and attending to my duty beside. And the skirmish-firing had capped the climax, so that when we were advancing in columns, the little wretch, scared by an explosion altogether too near for her sensitive nerves, bolted with me out to the front, far beyond our line, and in disagreeable proximity to where I knew the enemy to be, creating a peal of laughter, at my expense, through the whole brigade, in which she and I were well known; and completely shocking my sense of propriety and military punctilio.

But worse was to come. The next close explosion (before the occurrence of which I had reduced her to terms, and again taken my place on the right of the regiment) set Miss Dimple off *"en carrière"* in a diametrically opposite direction. This was insufferable, it looked so very like running away, which, in a physical point of view, it in truth was. This "bolt" occasioned another laugh, at which I began to get nettled. But fortunately, on again rejoining the regiment, Dimple covered with foam, and, I fear, bearing some severe punctures from my heavy spurs on her pretty flanks, I saw that all the mounted officers of regiments in our division were dismounting (a by no means unusual, but, I think, vicious habit before going into action); and I, nothing loth, though at the same time disapproving of the principle, gave over Dimple to a stray drummer to take to the rear, and resumed my duties on foot.

As to this habit of dismounting in action, I consider it a very bad one. It is good in one way, for it saves many of the superior officers from being disabled, thus preserving their utility in their respective commands; but unless, when behind breastworks, or in a decidedly defensive attitude, it is much more apt to do harm by showing the men that their officers are seeking to protect themselves, than good in saving them from wounds. A mounted officer can do more to keep his men steady, than if he were on foot. However, the instinct of self-preservation is generally sufficient to induce one to dismount, if he sees the example set by competent authority.

And so here I was on foot, in rear of the right of the regiment, shouting encouragement to the officers and men, and trying to keep the line steady, for already our skirmishers had been driven in by the enemy, and came falling back towards us, exchanging an occasional shot as they retreated.

Passing through our ranks to the rear, they soon discovered to our view the rebel sharpshooters, who, in their turn, were soon withdrawn to make way for the advance of the rebel line, which was ordered to attack us and drive us through the town.

A moment or two of breathless anxiety and impatience, and the irregular line of butternut and gray hove gradually in sight—their officers all mounted, waving their swords and cheering on their men. It had been hard, hitherto, to make our men reserve their fire. In a new regiment, there are always a few nervous fellows, who are sure to pop off their pieces long before there is any thing to aim at, and unless great care is taken, and the men constantly cautioned, half the rest will follow suit, and waste their ammunition, courage and morale, in worse than fruitless firing. And now, of course, there was the usual proportion of stray shots, each followed by a volley of oaths from the delinquents' superiors, and not a few by a sound rap over the head, administered to the offending son of Mars by a testy file-closer.

The danger of a premature general firing came, however, speedily to an end; for when the rebel line had arrived to within some two hundred yards from our own, the command was given, and a spirited fire by file rattled down from the right of each company.

This in no way checked the enemy's advance, but it drew their fire; and they continued slowly to push on, keeping it up in a desultory manner as they drew near, while ever and anon, as the smoke would clear away, in some spot, you could see their officers rushing to and fro in excited endeavors to keep their men braced up to their work.

At about a hundred yards' distance they halted, and as their fire became more steady, it began to have more visible effect upon our ranks. Every five or six seconds some poor fellow would throw up his arms with an "Ugh!" and drop; then pick himself up, perhaps, and start for the rear. Another would drop flat on his face, or his back, without a sound; another would break down, and fall together in a heap. Still another would let drop his gun, and holding his shattered arm, would leave the ranks; or, perhaps, stay by to encourage his

319

comrades. One brave boy near me, I remember, shot in the leg, sat there loading and firing with as much regularity and coolness as if untouched, now and then shouting to some comrade in front of him to make room for his shot; while some scared booby, with a scratch scarce deep enough to draw the blood, would run bellowing out of range; or some man, who had completely lost his head in the excitement, though mechanically keeping his place in line, would load his musket and deliberately fire in the air.

Before ten minutes of this work were well past, a good quarter of the men were lying about dead or wounded, or were limping back to the surgeons; but still the firing went on, neither side showing symptoms of wavering. Under the never-ceasing encouragements of the officers, generally taking the form of "Give 'em ——, boys!" or, "Knock spots out of them, boys!" or, "Rake the —— out of 'em, boys!" this familiar synonym for heat creeping into almost every admonition, our men, though with thinned ranks and ghastly wounds staring them in the face on every side, kept unflinchingly up to the mark.

After about thirty minutes of this withering fire, the rebels made a charge. It was not a charge on the double-quick, but a simple advance, firing as they came on. At the same time a rebel battery, which somehow had crept up on an eminence to our right, some half mile distant, began to pepper us with grape and canister. This was very annoying, for although the fire of a battery is much less deadly at a distance than musketry close at hand, the noises are so much more appalling that men will get uneasy under a harmless shelling quicker than under a murderous fire of small arms. And this battery was unfortunately almost in rear of our flank.

But our line preserved its steadiness, nevertheless, until the rebels had approached to within sixty or eighty yards, when it showed signs of becoming unsteady. We officers redoubled our exertions, shouted, waved our swords, swore, struck the men most inclined to give way, went to almost every extreme, but with no avail. Our line had already fallen back twelve or fifteen yards, we could see the division on our right in full retreat, and there was no disguising the fact that we were fairly driven off the field.

Just at this juncture, while rushing about, ordering and entreating, gesticulating and threatening, I was knocked clean off my feet by an excruciating blow (so it felt) on my right foot; our line passed over me in retreat, and I found myself in the disagreeable position of being between two fires (neither side having ceased their fusillade), and with redoubled prospects of being taken prisoner. The whole thing was done so quickly that I had no time to get any of our men to carry me off, and having no desire to be shot again, with "discretion is the better part of valor" on my lips, I lay down where I fell, among the dead and wounded, until the rebels, after a rousing yell, ceased firing, and advanced in pursuit of our retiring men. Then I sat up again, the rebel line passed over me, and I was captured.

A moment after, a rebel straggler, unkempt and powder-begrimed, came along seeking whom he might devour, and seeing an officer sitting before him in the hated blue coat, demanded my arms. As no one but an officer had a right to disarm me, I told him to "Go to —— "; improper language, I confess, but pardonable, perhaps, on this occasion. But instead of minding my admonition, he raised his gun, as if to club me. Luckily for my brain, however, as I was grabbing at my revolver, an officer on General Gordon's staff, as I afterwards ascertained, happening to notice my dilemma, gave a shout to my would-be immolator, which arrested his blow, and, on his turning about and ascertaining its source, had the effect of sending him about his business with a "D—d Yank, anyhow!" and I was saved from a broken crown. The officer rode up to me, demanding my arms, which I reluctantly surrendered, especially the sword—a gift, and a very handsome weapon. However, it was the fate of war. The officer told me the attacking brigade was Gordon's, asked my Corps, and before I could ascertain his name, with a view of subsequently recovering my sword, he rode away about his duties.

I then set to work to examine my wound. Cutting off my boot and stocking, I found that a minié ball had gone through my ankle-joint. This was not my first wound, but in neither of my prior ones had bones been broken, and I had no idea how painful such a shot could be. Tearing up my handkerchief, I made a compress for each side of the wounded ankle, using my canteen-water to moisten it, and bound it up with a bandage I had long carried in my pocket; then, with the aid of a sergeant of our regiment, who had been captured, and a Confederate tatterdemalion, who was disposed to be accommodating, and, I dare say, glad to go to the rear instead of the front, I limped away on one foot, holding the cumbersome limb out before me.

My progress was not speedy, but any change was pleasant; for the place where I had been shot was literally strewed with killed and wounded, and, withal, a worrying little skirmish was still going on between advancing Reb and retreating Yank, just far enough away for fifty per cent of the balls to whiz round our heads in undesirable proximity.

Still, in about an hour, by dint of frequent rests, I had limped some quarter of a mile to the rear, into a grove of trees, through which ran a good-sized stream. At the side of this I took up my stand (figuratively speaking), and pressing a drummer-boy into my service, by the aid of a tin cup and considerable urging of the youngster, I kept my wound in a cool and uninflamed state by dripping an almost constant stream of water upon it. And to this habit, in which I persevered all day and most of the night during the five days I was without medical treatment, I ascribe the fact that very little sign of mortification ever showed itself.

Before arriving at my brook-side resting-place, I had passed over the spot where the rebel line had been posted during the engagement, and I perceived, with a grim sort of satisfaction, that apparently more gray jackets were lying about than blue jackets in the place I had just before left; which was a partial, though perhaps inhuman, reward for the laborious drills in which I had participated during the previous nine months. But, in the main, my animosity had merged into selfishness, and all my thoughts, for the time being, were concentrated upon the ankle.

I had sat but a few moments by the brook, when an officer rode up, dismounted, and entered into conversation with me. He knew my corps by my badge, but was anxious to know as much of the movements of the rest of the army as possible. I knew little, and was conveniently ignorant of that, in my talk with him; and soon tired of pumping, he asked me if I would as lief give him my spur, as his jaded animal needed its incentive as much as forage. I complied with his request right willingly, as a spur was likely to be of little use to me now.

While on this subject, I may as well relate the singular adventure which befell my other spur, which I had cut off and thrown aside with my boot. It was a large Mexican spur, with two inch rowels and jingling pendents, the sort of spurs any one in search of "style" is apt to indulge in out in the field. Its well-burnished brass, as it lay on the ground, had caught the eye of a stray Reb, who picked it up, and carried it off as lawful booty. He had not gone far, dangling his prize, before he came across Colonel ———, who had likewise been wounded and left on the field, but although within twenty rods of each other, owing to the number of casualties in our immediate vicinity, neither he nor I knew of the other's mishap.

The Colonel at once recognized the spur, and asked the man where he had found it. "Aboot forty or fifty yards over thar!" quoth he, "on a boot—the cursed Yank was shot through the foot, damn him!" The Colonel at once demanded the spur as the property of his adjutant, and backing up his demand by the judicious display of a greenback, possessed himself of the article, which he subsequently returned to me. He thus knew I was shot, and rested not till he had reestablished communication with me.

I had frequent visits from lesser Confederate officers, generally of the medical, commissary, or quartermaster's departments, and many really agreeable talks with them during the remainder of the day, at my station by the brook. Most of them I found courteous, good-natured, and intelligent; few of them assuming, and the majority decided gentlemen. All were very confident of success in this move, sure that it would result in a peace favorable to the Confederacy; their usual argument being that the Northern Democrats would soon see an end put to the war, and an honorable peace secured to their brother-politicians in the South. Any dissent from this view was apt to be treated as short-sighted and biased, so that I soon learned to keep my opinions on the war-question to myself. But I have no cause to complain of my treatment by Gordon's Brigade. It was uniformly kind and considerate, and fully justified the high reputation the brigade enjoyed throughout the rebel army for its good discipline and material.

About 8 P.M., through the kindness of a rebel surgeon, I was carried into a neighboring house, and given a much more comfortable place than I had a right to expect, a bed and mattress. This was an entirely unlooked-for luxury, and duly rejoiced over; but when the surgeon in charge assigned one of our captured men, François by name, to me and my comrades as nurse, my delight knew no bounds. I considered myself made.

One of our General officers, a division commander, lay in the next room to me (my bed was in a little room, where I was all by myself), severely shot through the body. His chance of life seemed very slim; but, like a brave man, he resolved he would not die, unless it was an absolute consequence; and as a reward for his valor in health and in sickness, he subsequently got well. I have often known such recoveries from sheer force of will; and I have known men with slight wounds that ought not to have kept them on the sick-list three weeks, worry themselves into the grave, *for fear* they were going to die. I only once caught sight of the General, as they were bringing him into the house on his stretcher, and as we could neither of us move, our communication was limited to messages through the medium of François.

The surgeon completed his kindnesses by giving me a morphine pill (a very precious thing in rebeldom), but had no time to examine my foot, as so many more severely wounded men were to be attended to. But the pill was a great boon, and under its drowsy influence I managed to get several hours' sleep during the night.

As morning dawned, an occasional gun gave notice of another impending clash of arms. It made us prisoners feel uncomfortable in the last degree; nor were we made less nervous by a report brought in by François, shortly after sunrise, that our house was in direct range of the Union batteries, which he could see posted on the hills beyond the town. Of all things apt to make you ill at ease is being wounded and under fire; and when the fire happens to be that of your own forces, the nervousness become painful in the extreme. François' report proved to be only too correct, as was soon after verified by the many shells which burst in the immediate vicinity of our hospital, and the three which went through it.

These last were missives from our friends, which could well have been spared. One of them set the house on fire, and only by considerable exertion were the flames extinguished. The other two contented themselves with scattering the plaster and such inmates of the house as were capable of being scattered, *pars quorum non fui*; and one of them brought the ceiling down upon my bed, much to my astonishment, discomfort and pain.

I have said above that I have cause only to remember my treatment in rebel hands as courteous and kind. I except one case. About noon of July 2d, I had managed to pump out of the owner of the house the weighty fact that he had a small barrel of corn meal and some half-dozen ducks hid away in the garret, sole relics of his "teeming flocks and granges full," for which, prior to the rebel occupation of his farm, he had "thanked the bounteous Pan." By earnest entreaty, and prompt payment of his starvation-price, I induced him to transfer his right, title, and interest in a portion of this meal, and three of these ducks, to me. I had at the time been fasting some 24 hours, was reduced by the loss of blood, and felt in great need of some nourishing food. On obtaining the precious edibles, with which I hoped to make glad the hearts of my comrades as well as my own, I committed them to the care of François, with orders to cook them without delay, and serve them up *à la militaire*, which means, generally, on a more or less clean board. Soon ascended from the kitchen below the savory smell of roasting duck and browning corn-cake; and I need tell none who have fasted as long under similar circumstances, *how* savory it was.

But in the delicious odor lay the danger. Not alone to our nostrils did it ascend, but it attracted to the spot a couple of straggling, voracious butternuts.

"Yank, what the hell you got there?" suddenly saluted the ears of startled François. Too late to hide even a portion of the viands, poor François stood rooted to the spot.

"Who the hell does them ducks belong to?" inquired the spokesman of the party.

"To the wounded officer upstairs."

"Confed. or Yank?"

Here was an awkward casuistic dilemma. Possibly, under all the circumstances, François would have been excusable in positive equivocation, if not absolute falsehood; but not versed in either of these useful arts, as soldiers are generally too apt to be, he unhesitatingly answered:

"Union!"

"Well, damn him, give me the ducks then."

And amid entreaties, protestations, and appeals, the ducks were borne away, leaving poor François not to be comforted, and we hungry mortals above, dinnerless, and without a chance of dinner.

This piece of foraging, even considering the source—a pair of *butternut stragglers*—I have always felt to be meanness personified. Perhaps I am biased. But to take food from a wounded man, be he friend or foe, must require a pitifully small nature.

François felt worse than I did; and shortly after endeavored to retrieve himself by bringing me some broken hardtack, which, though on a searching cross-examination, I elicited to have been gathered from the haversacks of sundry dead men hard by, I nevertheless ate with such relish as my physical condition and the not very great sweetness of the morsel allowed.

My diary for July 2d contains little. I was too weak to write much. I had lost considerable blood, and felt listless. Among the jottings occur: *"Long, weary* day"—"Wound very painful"—"Wonder how long before my ankle will get well again."

This last is curious. I might have known that with the ankle-joint shot all to splinters, I could never have any thing but a stiff foot, even if I could keep the foot at all; but all my life I had been a great runner, jumper, gymnast, cricketer; my legs had always been the best part of me—not so much in the handsome as in the useful line; and I never once dreamed that all these habits were of the past, and that in the future I should limp along through the world—a cripple. I can give no idea of the heart-swelling shock I felt when told I must *lose* my leg. I do not remember that I ever had any thing so entirely crush me for the moment, as this unlooked-for bitter news.

On Friday, July 3d, I was evidently still more listless, partly from inaction, but mainly from the drain on my system occasioned by the loss of so much blood and the constant pain. I had had no medical attendance whatever; surgeons were few, patients many. Only "Rebel Commissary" is jotted down in my diary. But this recalls a pleasant reminiscence.

About 3 P.M. of that day, a Confederate officer came into my room, sat down, and began talking with me. Suddenly he stopped, and said:

"You look as if you wanted something to eat and drink. Have you any one here to wait on you?"

I called François, to whom the Commissary gave a hastily scribbled note on a page torn from my diary, telling him where to go and bring what was ordered therein. In some twenty minutes, François returned with a tin-cup of hot coffee, and three or four nice buttered rolls. Little did I ask where such delicacies came from. I only thanked the Commissary, and did immediate justice to his bounty. A brighter spot in the whole of my life I do not remember than this little courtesy.

The Commissary told me that our forces were getting badly beaten, despite their good position on the hills.

This I took *cum grano salis*. He also told me that they expected the Union army to retreat during the coming night, in which case there was no doubt the war was at an end. I did not pretend to argue with him, but I nevertheless had my own notions on the subject. Most of our conversation was on other topics. We had both been students at Heidelberg, and found no lack of pleasant memories to chat about. Since then I have cherished a warm friendship for this gentleman, though his name has escaped my memory, and I have no idea where his lot may be cast.

Under Saturday, July 4th, I find only the word "ambulances" noted in my diary. This I remember to have been the information, scarcely credited at the time, that some Union ambulances had driven up the road within quarter of a mile of the house. François said he had seen them; but I feared he was mistaken. To be sure, there had been an almost universal cessation in the firing, the rebel pickets had been withdrawn to near our house, and large masses of the enemy's troops had left the vicinity; but so little idea had I that the enemy would leave us behind, that I could scarcely credit such good news. I was not aware that they could not carry off one out of five of their own wounded, for lack of transportation.

And when on Sunday, the 5th, we woke up to find that the rebel army had actually left, that we had won a great victory, that the enemy was in full retreat lest he should be cut off before he could cross the Potomac, who shall depict the joy which made warm our hearts and shone in our faces? We were recaptured, victorious, not doomed to starvation in Libby or Andersonville. Happiness was not our condition— we were in seventh heaven.

But this ends my subject. I need not tell of my being carried into town, in the same ambulance with the Colonel, who, when he had found where I was, rested not till he had got me beside him again; or our procuring a private room in Gettysburg, through the kind instrumentality of a friendly General officer; of the lovely care of our good hostess; of the Colonel's pretty wife coming to rejoice over his safety; of my suffering amputation; of my being carried home; and of my living to know that a one-legged man is not necessarily a *cripple* in its worst sense—all this I need not tell. My story ends when I was recaptured; and I doubt not my reader has already found out that I was one of the luckiest, take it for all in all, of the poor fellows who, during the war, were so often "left wounded on the field."

Index

About the Editor

Stephen W. Sears is the author of *Landscape Turned Red: The Battle of Antietam; George B. McClellan: The Young Napoleon; To the Gates of Richmond: The Peninsula Campaign; Chancellorsville;* and *Controversies & Commanders: Dispatchers from the Army of the Potomac.* He is the editor of *The Civil War Papers of George B. McClellan; For Country, Cause & Leader: The Civil War Journal of Charles B. Haydon;* and *Mr. Dunn Browne's Experiences in the Army: The Civil War Letters of Samuel W. Fiske.*